Praise for Tim Mulherin's essays:

Some can visit a place a thousand times and never get to know it, while others go deeper, beyond the tourist lookouts and marked trails, until they've learned the place by heart. Tim Mulherin is one of the latter. He "gets" northwest lower Michigan, and his book is a rich and entertaining celebration of it.

—Jerry Dennis, author of *The Living Great Lakes*

To read Tim Mulherin is to be informed, entertained, and challenged. It's rare that one book can do all that, but *Sand, Stars, Wind, & Water: Field Notes from Up North* achieves all three and more.

—Philip Gulley, author of the *Porch Talk* and *Harmony* series

Tim Mulherin takes us on a memorable walk through one of the most beautiful places in America, a place he cherishes and honors with acute observation. In telling his tales of Leelanau, he gets the biggest issue of all – the need to live with respect for the water and all living things. In accessible prose, he teaches, delights, and entertains.

—Dave Dempsey, author of *The Heart of the Lakes: Freshwater in the Past, Present, and Future of Southeast Michigan*

Anyone who's ever had a face-to-face connection with nature, or a passing interest in the Lake Michigan wilds on the Leelanau Peninsula, will relish Tim Mulherin's *Sand, Stars, Wind, & Water: Field Notes from Up North*. With captivating use of word and language – and an engaging blend of per~~~~l recollections – Mulherin brings readers up close and personal with t gion's people, places, and nature, from Sleeping Bear Dunes throu₃ land, past Lake Leelanau to Traverse City.

—Steven Higgs, author of *A Guide to Natural Areas of Southern I* and *A Guide to Natural Areas of Northern 1*

In this next best thing to an actual visit, readers will find good coɪ Tim Mulherin's amiable, intelligent, affectionate essays evoke the ƥ and interest to be found Up North as it is now, tourist throngs and

mussels notwithstanding. In *Sand, Stars, Wind, & Water: Field Notes from Up North*, Mulherin, a Hoosier visitor, offers a personal, intently observed collection of experiences in a place that so many, however long they may stay, do love.

—Stephanie Mills, author of *Tough Little Beauties* and
Epicurean Simplicity

"We are born to love the planet." So says Tim Mulherin, and I agree with him. Indulge yourself in a little Northern Michigan planet love with this vibrant collection of essays.

—Heather Shumaker, author of *Saving Arcadia:*
A Story of Conservation and Community in the Great Lakes

SAND, STARS, WIND, & WATER

Always keep that "Up North" state of mind. Peace.

Tim Mulhern

SAND, STARS, WIND, & WATER

Field Notes from Up North

TIM MULHERIN

MISSION POINT PRESS

Mission Point Press
2554 Chandler Road
Traverse City, Michigan 49696
www.MissionPointPress.com

Printed in the United States of America

ISBN: 978-1-954786-17-2

Library of Congress Control Number: 2021906132

For Janet, always

Each night before bed I step out and look at the stars. It's good for humility.

—*Jim Harrison,* The Big Seven

CONTENTS

INTRODUCTION

Dad's text message to Matt in early March 2020: "Any interest in opening up the cabin in Cedar w/me in early May, second weekend?"

Matt's text to Dad: "Yeah I'd like to go. Let me talk to Kelli and look at my calendar and get back with you."

Minutes later, Matt's attack-of-conscience text to Dad: "That's Mother's Day Weekend."

Dad's voice-of-experience text to Matt: "Not a problem on my end. Having me away for a few days is the perfect Mother's Day gift for your mom." Crazy happy emoji.

Matt fails to respond.

Dad nudges Matt: "Could be an issue for you, I'm suspecting."

Matt eventually texts Dad: "Haha well that was the first thing Kelli said when I told her. I mean asked."

My darling wife, Janet, upon learning of the possibility of this rare father and son trip being scuttled due to the Hallmark holiday entrapment on Matt's end, says she'll work on it. "I can help Kelli with Brennan and James," she offers.

Grand-mothering is pure joy for my wife, and she takes every opportunity she can to spend time with all eight of our grandchildren. Unlike me: Florida-type attachment-disordered grandfather who makes himself scarce; i.e., to keep some healthy distance between us. That absence cultivating fonder hearts thing.

A day later, Dad texts Matt: "No pressure. Might even go solo. Can't wait to head North."

That's all it takes. Although I'm perfectly fine to have a short monk-like sabbatical all by my lonesome while handling opening ceremonies, Janet is definitely not okay with that arrangement. "You're too old to go by yourself, honey. I'm calling Kelli now."

Later that night, Matt texts Dad: "I'm in for Michigan."

Go figure, I think dryly. And yet, Dad is very, very happy.

But that happiness would be short-lived....

❋

Every March I find myself daydreaming with increasing frequency about re-turning to my adopted motherland, Leelanau County, Michigan, sometime in May, a now 15-year-old custom. As I open in this collection of essays, *anticipation* may well be the best part of the process—next to being there, that is. By mid-March 2020, however, the Covid-19 pandemic would take the wind out of my sails, with emergency shutdowns rippling across the country, including Michigan and Indianapolis, and a trip north with Matt would have to be postponed at least until late spring of 2021. My wife and I are older now (how that happened is beyond me), and we have taken the necessary though heart-wrenching precautions during this long viral crisis, keeping our distance from our loved ones and friends. So our anticipation for our eventual return to normalcy Up North, to enjoy our time there with friends and family, aches more than ever before. And that's okay—that happy day will come.

My family and I have been visiting Leelanau County and the Traverse City area since the early nineties. I first experienced the legendary beauty of the region in the late eighties: lovestruck at first sight. This condition never leaves me, and my longing is most acute while away. Sometime in February, while standing on our backyard deck and peering up through the bare limbs of our towering black walnut tree into the starry winter night, I ponder my eventual return Up North. As spring begins to make its eventually con-vincing argument with winter and the crocuses start to pop, I emerge from my hibernation far away from those woodland haunts near the Big Water, Michigami ("Great Water"), as the Ojibwe Indians named it, and initiate my very preliminary preparations for my early May northbound road trip. With something of a sense of reverence, I gather a four-pound test fishing line spool, a new deck-tinting pad, a set-aside book of poetry I've yet to crack. This simple ritual alone lifts my spirits.

My decades-long love affair with Leelanau and Grand Traverse counties and many other points north throughout northwest lower Michigan owes its origin to my longtime associate in sundry unforgettable and mostly out-door adventures—and occasionally sinful yet hilarious activities—Craig, a Traverse City native. (And Craig it will remain, to provide him some rela-tive anonymity.) Nearly 40 years ago, as bartenders together in Indianapolis, we forged a friendship that even today, despite our political and worldview differences formed by myriad influences—most notably including family heritage, upbringing, and political tribalism, as well as from unique interpre-tations experienced in higher education, the school of hard knocks, and the workplace—still holds true. Craig opened the north country to me through his unique lens as seen through the eyes of an artist, and I can never repay this life-altering kindness. Occasionally I try an insufficient gesture, like seiz-ing the check at a local drinking establishment after a few precious hours together laughing heartily while reminiscing about some of the crazy you-wouldn't-believe-it escapades we had when we were young bucks. Youth may indeed be wasted on the young, but the memories are a precious dividend.

These personal essays—stories—are about this special place that has drawn me back into the enveloping arms of the Great Spirit Manitou, as the Ojibwe people's theology names the omnipresent life force ultimately experienced in nature. I live in a densely populated Midwestern metropo-lis; it drains me. I return to open country Up North; it sustains me. It is my hope that these pieces—homage to the experiences the area has given me and mine these many years—invite you to make your own beautiful memo-ries here in northwest lower Michigan. And to do so with the utmost respect and reverence for this environmental treasure. Visitors, too, are stewards of the land and are called to leave no trace, unless it's for the better. The lo-cals—flora and fauna, including the humans that inhabit the area—greatly appreciate it.

— Tim Mulherin, Winter Solstice, December 21, 2020

SAND, STARS, WIND, & WATER

JORDAN VALLEY FISH

THE YEAR OF THE SUCKER HOLE
KNOW YOUR LIMIT

NO MORE THAN 3 SHOTS OF WHISKEY BEFORE SUNRISE. 1 GALLON OF RED WINE IS FINE BEFORE LUNCH. VODKA IS FINE ALL DAY. NO LIMIT INLAND RIVER ONLY. NO DRAMBUIE ABOVE WIER. NO MORE THAN 3 MUD GUPPIES BELOW ROBECOS BRIDGE WITH COGNAC FRESH SPAWN AND IRISH MIST ON GREEN RIVER ONLY. NO ORANGE VODKA ABOVE PENNY'S BRIDGE. NO SINGING TO THE FISH, OR GIN, AT MOUTH OF JORDAN RIVER. YOU MAY PISSSSS 3 BOTTLES OF GIN, AT MOUTH OF JORDAN RIVER NO CHAMPAGNE WITH ARTIFICIAL CRAWLERS. NO TROLLING IN BEAVER PONDS. KEEPING A TOOWANIGAN EQUIPPED WITH A PONY KEG IS UN- LAWFUL. SPAWNING STURGEON CLUB IS STUPID IT IS UNLAWFUL TO RIDE ON BABY KITTENS IS ALLOWED BENEATH SUCKER HOLE TEQUILA MAY BE USED ON FLY ONLY STREAMS. OTHER RULES MAY APPLY

IF YOU SEE THIS FISH CALL THE DNR.
TROUT

CAMP

PART I

Spring

ANTICIPATION

Three hundred ninety-eight miles away, I can see it vividly in my mind's eye: *As I turn my pickup truck into Manor Green, my youngest brother and I embrace the late afternoon spring ambiance of the sun-painted trees, yet bare, though not for long. The pumpkin-colored and evergreen-trimmed A-frame cottage seems to acknowledge us with its quarter-moon-windowed visage as the climbing truck tires bite the gravel driveway's steep grade. There's that clutch of white trillium in the front yard again, growing in the same spot year after year. No doubt the leeks are sprouting on the woodland floor beneath the sky-reaching sugar maples in the backyard. Truck door open, I stretch toward the afternoon sun, take a deep breath, and sweet, clean air swells my lungs.*

"Honey, we're home!" Chris shouts in his pretty-damn-happy state. Home as in Cedar, Michigan.

Anticipation. It's the best part.

Chris and I will be traveling from Indy to Cedar on Thursday morning in front of the second weekend in May, our cabin-opening tradition for nearly the past decade. This time, he'll do the driving, sparing me one lengthy road trip of the five or six my wife, Janet, and I will make this season. He's a talker—an animated, hand-gesturing talker—so I'll have to watch the road for him as he gets so involved in the topic being entertained that paying attention to the highway will take a back seat to the conversation. The only downside to Chris kindly using his Honda Pilot for our northward trek is the potential of us smashing into the back end of a semitrailer during a particularly engaging—and blinding—part of our discussion. Other than that, we're good.

He and I have been emailing back and forth for the past week about our plans and preparations. We seldom chat in person or online during the course of the year. But our interaction heats up in mid-April as I confirm his availability to head north and we begin thinking about the trip.

"It's almost time to get the hell out of here," he says during a phone call a week out from our departure. "I can't freakin' wait."

"I'll second that."

I've told him to be at my house by 7 a.m. so as to avoid the peak of morning rush hour traffic, his on Indy's south side, mine on the north. He says he'll be here by 6:30 a.m. I'm betting on 8 or so. I've learned not to get upset when he predictably misses our agreed-upon departure time. It's good for my blood pressure, and good for preserving our brotherly love.

I discovered last year that Chris is a Starbucks coffee snob: just has to have a Grande cup of that bitter, hand-tremor-causing brew they call dark roast before life can go on. "How about that truck stop?" I suggest about 30 miles out of Indy. "Truckers drink lots of coffee, so I'm sure it's decent." He eyes me as if I were suggesting he try some hemlock tea.

"I ain't touchin' that swill," he declares, sounding offended. Eventually, we locate a Starbucks, thanks to Siri on his iPhone, about a 10-minute drive off the U.S. 31 North exit. Our drive time is already suffering a setback, I complain to myself, wanting to avoid sharing my frustration so early into the trip.

We end up finding the Starbucks in a mall. I wait outside and stretch my hamstrings, leaning on the SUV for balance, while he goes off on his preferred-blend hunt. I take a series of deep breaths. I check my phone for messages from work. I check it again. Twenty minutes later we're back on the road: his headache averted; his customary morning-caffeinated buzz keeping him reasonably sane and easier to get along with. I turn off my watch's chronometer. Sigh in resignation. We'll get there when we get there. Only Zen thinking will save me now.

My custom in preparing for all of our trips north involves setting aside a cardboard box in the corner of my home office as the collection point for provisions, which is good for my morale. I especially savor my growing destined-for-out-of-state stash over the winter, as I long for our return Up North. I pull out the notes I took when closing the cabin last October for items to be sure to bring next season. This year, after so much practice, it's a fairly short list:

- **Long shaft Phillips screwdriver:** Why, I can't recall, but I won't question the wisdom of the reminder. It will come to me when I get there.
- **Small flashlight:** The new one I purchased last year, and loved, with its hard-rubber impact-resistant surface and high-powered lumens, somehow walked off, a typical phenomenon in vacation homes with frequent visitors, especially of the pint-sized variety.
- **Gallon of paint for the new outdoor shed:** We never did finish painting the white trim—time was not on our side last October for chores—fun prevailed.
- **Lake Michigan photo wall calendar:** Janet prefers it there rather than have it here in Indy to remind us of our little piece of Up North paradise. After nearly four decades of marriage, I no longer ask questions about logic, for I am finally trained according to my wife's domestic behavior standards and, as Red Green (Steve Smith) used to say when concluding his Canadian TV comedy show with the Possum Lodge members' Men's Prayer, I admit it: "I'm a man…but I can change…if I have to…I guess." Forever *reluctantly* well trained, that is.
- **Ibuprofen:** For eating when my overexuberance from hiking, biking, walking, and working around the house takes its toll. These days, Gumby I ain't.
- **32-inch digital TV:** An older LG model from our home in Indy, which we replaced with a smart TV this winter. This will be used for watching movies on DVD and catching one or two of the local channels whenever the wind isn't blowing, and we are seated perfectly still—when the reception is as good as it gets. We will never have cable or Wi-Fi in the cabin, which is disappointing to our adult children. We are here to get away from it all, not to bring it all with us.

Once in Traverse City, my brother and I will stop at the Oleson's Food Store on our way out to Cedar to procure our long-weekend store of food and beverages. As learned from previous trips, I will let Chris do his thing and not try to influence his purchases. He will buy steel-cut oats, lots of cheese and eggs, perhaps a four-pack of Michigan's own Founders Breakfast Stout (he's not much of a drinker but will have a beer with me during happy hour each early evening), coffee beans of some exalted variety, electrolyte-restoring health drinks, and other personal essentials. One item he won't buy is Great Lakes Potato Chips. I like to indulge in them as a special treat when visiting the area. "Care for some chips?" I'll ask. I always get a large bag of the Michigan Cherry BBQ variety.

"No man. I stay away from that crap. You should too."

Right.

Once I open the bag, usually later on night one, he will be drawn to the counter by the sound of my crunching and hearty satisfaction, reach in the bag, grab a giant handful, and tell me how tasty they are—"Hey, these are pretty damn good"—and devour the bag's contents in a sitting or two. Happens every year. Which is perfectly fine, as we are here to be foolish and enjoy ourselves without any adult supervision.

Once we arrive at South Green Court, we'll unload, then I'll head upstairs to rest a bit on the incredible memory foam mattress my wife purchased from a doctor friend who bought the king's-ransom-priced bed, slept on it once, didn't like it, and sold it to us at half the price. I'll power nap for 10 minutes, wake up from my snoring, and chuckle at my old-guy-ness. Then I'll sit up, pause, and think, with a smile on my face, *I'm so glad to be here.*

❀

A few years ago, I asked some local friends to open up the cabin for me. Used to be, I would say a few prayers as I turned off South Good Harbor Trail onto Bodus Road, about a quarter mile from the house, that everything would be in good working order: the power, the well pump, the water, the furnace, etc. Then I would check things out, which included dropping down into our crawl space to turn on the water. Our good Cedar neighbors Marie and Paul now do the honors for us. And Paul, a pious man who is deeply involved in the local Catholic church, Holy Rosary, brings an extra spiritual dimension to our prayerful hope for the house to play nice with our wishes for a clean opening. Thankfully, the report I received from Paul a week ago, in anticipation of this trip, was that all systems were go. For years I would handle all of these chores, and happily so. Being a desk jockey keeps my hands soft, so being able to get dirty every now and then is a matter of personal pride: a real man thing. But then, my painful arthritic right hip discouraged me from venturing into the crawl space. Pride aside, we all get by with a little help from our friends.

One year, during opening ceremonies, the fill valve of the toilet in the loft bedroom's half bathroom blew apart, and since the tank lid had been removed, it sprayed water all over while I was in the crawl space, just after I turned on the service. Janet shouted in emergency mode: "Tim! Tim! Get up here quick! There's water pouring down the inside of the walls and it's spilling onto the floor!" I hoisted myself out of the crawl space, dashed upstairs to the loft and shut off the toilet supply valve. Within seconds, the power went out. Janet put two and two together: "Wow—the water leak must have shorted out the power!"

This was clearly impossible. What did, in fact, happen, was that high winds had coincidentally knocked out the power for much of this part of Leelanau County, as my call to Consumers Energy revealed. So we took a stress-relieving break and went over to the Sugar Foot Restaurant, a two-minute drive from the house, and settled our nerves with beer and wet burritos (remarkably, the Sugar Foot had power; outages can be so unpredictable and mysterious when it comes to the extent of affected areas). Much to our surprise, by the time we finished our impromptu dining experience, the power was back on. Usually up in these parts, a windstorm or traffic accident that takes out the power results in at least a half-day wait.

Now, thanks to Paul and Marie, our return is like booking through Airbnb, and all is in readiness for the guests. A much better arrangement, to be sure.

✳

In the evening, I will cook for Chris. He enjoys my "chunky" spaghetti sauce—an Italian sausage and turkey burger-dominated concoction—and ends up wolfing down most of the pot of pasta over the next several days. Supper over, a cold beer within easy reach on the coffee table, and Chris toying with his catalogue of seventies rock for our listening pleasure, I will re-line two of my favorite ultralight spinning reels—a Pflueger and an Okuma—with Berkley Trilene four-pound test, my go-to fishing line brand for years, selecting from one of perhaps a half-dozen spools stored in the closet. I buy new line each year just in case, a ridiculously irrational habit, and so my backup 4-pound test spool collection continues to grow. I'll prep my small tackle box, filling it with new #10 hooks, split shots, a few lures that I'll most likely never use, a few small bobbers that I'll hardly use, and some swivel snaps that I'll seldom use. Just got to have a well-stocked tackle box to impress my fishing buddies, and to help out a brother who seldom brings enough tackle and relies on his big bro to replenish his supplies whenever a needy situation arises. I'll retrieve my khaki fishing vest from the closet, get out my net and hip waders, and pick out some clothes based on the weather report for the following day. Then come morning, we'll fish the Jordan River in Antrim County and have yet another spectacular day in nature for the record books. We'll catch fish too. Mostly brook trout, along with the occasional rainbow and brown. I'll calm down, temporarily released from the ties that bind. For this interlude of reprieve, all will be well.

But the best part of the whole Up North visitation season for me begins way before arrival. It starts on some bitterly cold late February night in Indy when I decide to grab a beer or glass of red wine, put on my down-filled nearly 40-year-old winter coat (which I wear only when the temperature is in the single digits or else I'll overheat), beanie, and gloves and venture outside on my backyard deck to gaze southward at the constellation Orion in the clear, dark winter sky. It is here, at this moment, that I allow myself to think about the approach of warmer days, of making preparations to open up our seasonal home that I miss terribly when away, of that anticipation-filled therapeutic drive north away from Indiana and into Michigan, and of white trillium dotting the woods, announcing spring to all who attend to its glorious declaration. It is always worth the long wait.

BEFORE THE (GOLD) RUSH

The folks at M22, the apparel outfit that has commercially branded the Leelanau County area, just sent me and everyone else on their email list another of their frequent promotional messages. This one is particularly interesting, with its tagline: "Ready. Set. Summer." It shows an attractive female model with her twisting blonde tresses draped over her right shoulder, sporting a new item: the M22 Classic Tank. She is standing in her trendy majorly distressed blue jeans while barefoot in the middle of a two-lane road in front of a covered bridge. Most notably, she is stretching the orange tank top down to highlight the "scoop neck" shirt and what it contains beneath: the woman is obviously braless. Her smile radiates pure Up North bliss. She must be imagining the sweet sound of cash registers going *ca-ching* this summer season as tourists swarm the M22 clothing stores in Glen Arbor and Traverse City.

I get it. Everybody needs to make a buck. But the M-22 countryside in Leelanau County doesn't need sex to sell it. For better, and, unfortunately these days, sometimes for worse, this special place sells itself.

✳

On Memorial Day Weekend 2019, I took Janet to Empire Bluffs for a hike. We've hiked almost all of the Sleeping Bear Dune National Lakeshore's "official" trails, but this one was new to her. As we pulled up to the trailhead, my heart sank. "Wow, that's weird," I murmured. Then verbalized more distinctly, "The parking lot is full. I've never seen that here before. Usually there are maybe three or four vehicles whenever I've made this hike. Summertime included." I kept the pickup truck idling as I looked on in disappointment, hesitant to engage the heavily peopled path.

"Well, it's nice that people are getting out in nature, don't you think?" my ever-optimistic, think-the-best-of-everyone, Love Wins T-shirt-wearing wife replied. I didn't budge. "We're here. So park the truck and let's get going. You don't have to talk to anyone but me."

As usual for the past 37 years, my bride's wish was my command. We hiked the trail, passing a number of other visitors along the way. There were retired couples who passed us quietly, acknowledging our presence by smiling or gently waving as they moved on. There were college-aged and somewhat older twenty-something couples who seemed to glide up the steeper grades with the eager muscles of youth. Then there were young married-with-children couples exposing their online-endangered children to the great outdoors. "See," Janet chided me. "It's all good." But it wasn't, really.

Here's where Janet and I differ: I didn't come here to see other humans happily enjoying their day-hiking experience; I came here to get away from my species, to get far from the madding crowd I live with in Indianapolis. And, there was another problem: many of our fellow hikers were noisy. Though I tried not to catch the substance, if any, of their conversations, they yakked loudly, disturbing the peace—my peace. They brought along their unthinking, self-absorbed, clueless selves, not caring about those around them and the space they were sharing in the woods and on the bluff.

Perhaps I'm being too harsh. Too judgmental. Too impatient. Too crotchety, as Janet labels my "okay, boomer" moodiness these days. Aging will do that to a fella.

A day later, two friends from Indy arrived to stay with us in Cedar for the long weekend, Randy and Susie. They, too, love being outside. Randy is quite the amateur birder and a much-in-demand carpenter steeped in the arts of old home and commercial structure restoration. When he retires, his humble ambition is to be a bird guide. Janet suggested we revisit Empire Bluffs, as the wildflowers were in bloom, carpeting the woodland floor, and they would enjoy the dramatic view of Lake Michigan. To top it off, the woods were teeming with warblers and songbirds in full spring migration to their nesting grounds.

As we drove up the long, steep hill to the trailhead, it was "deja vu all over again"—with a vengeance: not only was the small parking lot brimming with approximately 30 vehicles, but just as many SUVs, pickup trucks, and cars were parked along the road, with more streaming in as we contemplated our next steps. I uttered some choice words, adding, "Sorry, but I can't handle this. Let's go where they aren't." Randy concurred: "I'm with you. Besides, you're driving."

"Say goodbye to Empire Bluffs Amusement Park," I growled, as we wheeled around and headed to Alligator Hill, another trail in Sleeping Bear Dunes National Lakeshore. When it came to tourists, it ended up being a much better destination, though the parking lot was nearly full, another first in my experience.

I can be reactionary. When I take a deep breath and calm down in such situations, I do ask myself, "Who am I to judge?" Yet the answer is always the same: *me, that's who.* Like most Americans, I tend to want to control my surroundings, my experiences, and I'm especially picky about whom I'm sharing them with. When I'm seeking relative solitude, any outsider in my proximity who isn't playing by my rules, which includes being quiet and no idle chatter, will get my blood pressure up. I guess, like the Sammy Davis, Jr. hit song declares, *I (just) gotta be me,* warts and all. My life coach, my personal bodhisattva, dear Janet, keeps me working at improving my karma, however. Like it or not. She'll keep me grounded throughout our hikes, providing walking therapy for me, such as: "Oh, those people aren't bothering us. Live and let live.... Hey, look at how blue the sky is.... Check out those wildflowers, honey; gorgeous, aren't they? I bet we could find some morels out here; let's look.... Oh!—is that an indigo bunting? There—at two o'clock...." If it weren't for the guiding influence of her saintly presence, I would truly be lost.

*

During our first week in Cedar for the summer (currently I get two, usually taken one at a time about a month apart; the good Lord willing, in a few years or so, my prayer is that I'll get several consecutive months), the week of June 17, 2019, we could sense that the annual tourist invasion was gathering. Biking along the Heritage Trail near the Dune Climb on Tuesday, our Cedar neighbor Paul and I saw the early tourists going up and down the heart-pounding sandy grade. "The advance guard," Paul mumbled as we passed. Perhaps 50 paying customers were on the slope. In a few weeks, the dune would be crawling with people. Literally. "I suppose it's inevitable."

The following morning, Janet and I took our dog, Benny, for a stroll through Leland. After an hour walking through the neighborhood east of M-22, we stopped by Carlson's Fishery in Fishtown. We had a craving for some fresh-caught lake trout, and Carlson's always delivers.

The young woman behind the counter pleasantly welcomed me, the only customer at the time. Then, as she began to wrap the lake trout I'd chosen, I had a change of heart. "Sorry, but I'd like that piece as well," I added, pointing to another particularly appealing filet.

"No problem," she cheerily said, forgiving my indecisiveness while ceasing her brown paper wrapping to grab the additional filet. "For now."

We both laughed. I understood. "Different story in a few weeks, eh?" I asked knowingly.

She stopped smiling and shook her head woefully. "They're coming. I'm bracing myself."

"It will be good for business, though," I encouraged.

"That it will," she agreed, regaining her business sense. She resumed smiling when she handed me the skillfully packaged trout. "Have a great day!" Fresh lake trout dinner now firmly in hand, I bid her the same.

❉

While on this respite from the rat race, I read Fr. Richard Rohr's book *The Divine Dance: The Trinity and Your Transformation*. In the foreword, written by author William Paul Young, he sagely advises that we should "live only inside the grace of one single day." I tried. But I was seeing signs of the coming horde everywhere. Signs that were hard to ignore. The area party stores were stocking up. The beer-soaked Polka Festival in Cedar would happen this weekend. And before we knew it, July 4th would bring the National

Cherry Festival and the surge of vacationers wanting their slice of Up North heaven. Let the games begin.

One evening during our first summer week here, Paul, his wife, Marie, and his brother-in-law Mike came over for cocktails and dinner on our front porch deck. While sipping a nice red French blend, Chateau de Fontenelles, and swatting the persistent mosquitoes this most pleasant time of year brings (nothing is free), I mentioned my exchange earlier that day with the clerk at Carlson's. Paul laughed. And related.

"Last night I drove down to Buntings Market in Cedar to pick up a few things," he explained. "The checkout lady is a friend of mine from church. I asked her how business was. She said, 'It's already starting.' I said, 'Already? Wow. I know how you feel.' And she shook her head and said, 'No, Paul; no you don't. We've already waited on some real doozies. And it ain't even summer just yet.' Poor thing. She's right. This is only the scouting party."

In 2017, 1.7 million people—downstaters, other Midwesterners, Americans from every state in the union, and people from many foreign lands—visited Sleeping Bear Dunes National Lakeshore, Leelanau County, and the Traverse City area. They brought their kids, their curiosity, their good and occasionally bad natures, and, perhaps most important of all, their money. But no doubt about it, that's a lot of people and a lot of pressure on such an otherwise pristine environment. Yet I tell myself that the window of opportunity for visitors and local businesses is small, the season short, and things return to their natural state on Tuesday following Labor Day, as if it never happened.

※

Doing our domestic upkeep thing, which must occur now and then during a vacation when one is fortunate enough to own such property, Janet and I went into town (Traverse City) to buy a closet door to swap out with an older one and some shrubs to plant around the front deck. We stopped at the Duncan L. Clinch Marina for a refreshing walk along Grand Traverse Bay. As we walked, we happened upon a pontoon boat putting in at the public launch. Normally, this wouldn't stop us in our tracks. However, this did. The dock was nearly underwater, the concrete drive had disappeared, and the parking lot was flooding, as was the road to the lot. Lake Michigan's water levels are up dramatically, approaching record levels. Beaches throughout the Sleeping Bear Dunes area have shrunk dramatically due to the encroaching water. Vacationers will be surprised, and some will be very disappointed. They will simply have to adjust. Or not.

I called Paul's older brother, Craig, my friend of many years, trying to arrange a day of trout fishing, just the two of us. Our schedules weren't in sync, though. So we spent some time catching up. I happened to mention the high-water phenomenon at Lake Michigan. Craig didn't hesitate to jump into a commentary: "It ain't global warming, the mantra of the libs. It's a cycle that's way beyond our hundred years or so of weather recording. The planet is old, bro, and it's not in the business of making humans happy. Someone has seen all this before. Remember back in the late eighties or so when Lake Michigan was at a 'record' low level? People need to get over it. This, too, shall pass." I can always count on Craig to give me his unvarnished take on the world, with little prompting. Up North candor is easy to come by.

❋

So it goes with the oncoming gold rush, tourists bringing millions of dollars to leave behind, injecting northwest lower Michigan with cash to cover operating costs for much of the remainder of the year for those in the tourist-catering business. As with farming here, tourists just happen to be another lucrative cash crop. More than a few of them are decent people, first-timers who will fall in love with the area and return as customers who will treat it preciously, reverently, and perhaps buy a seasonal home or a vacant lot full of dreams about future days here in God's country. Someday, some of them will even find themselves like the locals, dreading the coming of the "Fudgies." The Fudgies that they once were. That Janet and I, admittedly, once were too. Conversion has a way of putting things into perspective.

GONE FISHIN'

Simon Peter said to them, "I am going fishing." They said to him,
"We will also come with you."

—John 21:3

My Up North partner-in-crime checked in with me at the start of our
summer vacation in mid-June 2017, wondering what kind of diversions I might be game for in trying to recover my soul from the trials and
tribulations of big city living in Indianapolis. "Well, how about a day out
on the Jordan?" Craig suggested. "Just you and me, though. Don't get me
wrong, I love Janet like a sister. But hey, we need some time together. I only
see ya a couple times a year, bro." My dear wife was fine with the guys-only
adventure. Having surrendered the threat of making her a golf widow long
ago, I typically can secure permission to go fishing with the boys once or
twice a year with little heavy lifting to convince her. And as every married
couple knows, there are things men talk about that belong out of range of
the feminine ear—and vice versa. We all need some distance between each
other every now and then. Janet treasures her downtime at our cabin in
Cedar. Benny, her Pomeranian, will rest on her lap while she reads a novel
on a sun-drenched deck, with birdsong the soundtrack, and no husband
around to disturb her timeout. Win-win.

I was up at 4:30 a.m., just ahead of first light, which comes fast as the
summer solstice approaches. Learning from many earlier mistake-laden outings, I put all my fishing gear together in one location the night before;

morning befuddlement can be the enemy of a forgetful fisherman. My preparations had one small dent, however: I forgot to pick up bait at the Cedar Hardware earlier in the day. "Ain't no biggie," Craig reassured me on the phone as I stood on the deck sipping coffee while consciousness slowly returned to me. "There's bait available all over Antrim County. We'll stop at Mancelona Sports; it's on the way. See you in about an hour." We rendezvoused in Traverse City at the Duncan L. Clinch Marina, where Janet and Benny kindly dropped me off. She was fine with driving into town: another chance to take in the splendor of Grand Traverse Bay on a morning walk along the marina.

We arrived in Kalkaska about 7 a.m. on Friday and stopped at the Shell station at M-72 and U.S. 131 to fuel up. They didn't have bait; but they did have donuts. "Want one?" Craig asked.

"I'll pass. Do you?"

"Nah. Just bein' nice. They aren't good for my girlish figure."

Nor was bait available at 7:30 a.m. on Friday in Mancelona. According to the door sign, Mancelona Sports would open at 8 a.m. "Let's just mosey over to Shirley's Cafe to kill some time with a manly breakfast. There's no hurry. The fish will be there waiting for us," Craig proclaimed.

While at Shirley's, catching up over coffee and corned beef hash, sausage, and eggs-over-easy (thank God for statins), my friend decided to climb up on his rightward-leaning soapbox about our political state here in the good ol' US of A. Maybe it was the sausage. Or maybe it was just having an audience. The young waitress, with a laidback air and easy smile, didn't flinch; I'm sure she has heard worse in these parts before, hunters and fishermen being, well, hunters and fishermen. Thankfully, the restaurant was almost dead, with just one other table of diners across the room. I listened politely to Craig, agreeing with his general state of dissatisfaction with "The Swamp," yet not quite aligned with him philosophically. The country was divided, to be sure. Liberals, conservatives; we're all at each other's throats. These days, it seems as though we're being drawn into making America hate again. When the echo of his righteous tirade eventually became obvious to him, he paused, then said in a low, apologetic, caught-in-the-act voice: "I'm sorry. I don't know what got into me. Hey, pass me the ketchup."

"It's okay, dude. I know how you are. Just eat your breakfast and let's go fishing." He laughed, we small-talked and finished eating, I paid the tab, and we went and picked up some bait and beer and lottery tickets. "And a small bottle of Baileys for a wee skosh, you know, when the fishin' is slow," he confessionally explained to the clerk. "And, well, why stop now: how about a pack of Marlboros." Turning away from her while thumbing through his roll of cash and looking at me, he said, "You may not believe this, but I haven't had a smoke in at least two weeks." I didn't. But what are friends for. We got out of there with just the essentials.

We drove through the Jordan River Valley's two-tracks, an obstacle course of muddy water-filled ruts and the occasional downed tree limb, navigating to our usual spot to park the truck. It was sunny, the wind was calm, and the temperature would eventually climb into the mid-70s. Craig dropped his pickup truck's tailgate and we sat and pulled on our waders: his, chest; mine, hip. We tied bandanas around our heads, wore long-sleeved shirts, and sprayed on several varieties of "bug dope" to try to keep away the no-see-ums and black flies. Always a losing battle. Yet for every Michigan trout fisherman from mid-May into June, it's just part of the program.

Craig and I are bait fishermen—no *A River Runs Through It* fly-fishing highfalutin'-ness for us. We got out our ultralight rods and spinning reels, tying on small #10 hooks and lead weights, Craig arranging his preferred three-way swivel setup. Not me. In the fast-moving late spring river water and with all the downed timber throughout the river, it would be "snag city," as we called it. I'd rather take a simpler approach in re-rigging to get my line back in the water ASAP. But Craig, a fine artist, a painter, is also an artist in all things. So having an elegant presentation for the wary trout mattered.

We were parked about 75 yards from a footbridge over the river, our favorite place from which to begin the day's fishing, then typically heading upstream from there. There was just one other vehicle, most likely day-hikers. As is frequently the case here, we had this stretch of the river to ourselves.

About an hour into my trout fishing trance, I looked up and Craig was no longer in sight. Usually, we work the river with each of us on opposite banks. I wasn't concerned by my apparent aloneness, for I knew he was nearby and kept me within sight. Craig is from a long line of proud outdoorsmen. He knows geology, geography, astronomy, meteorology, water, fish, birds, mammals, firearms, bait and tackle. Uncannily, he also knows precisely when to have a smoke; when to crack a beer; and just when to pierce the air and sweeten the moment with a hearty laugh. Perhaps trout fishing with Craig would qualify with the late psychologist and philosopher William James as a fitting selection of one's variety of religious experiences. For me, on a trout stream with Craig, it always is.

※

I was running out of bait. Early on I could tell that I had been shorted, as the living ball of leaf worms looked to be considerably under the promised 30 per container. Then again, I had been frequently losing bait from missed hits. When in doubt while fishing, blame it on the bait shop.

I had landed a few keepers, several 10-inches-or-so brook trout. I had also enjoyed two major strikes, momentary adrenaline teases, missing them both. This caused me to reactively swear "damn it" or "shit" in hushed tones, followed by a chuckle of resignation, then back at it. That's fishing. So to replenish my bait, I started back toward the bridge, casting now and then along the way as if making wishes. As I approached the footbridge, I could hear Craig's unmistakable hearty voice and gales of laughter carrying along the stream, then saw him standing on the bank beside the bridge talking with two old-timers. I stopped within earshot beneath a canopy of tall cedars and fished a bit. Apparently, they had taken some brag-worthy browns last night.

"Wow. You guys did good," Craig expressed admiringly. "The big browns tend to come out at night; it's the best time. Congratulations on your catch. God love ya. Have a good day, men."

Moments later, I joined him. "They caught some huge browns night fishin'. In the 5- to 8-pound range. Whoa," he emphasized. Until my personal record rainbow catch the previous year, such talk had been the stuff of myth to me.

It was almost noon. "Time for a beer," I suggested as we walked toward the truck.

"Already got you covered," Craig said, reaching into his canvas shoulder bag and handing me a pint can of Bell's Two-Hearted Ale. The wet shriek of aluminum pull-tabs was music to our sunburned and black-fly-bitten ears. Though the beer was on the warm side, it was pure refreshment.

And so we began to converse as we resupplied, covering the usual territory. Craig lighting a cigarette and confessing how much he would like to quit. *Bullshit.* Craig talking about women and the loves of his life and trying to get some satisfaction, like Mick Jagger can't. *More bullshit.* Me talking about how much I want to live in northwest lower Michigan and don't want to return to Indy, ever. *Definite bullshit*—that is, unless I get a divorce. Even though my dear wife says she'll move away from her ancestral central Indiana home, she won't. That's just love talking. Too many grandchildren have arrived, and too many family members rely on her for insightful, no-nonsense guidance and encouragement as they struggle with stuff large and small. Me quitting my leadership role in an urban charter school and doing something less stressful, less rapidly aging? For now, well, that's *total bullshit.*

How I miss these bullshit sessions. Fishing is the perfect backdrop for them. It gives us permission to be our damn silly male selves, with no witnesses, and no regrets.

Turning to his bag of tricks, Craig tied on a wet fly that a fishing guide friend who works the Manistee River swears by for trout, and can be used with spinning reel and rod. "I missed two monster hits earlier," I offered. "Me too!" he exclaimed. "They're out there, amigo. I'll see what this rig can do. Meanwhile, let's have one more beer and then we'll quit screwin' around, and go catch some fish. What do you say to that?"

"Hit me."

＊

The fishing slowed in early afternoon as the clouds lessened and the sunshine blazed. So we jumped in the truck and traveled along the river on the two-track that shadowed it. Without warning, Craig braked the Chevy Silverado and pointed to a large culvert emptying water into a tributary stream off the Jordan. "Looks like hot brookie territory to me. Why don't you give it a shot here and I'll go over to the river," which was on the other side of the road. Craig always puts his fishing buddies on the most promising spots without first taking them for himself. Gentleman, scholar, scoundrel; what's not to love.

My first cast from atop the metal culvert resulted in a keeper—an 11-inch brook trout. After a few more casts, I moved downstream then slid down a birch-and-cedar-wooded embankment to a small clearing on the water's edge. I gingerly felt the stream bed for purchase; it was black and silty, often a sign of quicksand-like mud. But it held me, and I waded out farther, casting around outstretched tree branches. Within minutes, I landed several more brookies just right for the skillet. I lost the biggest one, though—almost 14 inches—when it flexed mightily and jumped right out of my left hand as I went to unhook it. You gotta laugh.

Ever on the move, we drove to another of Craig's favorite holes. "I want to put you on a monster brown, and here is the place. My brother Freddy nailed one here on opening day this year." It took some doing to get to this bend in the river, pushing through chest-high scrub while holding our rods aloft to avoid the lines catching. In a few minutes we arrived. There was plenty of open space to cast. Craig sat down on a log for a smoke while praying for me to hook a Michigan Master Angler trophy trout.

I sent the leaf worm gliding downstream, and it disappeared as intended in the dark hole in the bend. "That's it," he coached. "Here he comes..." Instant action: lots of small trout aggressively competing for food. In minutes, I caught a half-dozen under-limit rainbows and browns. However, try as I might, no monster this time. No doubt the big one was watching and fish-giggling at my folly.

"Anyway, it sure is nice here," he commented. Indeed it was. Tranquility. Indianapolis was nowhere within sight. Nor was my vexing constant stream of decision-making and problem-solving, what I get paid for. "Workin' for the man," as my five-year-old grandson says so comically and so way beyond his years, the term mischievously planted by his father. Yet here, along a trout stream, free at last.

"Next time," Craig said in hopeful conviction. "There will always be a next time, bro. Ready to head out?"

We gathered our gear and turned to go, to hike back through the shin tangle and return to the truck. Two minutes later, Craig suddenly yelped and went totally airborne as if he had just jumped out of a skydiving plane, arms and legs outstretched. Then just as suddenly, gravity pulled him to earth, where he face-planted with a groan.

"You all right?" I called to him.

"Sonuvabitch," he cursed. "Yeah, yeah, I'm fine." It was his stock answer whenever he did something potentially hurtful to himself. It would be futile to tell him that he needs to be more careful, especially at his age; he would never listen anyway.

As he wiped the mud from his jacket sleeves and spit out marshy detritus, I wisecracked, "I scored that an eight out of 10. Excellent degree of difficulty, but you didn't stick the landing at the end of the routine."

"Kiss my ass," he grumbled, then started laughing until he winced.

❄

Ever the excellent fishing guide bearing the best interests of his client— friend—in mind, Craig drove us to a nearby creek for me to do some "crickin'," as folks Up North call it. It's hard to believe that such a small body of water—five or six feet wide and no more than four to six inches deep—holds fish worth fishing for. Yet as I waded in, I nearly stepped on an eight-inch brook trout that scurried off into the safety of an undercut. "See!" Craig exclaimed, laughing.

As I held onto a maple tree and reached over an undercut in the bank and dangled a leaf worm in the babbling water, I glanced over at Craig. He was stripping off his chest waders and soaked blue jeans (from the sweat of fishing exertion and not from a leak in the rubber) and putting on some shorts. Then he pulled out a folding chair from the back of the truck and settled in for a rest. He was smarting from his earlier unplanned aerial acrobatics. But despite the pain from his fall, he was intent upon squeezing out as much time as possible here in the woods together, fishin'.

While trying to walk quietly in the leafy deadfall so as not to startle any brook trout, I successfully spooked some woodcocks. They whistled close by at the altitude of my head, flying upstream. I looked back. Craig was smoking another cigarette, laughing at me flushing the birds.

"You ready to head out?" I asked knowingly.

"Yeah. I'm toast. That spill took it out of me. Gettin' hungry too. I could really go for a burger. How 'bout you?" We stopped at McDonald's on M-66. Craig ordered a Big Mac Meal; I had the same. "I would have ordered a Sad Meal, but it just wouldn't be right for the occasion, you know? And hey, don't worry, I won't tell Janet. It must be tough living with a health-nut nazi."

Ravenous from my exposure to fresh air and the intense attention fishing required and the river wading here and there, I quickly dispatched the gut bomb. Craig took his sweet time, savoring every bite. "Wish I would stop eating this junk," he said candidly. But, like smoking, the best treats are the forbidden ones. And though I didn't confirm it aloud, I enjoyed my Big Mac too.

❋

The drive back to Traverse City was fun, despite the inevitable sadness that comes with the conclusion of such rare and precious events like trout fishing with your best friend. Craig held the steering wheel, and so he held court. Deeply conservative, he shared his views on America. Deeply Catholic, too, in his own quirky orthodox way, he shared his views on everybody else. The ghost of Barack Hussein Obama II continued to haunt him. Liberals were migrating to Traverse City as if an invasive species overtaking Lake Michigan. Socialists—make that Marxists—were threatening America. Radical Islam lurked as a growing menace. All seemed to be lost. But then the talk turned—or returned—to women, creatures of great mystery and imagination to us. The female form has naturally long attracted his artistic attention. And my more pedestrian appreciation. Like catnip.

The last half hour of our return to TC was uproarious. X-rated. Juvenile. We had tears in our eyes from the ridiculous quality of our conversation. The obscene adverbs and adjectives, the nasty nouns and verbs.

"Oh my God," Craig said exhaustedly, "this is bad, really bad. I gotta go to confession this week. Fr. Jim will have to brace himself. I think this one sealed the deal for me doing a billion years in purgatory. Jeez." Sinning and paying the price for it is a weirdly attractive cycle for us Catholics.

"You like to remind me that Christ was a fisherman, as were his apostles," I said, catching my breath. "I wonder if their talk got a bit racy from time to time. Guess we'll never really know."

"No, we won't," Craig responded, looking straight ahead, wondering along with my train of thought. "But I think He'd be okay with us being silly. We should just keep this between you and me and The Big Guy. Know what I'm sayin', Vern?"

"Amen."

Our windows were down and the wind whistled in the late afternoon warm June air as we drove on M-72 through Traverse City to our prearranged meeting with Janet at the Tom's Food Market parking lot on West Bay. We had fresh fish in the cooler and a few empty pint cans: evidence of a day well spent on the river. In minutes, this adventure would be over. Yet the afterglow would linger well into the evening, until a heavy sleep would come upon me, the old guy who doesn't get out much or nearly enough. And perhaps the large dose of outdoor stimulation and deliciously poor dietary choices for the day would cause me to dream of dying, and rising, at a glorious trout stream like the Jordan. That would be Paradise.

The One That Didn't Get Away

These days, most of us tend to carry photos of things that are important to us on our iPhones and Androids—like our children, grandchildren, vacation spots, pets—and most of us tend to forget we ever took millions of digital pics in the first place. But for me, since May 13, 2016, there is one photo I have pulled out every time the subject of fishing has come up. And I'm often the one to bring it up in the first place, with good cause.

My youngest brother, Chris, and I traveled to northern Michigan that weekend to open up my seasonal home in Cedar, which is about 13 miles northwest of Traverse City. The drive from Indy to Cedar is roughly 415 miles, so we had plenty of time to catch up on our annual trip together. Chris is a Six Sigma Black Belt trainer for Eli Lilly & Company, and along the way he interrogated me in his painfully meta-analytical way about some of the challenges I was facing as the then-interim CEO for an urban Indianapolis public charter school. That killed a lot of time while putting me in the mood to distance myself not only geographically but mentally from my administrative toil.

Once in Traverse City, we stopped at Gander Mountain (which has since closed), and Chris quickly blew through a $100 gift certificate, buying a Shakespeare ultra-light rod and reel combo, a pair of chest waders, and some Mepps spinners. These days I only fish in Michigan—clear, clean water snob that I've become from my exposure Up North. The chocolate murkiness of bodies of water here in central Indiana, habitat friendly to catfish and carp, no longer cuts it for me—and my ever-stocked tackle box was good to go, aside from some #10 Eagle Claw hooks and split shot weights I needed for when Chris would run out, which was inevitable.

When fishing with my local buddy Craig, we typically drive to the Jordan River before first light so that we're wetting our lines just after sunup. But after the long drive from Indy, Chris and I didn't get to the river until noon. Not that I cared. Since I turned 60 in 2016, I find rest has moved much higher on my priority list. Taking things slowly is taking things in.

We parked at the usual spot near Pinney Bridge. I first came here with Craig about 15 years ago. Ever since, I make at least one pilgrimage a year to this holy place in the heart of the Jordan River Valley. We stepped out of Chris's SUV and stepped into a state of bliss. Our city-boy senses were flooded by migrating warblers and other songbirds, mourning cloak and spring azure butterflies mud-puddling for minerals, cedar and tamarack trees lining the riverside, and the burbling picturesque stream filled with trout awaiting just the right presentation of bait to hook their interest.

"Damn, I love this place," Chris said, saying it all. I smiled in agreement as we prepped to approach the river and test our luck. We pulled on our waders; loaded up our fishing vests with bait and mini-tackle boxes, gum, and energy bars (to stave off hunger and keep us on the river longer); and headed for the bridge. Crossing an adjacent creek, we then hiked upstream along the slightly worn path of fishermen who had been out two weeks earlier for opening day. After about a quarter mile of hiking, it was time to fish. Chris paused, then kept going…right out of sight. I like to keep my fishing partner within eyesight, just as Craig had taught me long ago. You never know when you might need a helping hand to land the big one or get pulled out of river-bottom quicksand. But Chris, well, he has a mind of his own; I wasn't about to stop him.

I trout fish maybe twice a year if I'm lucky. Oddly, I seem to catch a trout—or minimally, get a strike—on my first cast. I've never understood this phenomenon. Am I relaxed and dialed in upon arrival, not yet jittery from a day of snags and misses? Is the good Lord doing me a cosmic favor for all of my hard work to earn my rare riverside reprieve? Whatever the case, this year was no different. First cast, and I hooked a 10-inch brown. Chris was long gone. Too bad. One-upmanship is a constant in our ongoing expression of brotherly love, so I missed the opportunity to rub it in—for now.

No matter where I went along the Jordan, every few casts generated a strike. I was fishing with leaf worms—my preferred bait here—and occasionally impaled half of a crawler on a hook to see what action that might attract. About an hour into it, a Walt's crawler floating downriver gave this flatlander the fishing thrill of a lifetime.

It was around 1:30 p.m., which is not typically the golden hour for fishing. The black flies were in clouds that day; the only slight reprieve was backing away from the water's edge for a few seconds before they caught wind of me again. I had two varieties of bug dope with me—Off! Deep Woods Insect Repellant and Avon's Skin So Soft—and sprayed them with abandon. The buggers would zoom in close to the surface of my skin and hesitate a bit, but eventually they would break through my defense and bite just below my baseball cap, leaving a circular trail of bleeding, itchy welts around my head by day's end. But my Zen mind overcame most of the carnivorous harassment, as I didn't drive all the way Up North from Indy to let the bugs get me down.

The Jordan was running fast, as it typically does in early May, swollen by the April showers and snowmelt. It's a technically difficult river to fish, riddled with downed trees and remnants—from the logging more than 100 years ago—that stabbed the banks and embedded themselves in the river bottom. The hydraulics from the rushing water working its way around and under these obstacles have created countless inviting dark holes, making for perfect trout habitat.

I stopped about 20 feet upstream from a large, mostly submerged tree trunk that stretched across half the river's width, perhaps 20 yards at that point. Intuitively, as are many things with fishing, I decided to go with the crawler. With the size 10 hook and two medium split shots attached, I cast the four-pound test line upriver, letting the line spool out once it passed me, and I watched as it slid toward the dark hole below the log.

Just as the worm disappeared into the black void beneath the tree trunk, I turned the reel crank slightly to stop the drifting bait. Instantly, I felt a strike and saw a fish-belly flash of white. It looked to be a decent-sized trout. I immediately jerked the rod up and set the hook. I made sure to keep the rod raised and tension on. (A year earlier on an early October outing, I missed a nice brown in the Jordan near Chestonia Bridge when the trout hit within 10 feet of me on a retrieve while I was wading the river. I was so surprised by the strike that I failed to keep the rod tip up—even as my fishing guide Craig was shouting at me to do so. I swore that would never happen again; lesson learned.)

I began to reel in the line. But even with the drag set appropriately, I wasn't making much headway, as the fish was fighting for its life. It was pulling hard, back toward the safety of the hole, so I added more drag tension. Feeling the resistance, the trout came hurtling out of the water. "Holy shit!" I said aloud in a fisherman's prayer, as I realized this was no ordinary trout. In my experience, it was a monster; I had never caught a trout anywhere near this size. And my self-doubt was suddenly expressing itself.

I realized that my net was nowhere near me and Chris was long gone. Luckily, the route the trout took to seek cover was toward the end of the log closest to the bank. I reeled as best I could to keep it away from ducking deeper under the surface and into the hole where I would be sure to lose it. The trout suddenly turned and made a run in my direction, then, whispering "Dear Lord," I somehow managed to horse the furious fish up on shore.

My heart was pounding and my adrenaline surging; I began taking deep breaths to try to settle down. The moment was so extraordinary that my body was trembling with uncontrollable joy. Days like this don't come my way often.

The trout was a rainbow, easily identified by the distinct pink horizontal stripe running the length of its body, and would measure exactly 24 inches and weigh nearly five pounds. Despite my overloaded senses, I managed to get the fish on a stringer and dropped it into the water. I stared at my catch, awestruck, reveling in this rare moment of fishing achievement. Over the years I had caught mostly browns and brookies in the Jordan, and an occasional rainbow. But I had never taken a trout over 14 inches. This was my world record.

At that point I stopped fishing. I shouted for Chris a few times, but got no response. So I waited, exultant. A lifetime nonsmoker, I would have lit a cigarette if I had one; the victorious moment called for it. About 45 minutes after I landed the trout, Chris came sauntering up. "I heard you calling, but I didn't want to leave my spots."

"Well, good thing I wasn't dying," I responded, but held no grudge. If you find a promising trout spot, it's not easy to pull yourself away. He was forgiven.

"Catch anything?" he asked. I could hardly contain myself.

"You?" I responded, without answering just yet, rather fiendish of me.

"Naw. Lots of bites—and just as many misses."

"Well, all I got is this," I said coyly as I slowly reeled in the stringer toward us. The rainbow's dorsal fin broke the surface, and Chris exclaimed, "Oh my God! Look at the size of that thing!" I pulled it out and held it up, and Chris took a few photos for me. "Damn, man, I need to catch one of those," he said, exposing his natural fisherman's envy. He suddenly started gathering up his gear to get back at it, all excited by my catch, and the promise it suggested for one of his very own. He just couldn't let me get away with this.

Chris fished for another hour with a greater sense of urgency, and I casted halfheartedly a few times, going through the motions in a contented daze. I was spent by the emotional thrill of my personally historic catch, which in hindsight was foolish, for why not catch a few more while I was there? I was overflowing with gratitude and just wanted to stay put in my moment of trout-fishing success. For years, for almost every opener in late April, Craig and his brother Paul would send me photos of big brown trout held with two hands for emphasis (if not exaggeration) and their triumphant fishermen's grins. Now I was finally on the board.

Thankfully, Chris ended up not getting shut out, catching a few brook trout that put a smile on his face. I was happy for him. And really happy for me.

"Was that luck or skill?" the Six Sigma Blackbelt inquired with furrowed brow as we drove toward Cedar with my trophy fish to show my Michigan fishing buddies and make my glory official.

"Both," I answered. And we both laughed.

Driving down the hills of M-72 near Traverse City when the sublime sight of East Grand Traverse Bay dramatically appears as if revealed in a Pure Michigan campaign TV spot, I informed Chris with my newly acquired lunker trout-fishing expertise, "Your fish is out there, man. It took me nearly twenty years to earn this one. Have patience." Like I never did—until now.

CRICKIN'

That first morning during my inaugural trout camp with Craig and his clan in 2004—comprising several brothers and their buddies, Craig's dad, some uncles and cousins, men all and only per tradition—he and I had just pulled on our waders and rigged our lines and were walking toward Pinney Bridge on the Jordan River. Though I had trout fished on the Boardman River with Craig on several summer canoe outings, this experience was special: being invited to fish camp was no small honor. "Only select fellas deemed worthy of the experience are welcome to join us," Craig noted on the phone when the offer first came, in the dead of winter, when fish long for mayfly feeds to come and trout fishers dream of fresh-caught trout in the frying pan. "This is always special for our family. Can't wait." And now the waiting was over, and our moods were buoyant with expectancy: soon, it would be *fish on!* We were sure of it.

As we approached the bridge, our point of departure to stalk the hungry spring-enlivened rainbow, brown, and brook trout, Craig pointed out the five-foot wide creek running off the river, just to our right. "There are fish in there—nice fish," he said in a low voice just above a whisper, as if in church.

"Seriously?" I asked, his disbelieving friend. The creek water ran about 18 inches deep.

"Hell yes," he said, raising his voice slightly, so as to make his point while not disturbing any trout within earshot. "A few years ago, my brother Fred was walking alongside me just like you're doing right now. He dropped a leaf worm in and wham!—a 14-inch brook trout nailed it. I kid you not, bro."

I veered over and stared at the modest little stream with a barely discernible current, imagining Fred hooking that brookie. I couldn't conceive of such an occurrence; it seemed like something out of a children's book. Nonetheless, the possibility appealed to my inner boy. The wily trout are well camouflaged in their environs. The longer I stood there, the more easily I could envision a brookie beneath an undercut along the banks of the river a few feet away, just waiting for the next meal to float by....

❄

Eleven years later, Craig and I managed to negotiate a day on the Jordan in early July. I manage this special occasion perhaps twice a year, my work schedule and vacationing in northwest lower Michigan with my wife who doesn't fish being the prevailing conditions of this life. And Craig gets in his chores the day before, when he springs the question to his sweetie. So the release time is sacred to us two fishermen.

It was 90 degrees and sunny and the fishing was slow. After a full morning of hiking up and down and in and out of the Jordan in our waders, Craig suggested we try something else. He handed me a bottle of Labatt Blue Light, opened one up for himself, we quickly killed this first beer of the day, consecrating our outing, and jumped in his Chevy Silverado and drove Pinney Bridge Road, a stretch which follows the course of the river, until we came upon a creek in the woods. "OK, let's go crickin'," Craig ordered. And once again, I was a doubting Thomas.

"Do you really think there are fish worth catching in there?" I asked. He looked at me like the crick-fishin' trainee I was.

"Absolutely. We just have to approach with stealth; trout are super sensitive to vibration and noise. You'll spook 'em if you're not careful. Hook a leaf worm through the nose and let the line glide with the current; no split shot needed. You'll see, grasshopper," he predicted, referencing a nickname given Kwai Chang Caine (actor David Carradine) by Master Po (Keye Luke) while in training to become a Shaolin priest in the *Kung Fu* TV show in the mid-seventies. Friends as characters; characters for friends.

The creek had eroded the land for who knows how long, and so the surface of the shallow water was about three or four feet below us. I looked for small holes shaped by water pressure directed by limbs and other obstructions in the stream, as well as undercuts where brook trout like to locate. Within minutes I had hooked my first brook trout while crickin': eight inches of feistiness. Craig heard the splashing made by my catch and we both laughed approvingly. "See?" he said in affirmation.

I caught perhaps a dozen 8-10-inch brook trout in the next 45 minutes and missed double that amount. Craig only stayed out for about 15 minutes, as he was sweating profusely and not feeling well. "I'm heading back to the truck; I think I have heatstroke. I need to lie down. You stay at it for a while." I was mildly concerned about him; but frankly, I was more concerned about catching fish. I was hooked on crickin'.

When I returned to the truck, Craig was sleeping under the tailgate, his chest waders pulled down to his waist. He was groggy but he would make it. "Did you slay 'em?" he asked weakly.

"Oh my God, yes," I responded. "You okay?"

"Chest waders in this heat was a bad idea. But hey, you got to go crickin' and that's what counts." Craig enjoys putting a buddy onto a prime fishing spot even more than improving his own fishing chances. I have found this hospitable trait common among Michigander outdoorsmen and -women. Sharing the fun brings its own special joy.

✳

Several years ago, I was visiting Craig's brother Paul, who lives on a hillside above County Road 651 North, about a mile from our seasonal retreat in Cedar. As we chatted, I asked if he had ever fished in Victoria Creek, which runs on his south-side neighbor's property and courses parallel to the road. "Nope. Probably some brookies in there, I'm guessin'. I'll ask my neighbor if you can have permission to wet a line." Whereas once I wouldn't have considered the creek fishable, having seen the light, I couldn't pass up the opportunity.

That night, Paul texted me: "Permission granted. Hit the creek in the morning and see what you can do. I expect a full report."

I didn't get over to Paul's until after 1 p.m. Had to wake up from vacation sleep, have my morning tea on the deck with Janet, review our current state of bliss and plans for the whatever-we-want-to-do day, go for a walk near the Old Course at Sugar Loaf and find some stray golf balls from unknown contributors, then motivate to go fishing. When a vacation is really working, the need to be somewhere other than in the here and now evaporates. But it was time to check my luck.

It was a sunny late May day, when winter is finally out of sight in the rearview mirror and the promise of summer is coming into view. I parked on Paul's long dirt driveway near the stream. Paul's farmer neighbor had thoughtfully cut a fresh path through the late spring growth with his Bush Hog, stretching from the two-track to a footbridge crossing the stream, making for an effortless approach.

The bridge spanned about five feet across and was decrepit, but still hanging in there, leaning into the water. I stood next to it, leaned over, and played out enough line to plunk a leaf worm into the current, watching as it slowly sank and got swept under the bridge. In seconds, my line suddenly went taught and the end of the pole bent with a hard strike. It was a short but electrifying tug-of-war as the 11-inch brook trout fought my retrieve. I landed the fish and unhooked it. Holding it against my palm, I admired the brookie's camouflage dark mottle-patterned dorsal skin, riddled with tiny orange speckles, and a fiery belly and lower fins, then placed it in my creel. Trout are fun to catch because of their spirit, delicious when properly prepared, and beautiful to behold. Next cast, similar result, this time a 10-incher. Third cast, lost a nice one. Fourth cast, nailed another keeper. Not wanting to be greedy, it was time to leave. Ten minutes of fun and a fresh trout dinner in hand.

Paul texted me: "Saw the action through my binoculars. Way to go, Hoosier Man!"

I took a photo of the three brook trout on a plate and had it framed a few months later. The 8x10 image hangs in our cabin's main hallway. I never pass it without taking a moment to look; it makes me smile every time.

❋

In a month or so, my son and daughter will be bringing their young families to a summer rental house just outside of Northport. My wife and I will be at our seasonal home in Cedar, about 25 miles south on M-22. Although our small cabin has three bedrooms, the thought of four more adults and five grandchildren staying with us gives me the willies. Close enough.

Full confession: I am not a doting grandfather, quite unlike the other normal grandparents involved in my grandkids' lives. Like Popeye, "I yam what I yam," as I've tried to explain to my puzzled children. I work in an urban public charter school with more than 1,000 K-12 students. When my two-week summer vacation arrives, I do look forward to spending time with my grandkids—but in short bursts. Nothing against the cute little rascals! I'm just recovering from my intense days in service to so many needy children and overworked, passion-driven educators. Stress must find a holiday. However, my daughter did text me some photos of the Northport summer rental. One image caught my eye: a brook directly behind the house. An accompanying note said, "There's a cute little creek running through the back of the property."

That changed everything. "Shawn, I'll be up as soon as you guys are all settled in. I'll bring my fishing gear too. The grandkids will get a kick out of it."

"A kick out of what? You think there are fish in that teeny creek?" she questioned; doubt is apparently a genetic trait in our family.

"Oh, I know there are," I answered with the air of a true believer. "You'll see, young grasshopper."

"Okay, whatever," she replied, with no interest in understanding the Kung Fu reference, dismissing the babbling of a loony old man. Oh ye of little faith.

HIKING

One foot in front of the other. Steps uncounted. Steps ever moving into infinity.

Not concentrating. Just being. An ambulatory meditation.

No timer, no clock, no appointment looming. Fitbits forbidden. Woodland consciousness is all.

The ground rises and falls: pushing inclines, pulling downhills. Other than our footfalls and occasional talk between two brothers, no manmade noise intrudes. Songbirds trill. Wind troubles the leaves, brushing our flesh, invigorating our way. The sound of Lake Michigan's crashing waves gradually recedes as we tread deeper into the woods. The occasional rustle of a chipmunk or black squirrel in the brittle leaf fall momentarily draws our attention. Shafts of sunlight pour through the woodland canopy, painting the beech bark golden-white. One step in front of the other, in front of the other, getting lost in the rhythmic pace....

Hiking.

＊

Three years ago, I was opening our seasonal cabin in the one flashing-four-way-stoplight town of Cedar, Michigan, with my youngest brother, Chris. He loves to hike; so do I. However, I had a bad hip that had grown increasingly creaky—audibly and painfully and piercingly so—by that mid-May of 2017. Yet, here we were, exactly where we wanted to be: far from the madding crowd of our hometown, Indianapolis. And we both wanted to get out and treat our lungs to that sweet northwest Michigan fresh air. In with the good air, out with the bad....

About an hour after we arrived and checked out the house, Chris was getting restless. (The cabin was in fine working order, having overwintered nicely, which I always say a prayer of thanks for, whether the Creator is paying any attention to our humble seasonal abode as our divine caretaker or not.) "You up for a hike?" he asked considerately. "But come to think of it, you're an old codger now, aren't you," conveniently adding a brotherly insult. "With that fragile hip and all, maybe I should just go solo, and you stay here and rest up."

I gave him a potty-mouth reply to his teasing, followed by a command to "get your boots on and let's hit it." I reached for my own trusty, seemingly immortal Merrell hiking boots, grunted while slipping them on, an arthritic habit, and grabbed another essential implement for this outing.

Years ago, a now long-lost friend who owned a Wild Birds Unlimited franchise in Bloomington, Indiana, presented me with an unexpected and precious gift: a walking stick carved from a sapling birch tree that a beaver had stripped completely of bark, its chew marks making an attractive pattern, highlighted beautifully when shellacked by my generous friend. I hadn't used it for hiking in eons, it seemed. The nearly five-foot walking stick stood next to the fireplace in the cabin, ever on call for an opportunity like this, when I could use the leverage.

We hopped on M-22 and drove over to Good Harbor Bay Trail, the flattest grade of the dozen or so marked trails in Sleeping Bear Dunes National Lakeshore. I had hiked this trail many times with Janet, often in the late afternoon, when the light angling through the trees is most vivid. Chris and I parked at the trailhead just off Lake Michigan Road. Fortunately, we were the only folks parked there. Solitude, as ever, is the real draw for me when hiking.

"Perfect," I exhaled. "Just us."

Chris nodded, smiling.

The north part of the trail affords sandy footing, with cedars, tamarack, and other pines and evergreens populating this section, close to the shore. Pushing off was painful for me, with every other step causing me to wince;

I had become accustomed to it as something of a penance to help me endure. My gait was limited too, and I had to exert myself to keep up with my fifty-something younger brother, an athletic six-foot-two fitness lunatic who struts like the Hulk (and, come to think of it, looks a bit like him, too). He did go a bit easier on me, though not too much, his pace energetic yet measured. Brothers keeping their relationship ever on the edge.

Eventually, the ground hardened as we left the lakeshore area and headed south into the woods, into the shadows. Chris kept ahead of me about six feet or so (an early adopter of social distancing before it was in pandemic vogue). He would talk over his shoulder, covering the recent landscape of his life, as I inquired about his kids and his work, the last time he spoke with mom, as well as our brother and sister. Soon the stressors that haunt me—my own workplace responsibilities—loosened their death grip and fell away for the time being, one of the real benefits of hiking.

This part of Leelanau County didn't escape the historic 100-year "bow echo" storm on August 2, 2015. Yet this particular section of the woods had fared pretty well in enduring the malevolent high winds. Instead of whole swaths of trees being toppled, as was the case in a number of places throughout the county, a 60- or 70-foot tree or two would be down in the midst of dozens more that appeared to be unaffected. Chris and I stopped occasionally when encountering one of the massive uprooted trees along the path, awed by its giant root ball ripped from its moorings. Of course, we had to touch each of them we came upon; a prayerful gesture. One life form paying homage to another's grandeur and demise.

The trail began to demand keeping one's eyes looking at the ground, as ropy roots erupted the surface, a hazard that can rudely break a hiker's reverie, if not a leg. I started watching more closely once I struck one with my right foot, sending a zinger through my hip. "Unh—dammit!"

"You okay?" Chris asked, though not turning around to check nor breaking stride.

"Fine, just fine. And hey, don't bother waiting for me."

"Hell no. Unless you want me to carry you."

"It would have to be a near-death experience before I took you up on that offer. Walk on, bro."

We crossed another of the several narrow boardwalks over the creek that courses through the area. Northern leopard frogs sprung here and there into the water, seeking cover from the intruders. About 10 minutes away from the trailhead, and just under an hour into the hike, the sound of Lake Michigan's waves making landfall beckoned us. We passed the trailhead and took a short walk on a path through the dune grass to the beach. West of us, perhaps a mile away, several people were spending time along the big lake's shoreline. Kindred spirits. Yet the distance between us was, well, nice. Bet they thought so too.

South Manitou Island to the northwest, Whaleback Hill to the northeast, and directly ahead an oceanic endless horizon. What we all see "out there" is something ill-defined that stirs the heart with a strange yet comforting longing. Maybe it's the ultimately indescribable sensation of existence.

Chris took a stab at summarizing the view: "Nice."

I followed his articulate lead: "Real nice."

Janet and I have been hiking for years. Spring would coax us out for April wildflower walks and May birdwatching jaunts as we grew in our outdoor appreciation, purchasing field guides to document our sightings. Before I had to be concerned about slip-and-falls (eventually, we all become less rubbery and more brittle), many a snowy Saturday or Sunday we emerged from our warm abode to feel winter's stark beauty, making tracks through the woods. For years we took our kids to Eagle Creek Park, as toddlers and into their early teens, the urban park being one of the largest in the country, with 3,900 acres of land and more than 1,400 acres of water (including Eagle Creek Reservoir and the creek that flows into it). For landlocked, environmentally challenged Indianapolis, this remains our local outdoor "wilderness," a saving grace. We went on day trips to Indiana State Parks, often visiting Turkey Run and Shades about an hour or so west of Indianapolis. At the time, this was all well and good. Then in our late thirties, we experienced northern Michigan, and our hiking enjoyment grew exponentially.

One of our early Leelanau County hiking experiences came about on Thanksgiving weekend in 1997. Janet and I were staying in Charlevoix at the Weathervane Terrace Inn. Her good friend Cindy accompanied us.

There we rendezvoused with Craig. He and Cindy had been playfully sweet on each other for a few years, and this was an opportunity for them to toy with that notion a bit further. We spent the weekend with plenty of indoor and outdoor recreation. Cocktails were poured or ordered earlier than usual, for we were younger and had the stamina to stretch a party situation out for hours, if the spirits moved us. Hiking, though, was an activity central to this mini vacation; we had to earn our libations. The day after Thanksgiving (a.k.a. Black Friday, an observation we roundly ignored) we drove to Sleeping Bear Dunes National Lakeshore. We hiked up the mandatory Dune Climb that tourists flock to in the summer months…and just kept going, for nearly the entire afternoon. It was cold and clear and once past the dune climb, deserted. We made it out to Lake Michigan in about an hour, a two-mile hike up and down some fairly steep dunes; i.e., as the crow flies. Reaching the shore on this inaugural hike, which we would repeat with our children many times in summers to come, was a happy moment, full of sighs and smiles and comments about the stunning view.

The return trip was fun though exhausting, and definitely less than linear. Craig's zigzagging meandering route reflected his innate desire to milk a good time for all its worth, regardless of the exertion. It reminded me of the film *Beau Geste:* there we were, French Foreign Legionnaires trudging through the endless sands of the Sahara....

After a few hours we found ourselves on a high dune ridge overlooking an expansive wind-carved depression about the size of a football field. The moonlike scene drew out my inner boy, and, simply because it was there, I galloped down the side of the bowl, howling madly. Arriving at the bottom, I seized a piece of walking-stick-sized deadwood and traced an oversized two-word obscenity in the sand, a message the size of which could be recognized by low-flying aircraft. Craig's laughter boomed across the landscape when he realized from the very first letter what I was spelling out, he being a likeminded lowlife like me. Once I climbed back up and rejoined the group, having finished my sand-scrawled graffiti, Janet chastised me, though weakly, for my grandstanding foolishness. Craig, on the other hand, congratulated me for my inspiration and creativity: "That was beautiful, man." And Cindy performed a balancing act, trying to suppress her laughter so as not to alienate her girlfriend yet signal to me that it had been an amusing stunt. Years later, I'm almost embarrassed at the thought of it. Finally, I have outgrown my class-clowning ways. But hey, back in the day it was fun. *Bless me, Father, for I have sinned....*

During that memorable dune excursion, Janet became famished. She tends to eat like a bird, even when coached prior to some exercising. I guess that's why she's been able to maintain her girlish figure across these many years and I, alas, have not; encouragement to eat never required in my case. "I didn't realize we would be out here so long, and I didn't bring any food with me. Did you, honey?" I shook my head. "Shoot. I can't believe we didn't think this through. I should have known that Craig would keep us out here all day."

Just then I revealed a Snickers Bar, which I had kept hidden in my coat pocket, knowing well the habits of the Diversion Master. A king-sized Snickers, of course. "Oh, wow! You didn't tell me you had this!" Janet shrieked, seizing the candy bar from my hand, ripping the wrapper open, and summoning Cindy to join in.

"It will taste better because I didn't," I responded. "And hey, save me a bite!" I interjected into the piranha-like feeding frenzy, as the Snickers was disappearing fast.

Craig and I had a morsel, while our female companions' flagging spirits from low blood sugar were revived. "Ladies—I have an announcement to make: I'm afraid we're going to make it," Craig said, chuckling wickedly. He knew exactly where we were and decided then, based upon Janet's ravenous hunger, to adjust our ramble and head toward the parking lot and go get some grub. A half-hour later, we arrived at our Honda Odyssey and climbed in. While driving away, I was reminded of the New Testament biblical story of the loaves and fishes miraculously feeding the masses gathered to hear Jesus talk. Our Snickers-sharing wasn't quite of the same magnitude—fed but four and just a taste at that, nobody came away full, and the fare wasn't quite as healthy as what the apostles doled out—but the candy bar materializing at just the right time did work a small wonder.

✳

It's an unseasonably warm sign-of-spring late February day in Indy. Janet offers to pick up three of our grandchildren for an afternoon hike through the woods along the White River at nearby Holiday Park. My daughter releases the hounds without hesitation.

Over the past several years, Janet and I have been seeing more young families than ever before getting out and walking with their children in our neighborhood and at local parks. Just when I thought that childhood was surrendering to Xboxes and PlayStations, this phenomenon suggests hope. But contradictorily, it also makes me cranky, as Janet doesn't hesitate to point out whenever we're hiking these metropolitan area trails and we come across a few too many people along the way. I mutter aloud, complain about the prevailing conditions, and wish I weren't here. "You need to relax, Tim," she commands encouragingly. "You're ruining my hike." I take a deep breath, try to get over myself, and hope that the herd (okay, I'm exaggerating—but just a bit) thins out dramatically.

Today, Holiday Park's overused trails are humming with people's voices and dogs barking, that city park ambiance. I cringe; Janet doesn't. She is immersed in the grandkids' enchanted state of being and is wholly enjoying their company, like any normal grandparent would. They chat as they go, with Mimi (her official title) serving as tour guide, explaining the sugar maple tree sap tap and bucket we come upon, noting the calls of the "pretty birds" (mostly the common robins, cardinals, and blue jays, as the more interesting species have all fled the riot), commenting on the "wonderful sunshine we're walking in," as she glows with that grandmotherly delight in the grandkids' discoveries, whether a muddy crawdad mud tower left over from the previous season or a freshwater mussel shell at the river's edge. Despite my cross mood I do watch with some grandfatherly satisfaction. Janet is such a loving grandmother; the grandkids have hit the lottery with this Mimi of theirs. And they really are sweet grandchildren, even sweeter when away from their parents. However, I can't fully settle into the moment, as the din, from nearby hominids who have been drawn outside by the decent weather and don't yet generally carry that Thoreau-like quietly intense appreciation for nature, overwhelms my fragile state of mind.

While the kids take a snack break on a ridge above the river, I take several deep breaths trying to center myself. A millennial mom and dad, their two tots, and a pair of full-grown and no doubt rescued greyhounds pass by. The parents politely wave and the mom registers a hello to our clan in an annoyingly lilting voice. Janet returns the greeting; I nod and try to smile. People can be nice, can be respectful. *So settle down, dude*, I tell myself unconvincingly.

I should be able to enjoy the grandkids and my saintly wife and being here along the riverside on this grand late winter day, public park or not. And I do, somewhat. But the experience is distinctly lacking. My irritability radar is up, and it's picking up all kinds of bogeys that consume my awareness.

To be truly happy while being in nature, I need miles of woods and open trails that are largely free of beings like me. I need to be able to walk in tranquility with the company of one or two choice others who appreciate solitude and what nature has to offer the attentive, and not overhear superficial conversations about workplace complaints and how someone's love life is going south. I need to be able to sight birds like wrens and flickers, hawks and bluebirds without some unthinking clods spooking them. And I really need to not hear the incessant whine of vehicles whizzing by on adjacent thoroughfares, like Meridian Street, which cuts through Holiday Park by an overhead bridge. I suppose what I really need is to calm the F*%! down, as my wife maintains, yet graciously never says it so coarsely. And yet, herein lies the silver lining: Meridian is also U.S. Highway 31, and reaches from here to Traverse City. With that epiphany, I smile indeed. Better now.

M-22

Years before M-22 became memorialized by a wearable destination-bragging clothing line launched in 2004, the 116-mile scenic road was fixed as a central component in our family's collective Up North vacation memory bank. Our kids and my wife's vehicles all feature a square black-and-white M-22 decal on their back windows to communicate to other northwest lower Michigan visitors in code that we have been there, done that, too. I always get a kick out of seeing the quietly semi-famous decal in other Hoosier vehicles' rear windows as I commute to work on Interstate 465. (I've never seen an I-465 sticker; nobody in his/her right mind would buy one; the 53-mile beltway around Indianapolis is a necessary evil for commuters.) It makes me want to honk my horn, roll down my window, and give some sort of secret sign. But I restrain myself, happy enough that there's someone else here in Indy who appreciates an M-22 state of mind.

M-22 is the highway that connects us to all of our beloved Leelanau County haunts, especially to my wife's favorite spot on the planet: the village of Leland, approximately seven miles from our Cedar retreat. Whenever we're staying in Cedar, we make a point of driving to Leland for a morning walk through town. We park at the beach on Reynolds Road. Janet walks over to the sandy path, down to the water's edge, and looks out at the Manitou Islands for her moment—reminiscing about happy summer memories of her children playing on the beach and in Lake Michigan. Then I pull her and our dog, Benny the Chronically Yapping Pomeranian (related to the Tasmanian Devil somehow, I'm certain), away from the always breathtaking view and we stroll down South Lake Street, passing the rental home that first brought us here in the mid-nineties for our inaugural Up North family vacation. We walk down to Fishtown, check out the impressive recreational boats if they're in the slips—the sailboats, powerboats, recreational trawlers and tugs, and the occasional multimillion-dollar yacht—head back and cross M-22, wander the neighborhoods near the Leland Country Club golf course, past Nedow's Bay Beach, then take the seldom traveled residential road along Lake Leelanau, always marveling at the owners' waterfront view and their good fortune, hoping they never take a moment for granted at their northland lakefront paradise. We meander our way down other quiet residential roads, eventually making our way back to the truck. Our conversation is occasional as we drink in the ambiance of Leland, taking a deep breath every now and then as we internalize the experience of being here once again. That feeling of home. True north.

Whenever I drive on M-22, I like to think that I drive like a local; i.e., the speed limit is a mere suggestion. Not that the Leelanau County residents nor I don't drive safely. It's just that I know the turns as muscle memory and can take them quicker than the conservative speed limits that constantly adjust along the serpentine roadway. I can always tell when I forget to invoke my Michigander-like driving style: a true local will be tailgating me, coming seemingly out of nowhere. This is always embarrassing. Then I'll put my foot into it and corner like a Formula One driver. And the trailing driver will respectfully back off, a salute of sorts. Although driving above the speed limit is not a recommended driving approach, locals will appreciate where I'm coming from. Not reckless or dangerous driving, but modestly thrilling.

Driving like a local on M-22 also means driving responsibly whenever in the immediacy of pedestrians. Especially when tourist "hatches" are on Up North from Memorial Day Weekend through the season's conclusion on Labor Day Weekend, for one must always be on guard for less-than-careful behavior. Vacation Brain Syndrome (a.k.a. VBS) and its telling lack of paying attention can and does get people killed: like trainees on rented bikes drifting out into traffic; like college-aged visitors walking across M-22 toward Fishtown while engrossed with texting on their smartphones; like out-of-town drivers suddenly braking and pulling off the highway, realizing they are hopelessly lost and no doubt exchanging unpleasantries with their significant-other copilots. Yet there are other dangers too.

One late July morning about 20 years ago, I was a firsthand witness to a death-defying incident on M-22, midway between Leland and M-204. We were staying at the Lake Street rental once again, our third consecutive summer vacation there. As was my habit during that special work-free Indiana-paroled two weeks, I was up and out of the house at 7 a.m. for a four-mile morning run, before any of my slumbering family stirred or the summer heat began to awaken. On this morning, however, it was in the high sixties and overcast, raining sporadically. I wore a hooded rain jacket, but my hair was soaked. I didn't care. Back then I loved running and would have made a dedicated mailman: in snow, rain, or sleet, nothing would prevent me from getting my heart rate up and pounding the pavement. I was on my outward-bound leg, about a mile or so from the house, when the rain's intensity picked up. To my left was Lake Leelanau, as I ran against traffic next to the guardrail. Suddenly, a Subaru Outback came whipping around the bend toward me, perhaps 200 feet away. It was going way too fast for the slippery weather and the sharpness of the turn, and predictably began fishtailing. Then the driver lost control, and the Outback went into a tailspin—twirling right in front of me, headed right for me. I was getting ready to leap over the guardrail when the vehicle flipped and rolled toward the other side of the road. I ran over to the now stopped and inverted car, its wheels still spinning like a beetle on its back with legs scrabbling the air, praying the driver wasn't injured. It turned out to be his lucky day—and mine as an amateur first responder. "You okay?" I asked while on my hands and knees, peering inside the open driver's side window. "Yeah, man," the teenage boy said, his long hair hanging down toward the top of the cabin's ceiling. He managed to wiggle out of his seatbelt and crawled out of the car with my assistance. "Oh, man, my parents are going to (f-bomb) kill me," he agonized frankly as he stood up, brushing strands of hair from his eyes. Other than the expected harsh parental verdict and sentencing, he was going to be okay.

A late model Ford Explorer was the first to come upon the scene. The woman in the passenger seat asked anxiously if anyone was hurt as she di-aled 911 with her flip phone. Many good souls stopped to offer assistance, moving on when informed of the non-injury crash. The boy and I directed traffic around the upside-down Outback monopolizing the southbound lane. Within minutes, the Leland Volunteer Fire Department responded. (I had been wondering about the volunteers' response time should we ever get in a pinch; it was impressive.) I continued directing traffic, as requested by one of the firefighters. Soon the boy's parents arrived. They didn't appear to be angry; they were definitely relieved. No killing occurred.

After about 30 minutes at the crash site and seeing that everything was well under control, I bade my goodbyes to the volunteer smoke-eaters who thanked me for doing my civic duty, and I resumed my run. The rain was still coming down, yet it was still a vacation day, and I was feeling pretty good about myself. Good about not getting killed; good about being able to lend a helping hand. When I got home, I shared my little adventure with Janet. She became wide-eyed. "You really need to watch when you're run-ning," she admonished me with unexpected grave concern. "You could get yourself killed." So much talk of killing that morning. And yet, no one had died in the vicinity. M-22 is such a scenic road. It's a shame that humans sometimes let their guard down and get reckless on this remarkable roadway, flirting with death. As some will do on all roads.

"We should check out that farmhouse and outbuildings someday," I say once again about the former farm west of M-22 about a mile from our Cedar retreat. I've made this comment for years as we've driven along M-22 in the Sleeping Bear Dunes National Lakeshore property. There are a number of these preserved farmsteads spread throughout the area. I've visited a few, such as the Kropp Farm near St. Paul's Lutheran Church. The property fea-tures a farmhouse, barn, granary, smokehouse, and small family cemetery. It quietly minds its own business while reminding passing drivers on Townline Road of the area's pastoral history. Someday, the teams of skilled tradesmen contracted by the National Park Service and trained in restoring buildings of that era—this home was built in 1890—will arrive with tools in hand. Eventually the Kropp Farm buildings will get the attention they deserve.

A few years ago we were just "meandering," a pastime Janet is fond of and encourages me to indulge in, while cruising along M-22. This activity included leaving my smartphone at home for a sanity-regaining respite. "You need to turn off all that noise in your head," she commanded. Although I resisted, an addict's initial reaction, I agreed to it—as long as she had her phone with her. How daring we all used to be, traveling without mobile phones before they were invented. We just didn't know any better.

We turned north on South Port Oneida Road. There are a number of farm buildings scattered about, vacant and well kept by the National Park Service. "Let's check that place out," Janet instructed me. I turned in what appeared to be a small parking lot for no more than six vehicles. The once-farmed fields in front of the old white-painted wood-sided homes were gloried with acres of blooming orange hawkweed, as if in a Monet impressionist painting. "Oh, my, this field is *gorgeous*," she gushed. It was indeed.

We traced the narrow asphalt walkway to the small compound of buildings. We walked unhurriedly, reservedly: This was hallowed ground, as generations of family farmers lived, worked, played, and died here. The front of the larger of the two homes faced away from the road and toward a thin line of tall trees that obscured the view of Lake Michigan. But we could hear it, the wind up, the waves crashing on the beach. I immediately thought how well the families must have slept here on spring, summer, and autumn nights, their windows open to the lullaby of the waves, a slight breeze ruffling the curtains....

I took a timeout on the porch while Janet continued toward the tree line, drawn to the lake. As best I could, I imagined what it must have been like living here at the end of the 19th century and turn of the 20th. As I sat quietly, I envied those who dwelled here in such a divine rural setting. I also considered how difficult life was then, devoid of the many modern conveniences we take for granted and the benefit of our modern state of medicine. Physical labor was the norm in those more-than-eight-hour workdays, six days a week. I envisioned trekking through the deep snow and bone-chilling cold to make it to the outhouse in the dark early mornings in the middle of a tough winter. Even though it was June, I shivered at the thought of it. My reverie was suddenly broken by Janet's shout: "Tim—I found a path down to the water!"

I rose up slowly as if from a pew in church. "Coming!"

The steps were formed of earth by settlers many years ago, with embedded timbers serving as the risers. Each step down was considerable, as if seven-foot tall people lived here once upon a time. A few minutes later we entered a sandy path bordered by tall wild grasses that reached to the narrow beach, the sand glistening from the advancing and retreating rhythm of the waves. Looking north then south, we were virtually alone, with a couple a good distance from us. Locals, no doubt. This was a farmer's private beach well over 100 years ago, now used by those in the know.

"They had it made," Janet says. In the context of the romanticized on-vacation moment we were enjoying then, I suppose they did.

Later, I got online and checked the National Park Service website for Sleeping Bear Dunes and the farms of Port Oneida. Our accidental field trip had been to what once was the Carsten Burfiend Farm, built by a German family, the first settlers in the area. Since then, Janet and I find ourselves returning every summer to visit the long-retired farm. There's just something about it....

❀

Almost every early May, my brother Chris joins me for opening ceremonies at our seasonal retreat in Cedar. As tradition has it, we head up on Friday morning, trout fish on Saturday, and go for a hike or two on Sunday before returning home the following day.

Several years ago, on that opening weekend Sunday, we were cruising along M-22 near the house, making our way to Sleeping Bear Point Trail for an afternoon hike. As we drove west, suddenly a large winged creature flew directly over Chris's Honda Pilot, just a few feet above the vehicle. "What the hell?!" Chris blurted, instinctively ducking from the pterodactyl-like presence in front of the windshield. A mature bald eagle flew so close to us we could almost touch it if we leaned out the window. Bizarrely, it stayed just above and in front of us for nearly a half mile, tracking M-22 as if tethered to our vehicle.

"Toto, I have a feeling we're not in Indianapolis anymore," Chris remarked as we navigated through the overhanging roadside tree canopy, following our national symbol. "This is crazy, man." The eagle then tired of the apparent game and flew up and away, out of our view. "What a sighting," he enthused. "Must be living right, eh?"

"Nah. I think it's the neighborhood," I dismissed. We both laughed. "It's that Leelanau County M-22 magic."

"There's no place like home," he concluded, still working his Oz theme. "Man. Little different than a crow, no?"

"Don't go dissing crows, now," I retorted gamely. "Most people don't know it, but they're some of the smartest birds around."

"That may be, but with all due respect, they aren't eagles," he responded sarcastically. Aside from the brotherly jousting the unexpected predatory bird flyby triggered (doesn't anything and everything?), it was certainly a once-in-a-lifetime treat.

❊

A few weeks later, on Memorial Day Weekend, my Cedar neighbor Paul suggests we try out the relatively new Sleeping Bear Heritage Trail for a bike ride. Although I've ridden many roads around the area, I had not yet tried the Heritage Trail. So we do.

We park at the intersection of County Road 669 and M-22 in the gravel lot on the southeast side of the intersection. Paul admits that he has not ridden a bike in a while—"years," he confesses. But knowing his brothers as I do, especially Craig, I figure Paul will be fine. These fellas don't belong to health clubs nor will you see them out jogging. They like their cocktails, are proud carnivores, and will savor a good Cuban cigar next to a bonfire after a day of hunting or fishing. They are bear-sized men and can exert themselves whenever an adventure shows itself. Paul joining me for a 20-mile ride without having peddled whatsoever this spring is such an occasion.

The Heritage Trail wends its way from the eastern trailhead parallel to M-22 until it veers across the highway near the entrance to The Homestead Resort. The trail is mostly asphalt, but there are long patches of packed gravel, so a mountain bike works best. Paul is astride a hybrid bike with thin tires ideal for hard surfaces, but he does fine. My 20-year-old Barracuda mountain bike, a heavy piece of machinery from the dawn of the mountain bike era, is perfectly suited for the changing bike path terrain.

The ride is smooth and not too challenging, until we get near Point Oneida. Grades as steep as 12% have to be attacked. Even though my bike is old and its rider considerably older, I have been riding year-round and am ready for these climbs, and I stand as necessary to gut them out. Paul, though, with his tree-trunk-sized thighs and never-say-die attitude, pumps right past me, sitting in his saddle, smiling at the road ahead. He would be hurting for a few days afterward, but it's good to see him riding with the unbridled enthusiasm of a young boy.

We chat much of the way, and the miles just slip by. Typically, I ride solo. But there is much to discuss with Paul: how he and his wife, Marie, managed during the gnarly northern Michigan winter; how his four brothers are doing; how his job at a local assisted living center's dementia unit is going; how his devoted involvement with Holy Rosary Catholic Church is working out; when is he ever going to break down and buy some padded bicycle shorts. And I share some of my own world of late: the unrelenting challenges of being an urban school administrator; how Chris and I made out a few weeks earlier at the Jordan River and came home with a mess of trout; how my cranky hip was doing; how the kids and grandkids are faring; and how much fun I'm having with him on this sunshiny late May day.

We stop in Glen Arbor, turning on South Lake Street and peddling down to the Lake Michigan boat ramp next to LeBear Resort. From there, the view of South Manitou Island is dramatic, especially under a blue sky, the water Caribbean-clear thanks to the filtering efforts of the invasive zebra and quagga mussels. I split a chocolate PowerBar with Paul as we stand along the shoreline, sipping water and gazing at the island. An interactive meditation.

Several millennials with their parents are on the beach with their large dogs, some fancy breeds that uppity folks like to promenade about to impress us lesser beings. Although the canines are obviously purebred something-or-others, their behavior is less than perfect. Catching sight of us, the dogs begin to bark menacingly; suddenly they hurtle toward us. We stay still, alert but unconcerned, prepared to send them to the dentist if not an early grave.

The millennials trot up behind the dogs, and one of the young women reveals sweetly that "they won't hurt you."

"No, they won't," Paul concurs coldly. They catch his drift, seize the dogs by their collars and drag them back to the safety of mommy and daddy. Paul and I exchange a knowing, amused glance. "I probably shouldn't have said that," he says, with little perceived remorse. "But I don't care for unruly dogs and their ignorant masters. Not sure which is worse."

Our peace reestablished, we decide to stay a few more minutes as we finish chewing our shared PowerBar and taking in the view. It's hard to pull ourselves from it. Minutes later, Paul volunteers, "Well, ready to resume, Kemosabe?" as he straps his helmet back on and shoves his water bottle into its cradle. We mount up. After riding near Big Glen Lake and the numerous new upper-middle- and upper-class homes in the area, many seasonal— new construction and rebuilds after the windstorm of August 2015 rolled through—we cross M-22 and resume the Heritage Trail, a steep climb greeting us immediately. Our hearts pound as we summit the hill. This time, both of us are standing as we hammer our way up the incline. Paul has lost some vigor now more than halfway into the trip, which is to be expected after riding for a dozen miles for the first time out this riding season. Nonetheless, we cruise at a nice pace on the return leg.

Before we know it, there's the truck. Bikes remounted on the tow hitch rack; helmets off; sweaty bandanas still on, pirate-like; water bottles drained. We climb in the truck and Paul, reading my mind, says, "Damn that was fun. Thanks, Tim. I needed that."

We roll down the windows and I open up the sunroof as we drive along M-22 north toward Cedar, in no hurry to get anywhere, replete in this splendid moment. The essence of M-22 can't be captured by a bumper sticker or T-shirt or pint beer glass, charming claims to visiting the area that they are. M-22 really is a state of mind. For me, the title of one of my favorite novels by Leelanau County's own, Jim Harrison, embodies the M-22 experience best: It's *The Road Home*.

Viral Vacation

The Pandemic of 2020 changed just about everything. The emergency shutdown in Indianapolis, which began quite appropriately on Friday the 13th in March, instantly switched off the lights of commerce and schooling. As a school administrator, I worked from home most days throughout the fourth quarter of our second semester, our three K-12 urban public charter schools suddenly braking to a halt with school life as we knew it. eLearning commenced, a poor excuse for education, but it would have to do. The streets of Indiana's capital city quieted. The skies cleared. People I'd never seen before would pass our house, pushing strollers, walking dogs, saying hello.

As May approached, I planned to drive up to Cedar to open our seasonal cabin on the second weekend that month, per my annual custom. Although I am perfectly designed for quarantine life—having a slight case of attachment disorder and being almost bald—I was getting claustrophobic. Living in a city of a million people while a new and hardly understood deadly virus lurked about made my longing to head north that much more intense.

My son, Matt, felt the same way. For the first time in 10 years, he wanted to tag along with me on a father-and-son trip for opening ceremonies. I welcomed his company. But as Friday, May 8, crept closer, my hesitancy grew. Although Matt is a responsible adult, I couldn't come to terms with riding up in a truck together for seven hours then sharing living space over a long weekend. At my age, the mortal threat of Covid-19 has my full attention.

"I get it, Dad," Matt said over the phone, a rediscovered form of communication, with more intimacy than texting, one positive development in all of this. "I just wanted to escape Indy and breathe easy for a while. Anyway, you'll have a good time."

I didn't. Go, that is. Extraordinary duties at school prohibited any getaway, for the time being.

✳

In mid-June, I visited my dentist after several pandemic-related postponements. I walked into a surreal scene as if entering a spaceship, with the dental assistants, hygienists, and dentists masked, shielded, and gloved. I could imagine them saying, "Greetings, Earthling," as I climbed into the dental chair. Instead, my dentist, who knows I work in the field of K-12 education, welcomed me by saying, "Have you been enjoying all your time off since the shutdown?"

I nearly fell out of the chair. "Oh my God, I haven't worked this hard in years," I responded. "The kids may be away from school, but we had to learn how to deliver eLearning instruction with five days to prepare. Since then, we've been trying to plan for a school year the likes of which we've never seen before. It's like walking down a pitch-black path for the first time with a weak flashlight, never knowing what truly lies ahead."

A sweet woman, she apologized immediately, expressing concern. "Oh, I'm sorry. I guess I didn't think of that." Not many people do. Americans have taken schools for granted for years. On the plus side, the pandemic might just turn that around.

"Have you made it up to Michigan lately?" she asked, knowing we owned property Up North.

"Yes, thanks. We did. Unfortunately, Governor Whitmer didn't close the border behind us when we got there." She laughed. I didn't.

Janet and I did manage to head north over the Memorial Day Weekend. Migratory instinct cannot be denied. But planning for this run north was much different than any previous trips there. Instead of counting on driving to Burritt's Fresh Markets or Oleson's in Traverse City and stocking up on provisions, we packed most items in Indy, and stocked up on plenty of hand sanitizer and Clorox wipes and face masks. I also visited the Michigan Department of Transportation website to see if rest area bathrooms would be open. "This feels pretty damn weird, Janet," I said, as we gathered our trip belongings and packed the truck.

"That's because it is. But hey, we need to get away from this house for a while. I'm going stir crazy," she commented, having been working from home since the beginning of March. "Everything will be fine," said my rock and my refuge.

On Thursday, May 21, we departed at 8 a.m., driving north on U.S. 31 through Indiana and into Michigan. Even though leaving on a Thursday before the holiday weekend would be a good driving day with minimal traffic, this time traffic was unusually spare. From Indianapolis to Grand Rapids, tractor-trailers dominated the highways. The rest of the sparse cars, pickup trucks, and SUVs largely traveled beyond the "suggested" speed limit of 75 miles per hour on U.S. 131 North. Once clear of Grand Rapids, we noticed an uptick in recreational boats being dragged to northern lakes. Governor Gretchen Whitmer had lifted some of the pandemic safety restrictions for the upcoming holiday weekend, and recreational boating was permitted once again. Moreover, the Traverse City area would be opened up further— a special dispensation for several adjacent counties, just in time for the usual start of tourist season.

We didn't stop in TC for any provisions, deciding to continue on to Cedar. "Do you mind if I stop in Buntings for a few things?" I asked Janet, once we rolled down the hill into town, Buntings Cedar Market to the left, the Cedar Tavern to the right. In non-pandemic years, we would be driving under the Polka Festival banner promoting the town's annual bash that draws people from all over the region to indulge in a long weekend of traditional polka playing and dancing, enthusiastic beer drinking, and gorging on kielbasa and sauerkraut and other Polish delectables. *In heaven there is no beer, that's why we drink it here....*

No banner greeted us this year, however; the festival, like so many other events, had been canceled due Covid-19. Nonetheless, as usual, I felt a wave of contentment wash over me when we drove into Buntings' parking lot. I know Janet doesn't get that same homecoming feeling as I do, but I do know she takes joy in my arrival euphoria.

"I'll wear my mask. They'll probably laugh me out of the store, but who cares."

"Stop if you want. Don't worry about what other people think," she said in her mom voice.

Buntings had read the memo. At the gas pumps, disposable gloves were available for customers. As the fuel flowed and I stretched my cramped legs, I watched folks going in and out of the store: masks covered every face. Inside, social distancing measures were in place, and the cashiers worked behind acrylic barriers at every register. So my shopping for essentials—a copy of the *Leelanau Enterprise*, a six-pack of cold Michigan craft beer, a package of cheddar-jalapeno-flavored brats made locally, and some vanilla bean-speckled ice cream for Janet— didn't appear to be a death-defying feat, much to my relief.

Now confident, my bravery went up a notch. Driving away from Buntings, I asked Janet, "Hey, do you mind if I stop at the Cedar Hardware? I need some leaf worms to fish for brook trout in the creek in front of Paul's house. And we could use some batteries."

"Go for it," Janet permitted. "But I'll wait in the truck." She's not much for shopping for worms, especially during a pandemic.

The hardware store had gotten the memo too. Enter-only through one door, exit-only through another. The owner had his mask on, as did the other customers in the small gotta-ask-where-everything-is store, as the sense of organization was something of a mystery, known only to the family running the business. There were even acrylic barriers at the cash register. Cedar wasn't fooling around.

I helped myself to the worm fridge in the small room where the fishing bait and tackle were kept. Out of habit, I opened the leaf worm container lid. Fingering the compost material for signs of life, I unearthed a twisting ball of healthy worms. Good to go.

But as we would soon learn, although the Cedar merchants were honoring the governor's orders, others, not so much.

❋

Like us, seasonal homeowners were reentering the area. Although quiet is what we sought, throughout the weekend, power equipment sang: lawn-mowers, weed eaters, and chainsaws kept up a din that echoed through the wooded lots. But at the end of the day, things settled down nicely.

Late that afternoon, while checking our street-side mailbox, I ran into a year-round resident neighbor. He kindly got me up to speed with how the neighborhood overwintered. He also shared a reservation he had about the upcoming weekend. "We're having some overnight company coming in from Grand Rapids tonight. They're hauling their boat up to put it in their slip in Suttons Bay for the season. Under the circumstances, I'm a little nervous about it," he confided. I would be, too, I thought to myself.

Janet stood nearby, waiting patiently for me to conclude my rite-of-spring check-in chat. "Well, looks like I'm being summoned for a walk to stretch our legs. Long drive up, you know. Take care of yourself." And I meant it.

Some other nearby seasonal home-owning neighbors from Grand Rapids, who tend to keep to themselves, and which we totally respect, had their recent college graduate-aged kids with them, their significant others, and a local relative, no doubt Uncle Somebody. Lots of self-determined coronavirus bubbles were appearing, although with liberal entry requirements. Another adjacent home had visitors over for a late lunch. This close interactive behavior during a public health emergency was all very puzzling. I suppose reading the memo was optional.

One evening, while all of this damn-the-pandemic visitation was going on, Janet and I sat on our front deck—our favorite location in the early evening. "I guess Governor Whitmer's guidance has been misinterpreted," I said.

"They think it's over," Janet responded. "Wishful thinking."

"Magical thinking," I suggested.

"Better yet."

"I'll try not to judge these folks."

"That's not like you, honey."

"That's true. Well, I'll try to keep my judgments to myself; how's that?"

"A worthy ambition. Now put your phone down, quit reading the news, and enjoy your beer. You need to forget about the world for a while."

Sound advice. Though impossible these days.

Our friend Marie, who also is the caretaker of our Cedar retreat, works in a health food grocery store in Traverse City. She stopped by early in our stay to say hello and give us a report on local happenings: "The snow-birds have returned. And although our employees are all masked up, there are a few too many customers who don't believe we're living in a time of pandemic. It's ignorant, and it's frightening. But, hey, what the hell. Not everybody received the common-sense gene when it was issued." Candid, she is.

＊

On Friday, Janet and I decided to start the morning the right way, to take our mind off things, with a hike up Whaleback Hill near Leland on a trail owned and maintained by the Leelanau Conservancy. The trek up the local landmark and glacially shaped elevation takes about 15 minutes or so, grad-ually becoming steeper. To the north, a large residence appears in this envi-able location, to the south, a vineyard. Otherwise, the hill is heavily wooded, and in May, wildflowers and migrating warblers abound. Once we made it to the top, we noticed the observation deck had two elderly visitors with their expensive spotting scopes taking in the view of Lake Michigan from the top of the 300-foot bluff. "Let's give them some space," Janet said, "and we'll come back in about 10 minutes."

As we walked along the path that follows the contour of the top of the bluff and overlooks the lake, I noticed a familiar northern Michigan spring birdcall, then saw a number of my favorite warblers trilling on nearby branches: American redstarts. The males are especially lovely, with their black feathers and streaks of fireball orange on their wings and tails and their white bellies. They seemed to be everywhere we looked. They also don't mind humans in proximity, and I was able to regard several of the redstarts from no more than five or six feet away. Being amidst these striking mi-grating birds adjusted my mental state, and I felt the shackles of workplace concerns slipping away. For now, the coronavirus seemed distant too.

About 15 minutes later, we returned to the deck. The old folks were still there, quite understandably hogging the dramatic panoramic view of Lake Michigan. I began speaking loudly so that they could hear me, popping their trance to give us our turn. With the hint, they moved on. Then, as we started toward the path to the deck, a teenaged boy and an older relative ran up on us, the boy in his zeal nearly touching me as he began to step on the observation platform. I didn't have to say a word.

"Excuse me—we've been waiting awhile to get on the deck. So if you don't mind, we'd like to take our turn," Janet admonished them as she surged ahead. The two stepped aside, nodding to us, smart enough not to mess with my five-foot-two and 100-pounds-soaking-wet commanding officer.

We leaned against the deck rail, took out our Nikon 10x42 binoculars, and looked out on South Manitou Island and the Manitou Passage. But I couldn't enjoy myself, as the young men stood chatting at the deck entrance, waiting their turn but a few feet from us. I just couldn't take it.

"C'mon, Janet," I said, gently pulling on her right arm and stepping off the platform. They barely moved aside. "Gents, in case you haven't read the news lately, there's a pandemic going on," I said disgustedly as I pulled up my neck gaiter, and we marched past the maskless, clueless duo.

"It's like being back in Indy," I commented as we walked downhill. About halfway down I stopped to put the glasses on some of the prolific number of redstarts and several rose-breasted grosbeaks, taking a few deep breaths to steady my viewing and calm my crankiness, seeking the birds' intervention.

"Just let it go, honey. Remember where you are. And remember: you're with me."

I pursed my lips, fighting her logic, and losing, as usual. I was so glad to be here with my soulmate; a perfect moment I was wasting due to my easily aggravated state. Thank you, Covid-19. Tourists behaving badly can easily get on one's nerves, but the hang time is minimal. Thoughtlessness or just outright selfishness and lack of concern for one's fellow man and woman here in God's country, when a dangerous and hardly scientifically understood virus was on the loose, well, that was hard for me to reconcile. But hey, I'm old, and therefore acceptable collateral damage.

❈

Later that day, we visited Houdek Dunes Natural Area, another Leelanau

Conservancy property along M-22 toward Northport. It had been a decade or more since we last walked the trails there. On a spectacular June day back then, Janet and I saw our first male scarlet tanager. For birders, this is an exquisite sighting. We also spotted a number of Baltimore orioles, one of Janet's favorite songbirds. It was a memorable day of taking in intensely beautiful spring migration avian color. Years later, on this Memorial Day Weekend Friday afternoon, we were completely alone here, just nature and us. The high seventies temperature and the nearly cloudless sky made for one of those "stop the clock, please" days. The following afternoon, Janet, tired from the drive and our outdoor exertion, gave me a pass to go for a solo hike. Given the rising number of people in the area—mostly snowbirds, but the advance contingent of the tourist season was beginning to appear—I decided to return to Houdek Dunes as a good bet for more solitude.

About 4 o'clock, I pulled into the parking lot. Two vehicles and mine; this my fragile mind could handle. I walked the same areas of the trail Janet and I had traversed yesterday, but added the Ridge Line Trail, which extended the hike to about three-and-a-half miles throughout the 370-acre nature preserve. The higher elevation trail winds through hilly but manageable terrain. I stopped on occasion to listen to the enchanting wood thrush song while watching warblers flit rapidly among the white birch, maple, and quaking aspen. No talking; no human distraction. Only birdsong and a cool breeze and the sensation of my heart beating harder from the inclines challenging me along the way. I took off my baseball cap, now wringing wet with sweat, and ran my right hand along my scalp as I once did when I actually had a headful of hair. I pushed on.

While in the foothills of the highlands, I unexpectedly came across a colony of yellow lady's slipper orchids, a wildflower first for me, growing adjacent to the trail. In early summer, I have found showy lady's slippers in boggy areas near Little Traverse Lake, but never this variety nor so many lady's slippers in proximity to one another. The yellow flower heads were just a day or so away from full bloom. I took several photos on my iPhone and sent them immediately to Janet, wanting her to share in this botanical moment of grace.

Once off the Ridge Line Trail, I was soon greeted by an observation deck above Houdek Creek. The creek's almost supernatural crystalline water, and the creekside dotted with clutches of marsh marigolds, adjusted my frenetic mental state. After a few minutes, my desire to stay indefinitely lost the argument with my legs wanting to keep moving.

With about a quarter mile left of my meditative trek, I came upon an older couple wending their way through the woods at their pace of enjoyment. I paused for about five minutes to give them time to put some distance between us and made sure they never saw me, honoring their privacy. Once back in my truck, I felt as if I were finally recovering a calm sense of self, which had escaped me since mid-March when the Covid-19 pandemic shut down Indy and put the whammy on us all.

Driving onto M-22, I cranked up the CD player, jammin' to Roxy Music's "True to Life" from the *Avalon* album, a favorite eighties tune of mine. Unexpectedly, a Subaru Outback pulled out from a side road, cutting me off. I braked hard. The Outback crept along, oblivious to other traffic, the driver and passenger in their own world. Perturbed by the poor driving technique, I floored the gas pedal, and my Honda Ridgeline's 250 horsepower engine surged, easily blowing past the sluggish Subaru. But then, the third— and this one unforgivable—transgression occurred: the female driver flipped me the bird as I passed her. My relaxed state of mind instantly vanished, and anger flooded my neurons. *Now I was pissed.* I veered in front of the Outback and immediately tapped my brakes. I watched in my rearview window as the young woman threw up both of her hands in a "WTF" gesture, as if I were the crazy person in this incident.

I was.

The boyfriend or brother or husband beside her talked on his cell phone. Perhaps he was used to her crappy driving and wishing himself elsewhere. Or, as my paranoia started to kick in, he was reporting a road-rage incident to the Leelanau County Sheriff's Department dispatcher. I resumed the speed limit, as the now-frustrated driver slowed down further to keep away from this lunatic—the lunatic who was perfectly fine until her careless driving triggered an immediate personality change like that of Dr. Jekyll to Mr. Hyde.

I drove south past Leland, and once I arrived at Good Harbor Bay Trail, instead of going left to head home, I went right toward the Good Harbor Bay beach parking lot, turned off the truck, and stepped outside. At that point, I realized my stress level was dangerously high. Covid-19 has many victims—even those who have not been physically infected by this novel virus. The stress it's creating as an awful byproduct is far more insidious than I imagined.

When I arrived home, Janet asked how the hike was. "I think I'll take a beer with me to the shower, and I'll tell you about it out on the deck with another one."

The hot water rained down my body, a therapy. I poured the cold light beer down my throat, another therapeutic measure. I tried not to think—perhaps the best intervention of all. Toweling off, I dressed, poured a pint of some real beer, went out on the deck, and took an Adirondack chair beside Janet. She was reading a novel, her preferred method of relaxation. I didn't interrupt her; instead, I watched the receding sun through the trees, taking it all in. My engine cooled.

"So how was it?" she inquired a few minutes later, looking up from her place on the page.

I showed her photos of the Ridge Line Trail, Houdek Creek, and the yellow lady's slippers. "Gorgeous. Great hike, then. You needed it."

It was time to come clean, as my conscience was gnawing at me.

"Well, it was an extraordinary hike. But then I discovered how stressed out I really am," I revealed.

But not quite so clean. I was too embarrassed by my road-raging behavior. And too shook up by seeing more clearly the upended state I was in. My account ended there.

Back in the big city, the Covid-19 pandemic is entirely real, at least to those of us who don't irrationally see it as the Chinese flu. Most people there know someone who has had the virus, has died of the virus, or both. Indy now had Covid-19 spreading in concerning numbers. Like here in Leelanau County, some folks wear masks in public; some don't. Some people have been brought up with regard for "the other"; others have not. Thanks to the pandemic, America is in the midst of an argument about reality. How utterly bizarre. And because I work in an urban public charter school and have enormous concerns about the school year and how best to safely prepare for the unknown, the pandemic's haunting threat has been slowly eating at me, eroding my sense of balance. I was the embodiment of harmonic distortion.

I sipped the beer. Kept quiet. Stayed next to Janet. Allowed the evening to soothe my senses, as I tried to return to my better nature.

*

On Sunday morning, I pulled my "ancient" black and silver Barracuda A2R Mountain Bike out of the shed. After I turned 40—24 quick years ago—instead of buying a Harley-Davidson like seemingly every other midlife-crisis-gripped guy I knew, I opted for something with pedal power. At that time, the hardtail Barracuda cost $1,000. Today, it's a heavy, outdated bike, and it could use a set of raised handlebars, as I'm not as pliable as I used to be. But I opted not to bring my much newer old-guy-outfitted Specialized 29er Rockhopper Mountain Bike from home, so this was as good as it would get.

I rode west up Bodus Road, a fairly steep grade, past the Sugar Loaf Old Course, and did that rotation a few times, staying close to home. Then I cruised up and down Good Harbor Bay Trail through a few miles of cherry orchards and farms and circled back through nearby neighborhoods. People working in their yards took a moment to wave. I rode about 15 miles, enjoying the "throwback" ride on my trusty old steed. The handgrip shifter was as smooth as ever, the wheels were surprisingly true, and the fairly new tires with few miles on them rode fine. The sun was out. And so was I. A boy again, reunited with his old friend.

On a back road, just past a small horse farm and in between acres of cornfields, I glided to a stop and put my feet down on the asphalt pavement. Late spring in northern Michigan. A deadly virus was raging across the country, but it hadn't yet made a hard landing in Leelanau County; perhaps it wouldn't. Maybe it would just go away, wishfully, as the Stable Genius tweeted. Yet right here, right now, the only currency there really is, felt right. No people anywhere near me. For the time being, I was untouchable, out of harm's way. "Good enough," I said to myself, and resumed my ride, smiling. Good enough.

PART II

Summer

FIRST LIGHT: LELAND

In mid-July 1996, we rented a home in Leland. I was 40 years young (but that seemed old at the time—which is humorous to me now). It would be our second family vacation. The first took place several years earlier. We stayed in a small hotel on East Bay that no longer exists, a name I can no longer remember, having been bought by a larger hotel firm. The hotel was perfect for first-timers to the area, for folks on a budget like us who just wanted to experience the slice of vacation heaven that Traverse City is to downstate and out-of-state (and now increasingly common, overseas) visitors. We spent much of our time hanging out on the beach and playing in Grand Traverse Bay. Cocktails in the evening; dinner on the Weber grill. We ventured no farther than downtown Traverse City, where we picked up our obligatory Up North-labeled T-shirts, baseball caps, and sweatshirts to ward off the chill of the cool summer evenings we Hoosiers weren't accustomed to, with our heavy humidity-shrouded summer nights. As vacation trainees, we thought we had it made. Little did we know what existed outside of TC: Sleeping Bear Dunes National Lakeshore. Empire. Glen Arbor. Leland. Northport. Lakes. Rivers. Brooks. Woods. Trails. Many years later, I can say that we were ignorant in our contentment during that novice vacation. If I had only known then what I know now about the area. Yet, no regrets. What good is that?

I was a late bloomer, starting college at 26, in a marriage that was less than a fragile year old; my wife and I spent the next decade pursuing college degrees and getting our footing in the white-collar world of work. We were self-made members of the middle class, and because of it, frugal. So indulging in some extended rest and relaxation was foreign to us. But Janet declared it was time. Back then, as now—though I was not yet a fully trained husband and would need some refining that would be years in the making—when the lady of the house decides to wield her influence, I do what I'm told. Eventually.

By accident if not miracle, she was perusing *The Indianapolis Star* classifieds one afternoon in the spring and came across an ad for a vacation rental on South Lake Street in Leland. Even way back then it cost $1,000 for the week, which was an obscene amount of money and would be a considerable indulgence for us. Or so I thought. Janet, always looking out for her family's best interests, made an executive decision, declaring, "Let's go. We are way overdue; we deserve it. Besides, it's only money." Her logic was sound, her heart in the right place, and it was time for me to try to learn how to relax rather than habitually work through my vacation time. We invited Janet's youngest sister's family, lowering the expense while filling the house with kids: two young nieces, my 11-year-old son, Matt, his best friend, Cory, my 13-year-old daughter, Shawn, and our 11-year-old foster son, C.J.

I awoke at 4 a.m. the early August day we were heading out, with first light emerging on the eastern horizon. The sky was clear. My mind was, too, as I was elated by the freedom, albeit temporary, that two weeks away from making a living affords. I had been to Leland once before, on a sailing expedition with Janet and my good friend Craig and his then-wife, Connie, in 1988. We motored out of Leland's harbor and soon put up the sails, making our way across the shipping channel to South Manitou Island for a long weekend of camping. We were charmed by quaint Leland—everyone is—with its historic "Fishtown" harbor and privately owned shops (no franchise of chain stores allowed) and the dreamy vacation homes along the Lake Michigan shore. Now we would be spending some extended quality time there, though a block off the water. Like a vampire dreading the sunrise, I was hustling to pack our new Honda van (the 1996 classic model with its distinct non-sliding side doors), get the bikes mounted on the roof rack, and get the kids belted in their seats before they woke up and the darkness had retreated. I just wanted a few hours of quiet before the Are-We-There-Yet Gang was up and motor-mouthing away.

We made it to Traverse City in about seven-and-a-half hours. Years later, when Janet and I became empty nesters, we would cut that time by an hour, easily. Those young bladders and insatiable appetites tend to slow progress on the open road.

Once in TC, we stopped at Craig's apartment on the southeast corner of East Front Street and Wellington Street. Stopping to be greeted by "Uncle Craig" would become an annual tradition for years to come as we made our way to Leland for summer vacation. Part of that tradition in following years would be dropping me off to have a beer or three with Craig and catch up during our yearly reunion, indulging in guy talk. But on this inaugural visit, we decided to head to Leland as an intact unit; Craig would join us later.

Once we arrived, everyone poured into the house, the kids claiming bedrooms, suitcases thrown open in a clamor for swimsuits. Matt and Cory took off for the beach just a short block away—or so we thought—as we settled in. Within an hour of their departure, we received a phone call on the land line from a local. The caller asked if the two boys jumping off the rock jetty into the Leland Harbor waters were ours. (How the anonymous caller suspected them as being ours still remains a mystery.) I thanked the woman, hung up, uttering a few choice words as I drove down to the harbor, catching the daredevils in the very act as they hurled themselves off the breakwater's tons of rock erected by the U.S. Army Corps of Engineers in the 1960s. Cory was fearless, and Matt was a loyal follower. Could have lost them both, as I explained in colorful Bobby Knight-like language. Fortunately, despite their daring, they came home intact. And I would be keeping a close watch on them, as apparently someone was on us.

Back then, I was an avid runner, keeping to an every-other-day routine of hitting the pavement for three- to five-mile runs, which by 1996 I had been doing for 15 years. I planned to be faithful to my fitness constitution while in Leland, and set my alarm for a quite un-vacation-like 6 a.m. awakening on our first morning there.

I had determined the night before that the best route would be to get out on M-22 and head a few miles south to the intersection of M-204 and M-22 and loop back, running along the winding scenic highway adjacent to Lake Leelanau. But my instincts insisted that I first visit Lake Michigan just down the street before heading out.

It was already warm enough for me to run shirtless (and in those days I could get away with it without embarrassing myself or being asked to put my shirt back on). I pulled on my running shorts, laced up my blue Brooks running shoes, and jogged down Reynolds Street toward the beach, exhilarated by that dawning vacation moment on the 45th Parallel and the promise of our two-week stay. I stepped down the short sandy path between the dune grass to the beach. The surface of Lake Michigan was completely still. The lake water gently lapped the shoreline, as if singing a soft morning lullaby. The Manitou Islands were prominent on the western horizon, a dramatic sight to this landlocked flatlander. To the south was Whaleback Hill, a landmark moraine glacially formed 11,000 years ago. As I peered at Whaleback, I saw two white-tailed deer standing in the water along the shoreline having a morning drink. No other human was present, normal vacationers still luxuriating in sleep. I was overcome with emotion: it was an "I can't believe I'm standing here" moment—a moment that recurs every time we're fortunate enough to be in Leelanau County. From Indianapolis to Leland seemed like a distance of light years. From then on, I would be frequently tempted by the thought of living here, like everyone who visits, i.e., during the summer. As I would come to know when traveling Up North for cross-country skiing outings a few years later, they have real winters here. And not everyone is cut out for them.

The wave-tossed stones dredged by the infinitely patient workings of this Great Lake over millions of years, now tracing the high tide mark in an undulating pattern, caught my attention, and for several minutes I picked through the wide variety I would soon come to identify, thanks to the inspired purchase of the *Lake Michigan Rock Picker's Guide* at Leelanau Books later that day. For now, though, they were simply captivating to this uninitiated newcomer.

When I looked up from my stone trance a few minutes later, the deer had disappeared, as if they were never there. I could feel the July heat on my now gently perspiring skin. A cold-weather runner, I needed to push off to get a run in before the temperature and humidity became stifling. When I returned about 40 minutes later, having run four miles or so, the house was still—other than the collective snoring. I went upstairs to shower, careful not to awaken any of my crew. Janet had been dozing and awoke groggily as sunbeams poured through the eastern-facing window above the bed. "How was your run, honey?" she asked sweetly, her eyes closed.

"Perfect," I said, sitting on the edge of the bed looking out at the quiet Leland residential neighborhood basking in the new day's summer sun. Between the endorphins flushing through my brain and the realization of my location, I was one happy camper. "You did good, Jan," I said, smiling, "really good. Better than I could have even imagined." And we have never been the same since.

AIRSHOW

I'm guided by the beauty of our weapons.
— *Leonard Cohen from "First We Take Manhattan"*

June 2017 has moved quickly—seemingly as fast as a supersonic Air Force F-16 Fighting Falcon. Six of the acrobatic warbirds—the Thunderbirds—are in Traverse City for the 92nd National Cherry Festival this week. Velocity is something that preoccupies me at the age of 61—that of my own in particular: the body creaks and slows, the mind wanders more in nostalgia, and time seems to accelerate. Yet sometimes I'm able to get it together and time things right, like today, when I'm planning on checking out the practice run for the airshow later this afternoon. The crowds won't be huge nor official. In fact, many vacationers—who are now descending on the area as a horde of overworked, stressed-out, ready-to-party people in need of some serious downtime, and who are more than willing to easily part with their hard-earned cash—will be strolling downtown this afternoon shopping along Front Street when suddenly the blue skies above will thunder with jet fighters, among other stunt-flying aircraft and the U.S. Coast Guard MH-60T Jayhawk helicopters, preparing for the festival's main event airshows on Saturday and Sunday.

I'm like a kid this morning, Friday, June 30, in anticipating the airshow practice. Part of my joy is because I believe I'm one of the few who know this is about to happen today. But most likely this over-the-hill kid is only kidding himself, as the festival website shows the schedule for this afternoon's practice run. Doesn't matter; this childish glee I can barely contain is what summer is all about.

My first exposure to the National Cherry Festival Airshow was about 20 years ago. Craig, a former bartending colleague and TC native, invited Janet and me to his apartment on Front Street to watch the performance from his second-story roof. We were running a bit behind on driving in from Indy and the city was teeming with thousands of people trying to find a parking place to get to the beach and stake their claim to some sandy real estate for the next several hours. Craig had a parking place reserved for us at his apartment, which faced Grand Traverse West Bay, but we were having a difficult time negotiating traffic. So many out-of-towners had no idea where they were going, but they were determined to get there. Somehow we made it just in time.

Seeing Craig's apartment door open, we eagerly mounted the uneven, century-old stairs. "You're missin' it! Get out here and see the show!" he bellowed from the roof as we hustled inside. I helped Janet maneuver out the window, handing her off to Craig. He was all worked up, as he usually gets when involved in any extracurricular activities. A Macanudo cigar in one hand, a Coors beer in the other, and he was good to go. "Grab a cold one," he invited, opening his cooler. "And oh, I almost forgot: welcome to Michigan," he said, laughing as he shook my hand. Totally prepared for our viewing pleasure, our master of ceremonies had several lawn chairs on the roof awaiting our posteriors. We gladly took our ringside seats.

Two stories below on Front Street, one of the Cherry Festival's parades crawled by. Craig called to acquaintances and friends alike as they passed beneath us, and they shouted back in acknowledgement. "Best damn seat in the house," he said to me minutes later as the airshow got under way. Back then, Janet liked joining us for these excursions and was patient when things became a bit much—boys being boys—as they usually either quickly or eventually did. Her job was to chaperone us while curbing our overly enthusiastic tendencies whenever Craig and I reunited, which was usually once a year. It was early, so things weren't close to being out of hand—yet.

We watched several preliminaries to the main-event Blue Angels, including the Red Baron Stearman Squadron biplanes, the Coast Guard aerial rescue demonstration featuring a swimmer plummeting into West Bay from a hovering Jayhawk helicopter, as well as several other pilots pulling major G-forces with their aircrafts' daring acrobatic routines. Once these warmup acts concluded and we were well into our beers, Fat Albert, the Hercules C-130 transport plane of the Blue Angels, came flying by at a low-and-slow crowd-pleasing altitude, its four props slicing the air, announcing that the Blue Angels were about to begin their set.

Moments later, the team of six F/A-18 Hornet jet fighters came from the west, shrieking low over the bay, having taken off from Cherry Capital Airport to the southeast, and raising a delighted roar from tens of thousands of Americans on the beach. "God Bless America!" Craig cheered. "Ain't they pretty?" I wasn't quite as patriotically moved as my dear Vietnam-era Army sergeant veteran friend. But the magnificence of these hurtling U.S. Navy technological wonders riveted my attention, as we marveled at the pilots' precision and nerves of steel. If anything can get an 18-year-old to sign on the dotted line for a tour of duty, seeing these warbirds do their thing certainly can.

"Look!" Craig instructed, pointing up. Directly overhead, a large corona halo encircled the sun. "The Big Guy's contribution to the airshow," he declared, smiling at me knowingly. "Ain't it somethin'? And that's not even on the program."

"Must be why nobody seems to be looking at it but us," I replied.

"Typical," he said. "Whaddya gonna do, eh? Might as well just beer me again, brother."

And the glorious afternoon just kept flying by....

❋

In 2015, Janet and I were sitting at the Good Harbor Bay Beach on Friday before the Cherry Festival weekend that featured the airshow. We were just off Lake Michigan Road, at the spot where Craig and his "sweetie," as he fondly refers to his wife, had their beachside post-wedding reception a decade earlier. The Lake Michigan water lapped quietly and soothingly near our feet. We were reading, soaking up some rays, having a get-away-from-it-all afternoon. I put my book down in my lap and peered at the panoramic scene. Pyramid Point was west of us; the Manitou Islands at roughly

10 o'clock; South Fox Island straight ahead way out on the horizon, and Whaleback Hill, and just beyond it, Leland, to the northeast. As my typically amped-up mind gradually slowed thanks to the dramatic change in scenery from my office in Indy to here, and as I took in the becalming view, I heard an unusual airborne rumble in the distance. Looking toward mist-shrouded Whaleback Hill, I located what I thought was the source of the sound. Suddenly emerging from the mist in low-altitude diamond formation were four F-16 Fighting Falcons: the Air Force Thunderbirds. The jets flew out over Lake Michigan, the diamond formation fixed at a 90-degree angle, as if a white cross were sailing through the sky. "Look, our own private airshow," I said to Janet, tapping her right arm.

"Oh, wow. That's cool, isn't it, honey," she said. As the jets circled back toward the shoreline, she returned to her novel, having only glanced at the aerial treat. I watched, transfixed, until they disappeared completely from sight. Janet and I are quite compatible in our different interests; it's our own version of marital bliss.

❋

So now it's just after noon on this splendid late June day here in the quiet Manor Green subdivision near Sugar Loaf. I'm going to quit writing shortly and close my laptop for the day. Then my plan goes into motion. I'll hop in my pickup truck and drive a mile or so on South Good Harbor Trail to the roadside stand we frequent at the end of June and pick up a few quarts of fresh strawberries for Janet, who will be arriving for a week's stay with me tomorrow, driving up from Indy with our son and his young family. The strawberry season is drawing to a close, so I'll hope for one last round set out at the stand. (When I think of summertime in northwest lower Michigan, strawberries immediately come to mind and the simple joy they bring my dear wife. The wallpaper photo on my iPhone shows Janet beaming while holding a fresh quart of the early summer berries in both hands in front of the roadside stand. It always makes me smile.)

Later, I'll travel south a few miles to Cedar and pick up some groceries from Buntings Market, making ready for her arrival. Then I'll drive toward M-72 and head for Traverse City, stopping at Oleson's Food Store on North

Long Lake Road, showing up about 2 p.m. I'll hand-wash my truck at the self-serve carwash just below the grocery store on the hill. As in years past, several Nam Vets will be situated just above me in the Oleson's parking lot, sitting in their portable camp chairs near their Made-in-America pickup trucks, wearing navy-blue or camouflaged baseball hats with gold trim distinguishing their military service, while shoppers go in and out of the store, ignoring their presence—the mixed blessing of being old—waiting for the Thunderbirds to put on their exhilarating show. I'll wave to these grandfatherly vets; they'll wave back. As I towel-down the wet, glistening truck, I'll occasionally check the sky for signs of fighter jets, only common in these parts during the National Cherry Festival. And when I hear the roar of the Fighting Falcons' supersonic engines, I'll join the war veterans in admiring the breathtaking display of military air power. I will not express aloud what seems to be a given to those claiming a certain sense of patriotism, *God bless America,* like that of my good friend, whom I hold in highest regard. I'm not sure these vets will either; who knows. They have more than earned the right to their own sentiments regarding God and country. But I will admit that we certainly have the finest war toys on the planet. And they truly are something to behold as they soar over Grand Traverse Bay…whatever one may think about their purpose.

Invasive Species

I've been reading *The Death and Life of the Great Lakes* by Dan Egan. The book was a finalist for the 2016 Pulitzer Prize. I'm about two-thirds of the way through, and it is an alarming read. But it only adds to my alarm, as since the mid-1990s I've been aware of the invasive species onslaught occurring in Lake Michigan. Anyone spending any time on the beach there can't miss the signs. Or, the message.

I began paying attention when hiking Good Harbor Bay beach in the late nineties with my great-outdoors spiritual guide who lives in Traverse City on Old Mission Peninsula just past Bowers Harbor. I became aware of these aquatic out-of-towners when I realized that the mounds of what I thought from a distance was sand tracing the pattern of the waves along the shoreline, were actually the carcasses of billions of little mussels. Craig, my guide, identified them for me: "Those are zebra mussels. Invasive species. They are slowly killing the lake's fish life. I don't think there is any stopping them."

"What will happen?" I asked tentatively.

"Who knows," Craig answered. "But it's possible that game fish like lake trout will lose their egg-laying habitat because the mussels are carpeting the lake floor. When that happens, it's curtains, man."

✳

Ever since that day of environmental awakening on Good Harbor Bay beach, each year during our May migration back to northwest lower Michigan I remark at the increasing clarity of the big lake, thanks to the zebra and quagga mussels' metastatic spreading across the lakebed. Their filtering of the water has given Lake Michigan a dramatic Mediterranean Sea-like appearance. No doubt, it's more beautiful than it's been in several hundred years, before Europeans entered the picture to claim the land, and our American manufacturing industry imprinted the environment with our noxious ways. But it is an ominous beauty indeed.

Craig created a mixed media installation for a modest art show in Traverse City in 1998. The piece was essentially an old metal road sign, its message faded away, attached to a post. He came across the artifact in Lake Michigan while wading the shallows for lumber shavings from the lakeside mills, which were active a century ago. The shavings, long smooth planks sheared from mostly white pine logs that would be sent to furniture manufacturers in Grand Rapids and destinations farther south, were well preserved by the cold lake water temps, and made ideal raw material for Craig's carvings and other works of art. (His striking rendition of four Modigliani-style nude female subjects etched into such a plank remains one of my favorite works of Craig's.) The creation came together quickly. He scraped the entirely zebra mussel-encrusted sign, leaving remnants still clinging to the edges, an organic matter picture frame. Then he spray-painted the sign and post a bright red metallic color. The finishing touch was a new message: **WARNING: INVASIVE SPECIES.** At the sign's base, another sign was mounted: **ZEBRA MUSSELS: IT'S ALL OVER BUT THE SHOUTIN'.** Funny, in a nervous kind of doomsayer way.

Craig didn't win any awards, and didn't expect to. "Just havin' fun makin' a statement," he said. But his disturbing point was hopefully heeded by all in attendance and not just laughed off as artistic whimsy.

Thereafter, I viewed the countless mussel shells on the beach, and those I would see covering rocks in the water, as no longer a natural occurrence but an existential threat to the Great Lakes. The invasive mussels have allies. The bodies of chubby round gobies are now fairly common when walking any Lake Michigan beach. And the past few years, the disturbing sight of dead loons and various waterbirds such as mergansers and even the reviled cormorants—trout slayers supreme—all killed by botulism caused by invasive species, is heartbreaking. Whenever I spot a dead waterfowl in various states of decomposition up ahead on the beach, I try to distract my wife before she can see it to avert her inevitable distress. A bird lover, she takes such catastrophic sights hard. And when an unbalanced ecosystem is to blame, her reaction is even worse.

But of course, one invasive species is far deadlier than all the others combined: humans—us.

※

Janet and I are long-time visitors to northwest Michigan and are fortunate enough to be property owners in largely pristine Leelanau County. We try to get Up North as much as possible from May through October. Because of our three decades frequenting the area, the two of us consider ourselves near-locals. We make it our business to keep Leelanau County beautiful. But the thousands upon thousands of tourists who are now attracted to the area— and understandably so, especially when they come from asphalt jungles like Chicago and Detroit and one of the world's largest corn and soybean fields known as Indiana—can be construed as invasive. Picturesque no-stoplight towns—villages, really—in Leelanau County such as Glen Arbor and Leland, can only survive due to the millions of dollars imported from downstate and surrounding midwestern states. And nowadays, it's not unusual to run into tourists from overseas. For example, during the second week of October in 2018, as Janet and I spent a week enjoying the vacant beaches and slower life of Leelanau and Grand Traverse counties once the tourists had mostly cleared out, we came across some folks from way outside of town. While on a walk with our Pomeranian, Benny, at Clinch Marina in Traverse City one morning, we passed an Asian couple taking photos of the scenic harbor and the remaining boats still in their slips, their owners understandably squeezing out as much time as possible on the water this dwindling boating season. A few minutes later we saw about a dozen large Chinook salmon swimming below the docks. Another young couple was leaning against the railing pointing at the impressive fish and commenting in a Scandinavian language. The young man looked at me and said in English, "Excuse me. Those fish, what kind?" When I told him, he repeated, "Chinook salmon" to the woman with him, as she then did. I suggested they go to the weir on the Boardman River to check out the hundreds of Chinooks and cohos congregating there. "Where is that?" I gave him basic directions—cross the street (West Grandview Parkway) and follow the river west a short way. "Can't miss it" (always a curse). I wasn't sure he understood or would make it, but he was grateful enough.

Inveterate beachcombers, last summer Janet and I were walking the Good Harbor Bay shoreline one fine June afternoon. For us, whenever time permits, going to the beach is always the right thing to do. "Look at that bird, Tim." She pointed to a spot about 25 yards in front of us. "Uh-oh," she said worriedly. "There's something wrong with it." A cormorant was swimming in a disordered manner very close to a woman and her two young children recreating there. Her son, perhaps 4 years old, was trying to get close to the ill bird. Mom, sitting on a towel, was encouraging the boy to try and play with it. "What is she doing?" Janet said to me, aghast at the mother's poor decision-making.

"Clueless," I summarized. We drew closer. I couldn't help myself: "You might want to keep your kids away from that bird," I suggested. "It's diseased and its behavior is unpredictable."

"Oh, really? That's interesting," she answered patronizingly, and let junior continue to approach the sick creature.

"Oh my God," I said under my breath to Janet, beseeching and not blaspheming, reaching for her hand. "Let's get out of here. I can't bear to watch."

Being present in nature and seeking to understand our place in it and to respect it seems to escape a few too many of us these days, even when immersed in it on a *Traverse Magazine*-cover summer day on a Lake Michigan beach in Sleeping Bear Dunes National Lakeshore. Go figure.

According to "Aquatic invasive species in Lake Michigan," a Michigan State University Extension website article, "As of 2007, there were more than 180 aquatic invasive species with reproducing populations in the Great Lakes." The article notes that "a new aquatic invasive species arrives in the Great Lakes at a rate of one every eight months." We can thank ourselves for this potentially calamitous degradation. Some of these critters come from home aquariums, their irresponsible if not criminal keepers releasing non-native plants and fish and crustaceans into the Great Lakes. The article goes on to reveal that "approximately 30% of new species are unintentionally brought to the Great Lakes in the ballast tanks of ocean-going freighters."

And now, here come the Asian carp. This invasive species has been identified in the Illinois and Mississippi rivers. These foreign fish can reach five feet in length and weigh up to 100 pounds. Aggressive feeders known to suddenly hurtle out of the water in large groups—and even injure fishermen—they could alter Lake Michigan and the Great Lakes' fish populations, out-competing native species, a major threat to the commercial and sports fishing industries. As of August 2019, Asian carp have been discovered in the Chicago River but nine miles from Lake Michigan, says an article published online by the Alliance for the Great Lakes. It could be just a matter of time until an ignorant or intentionally malicious fisher takes a few of these monstrous bottom feeders and drops them into Lake Michigan. Then things will really get interesting.

※

Grandpa Tom Walker, Janet's beloved kin, while in his nineties and feeling his life ebbing away, feared not. He was a Kentucky Church of the Nazarene preacher and believed to his core in his Lord and Savior Jesus Christ. Having served in the U.S. Army during World War II and a veteran of a long life, he would say to me in his last years, "I've seen enough. I don't want to be around for what's coming. Death won't be so bad. Besides, I will dwell forever in the glory of the Lord." His abiding belief in the afterlife made it easier to leave his earthly gig. If I happen to make the cut, I'll be right behind him, with a great hope for window-clear fish-filled trout streams and lakes (with only native species, of course) in Paradise.

As things seem to be going in this world—global warming and a population explosion and the corresponding climbing rate of poverty and hunger; war being waged somewhere on the planet at any given time, despite the catastrophic lessons of two World Wars; and a self-proclaimed "stable genius" in the White House, whose actions don't exactly support that immodest self-assessment nor inspire confidence during such a challenging period of American history in the making—I'm afraid I'm with Grandpa Walker. My greatest contribution to the Earth's health may well be my death. My cynical friend, Craig, who has little confidence in the general intelligence of humankind, a position that is increasingly hard to argue with, likes to say that "it's always dark before it goes pitch black." Things do seem to be getting dimmer all the time. And yet....

Janet and I are cruising homeward after a late Saturday afternoon walk in Leland with Benny. Smooth jazz is playing on Pandora, the temperature is in the always-welcome seventies, the sun is canting westward, though with plenty of light left on this late June day. The village is our very happy place. Even with the increased though manageable traffic of the vacationers' "shift change"—the excited incoming visitors, the near-tears homebound folks—nothing can detract from our buoyant mood. Benny always favors this walk, too, darting to and fro on his leash, checking out all of the scents that command his attention. Driving south on Good Harbor Trail, we pass the decaying general store from once upon a time. One afternoon several summers ago, I sought the cover of its porch when I lost a race with a pop-up thunderstorm that caught up to me and erupted overhead while on the last stage of an afternoon bike ride. I stood there for 15 minutes or so waiting for the storm to pass, in no hurry, curious about the building's former life. During the downpour, I served as a witness to the structure slowly slipping into oblivion. It was an oddly reassuring feeling; don't we all fade away, eventually?

As we drive toward our cabin, doing the speed limit, which reflects my reacquired calm, which is the goal of our Up North vacations, and what dear Janet works to make happen for me, we pass cherry orchards lining both sides of Good Harbor Trail. The farmers continue to expand these fields, planting acres and acres of new fruit trees to meet rising demand. This land so nobly worked and of great purpose is relatively safe from "foreign invaders" downstate and beyond, as the summer season is short and the tourists must soon return from whence they came.

Once back at our seasonal home in Cedar, we relax on our front deck, surrounded by the towering sugar maples under a sunny sky. After a few minutes of silence, gazing at the gravid ruby-throated hummingbird tentatively flitting by the feeder I put out a few weeks ago in hopes of seeing a hummer or two, this one a regular now, I announce, "They're here."

Janet, watching this avian wonder along with me, responds, reading my mind once again, as long-married couples often do, implicitly knowing I'm not referring to hummingbirds. I'm talkin' 'bout "Fudgies," that most dreaded invasive species in these parts (i.e., tourists who have a taste for fudge and other similar inclinations who tend not to glory in the great outdoors). "Yes, but most of them don't go where we go. And they bring money to help out the locals so they can make it through the winter. It's an ecosystem. Someday, with enough practice, they might even figure it out. We did."

Yes, we did. And yes, they can.

FUDGIES

Perhaps 25 years ago, I had my first experience with the dreaded "Fudgie." It was me.

I had been in downtown Traverse City, having reunited with a former bartending colleague and carousing a bit on a late summer afternoon, during the years when the body and brain would permit such ridiculously fun behavior. We were visiting a local establishment and bellied ourselves up to the bar. After a couple of beers and a shot of something to boost our buzz and toast the occasion of getting together again, we were becoming jolly. As we imbibed, my buddy introduced me to one of his acquaintances who happened to be in the bar as well. From the looks of his googled eyes and slightly slurred speech, he obviously had been at it quite a bit longer than we. Rather early in the day for such a condition, but he seemed a nice enough fellow.

After the two of them got caught up, my friend and I drained our beers and left. We were headed to his car across the street. So I did what comes naturally to an unthinking vacationer in northern Michigan who had a nice afternoon glow about him: I crossed at the middle of the street, my heading conveniently direct, as the crow flies.

One vehicle slowed for me then waved me on as I already had cut into traffic. The local my friend ran into, who was outside having a smoke, went ballistic. "You shit-for-brains jaywalking Fudgie!" I stopped—realizing he was shouting at me—aborted the street crossing and reversed my tracks.

"What did you call me?" I asked, inches from his face.

✱

"A Fudgie. A goddamned Fudgie." My friend quickly interceded, separating the two of us with his hands on our chests as if he were the referee in a boxing ring—another of the many talents of a seasoned barkeep. He settled us both down, explaining to his acquaintance that I was new around these parts and really didn't qualify as a member of the despicable invasive species of Fudgie. The amperage surge curtailed, we two near-combatants shook hands and called it a day.

"So what's a Fudgie?" I asked as we drove off.

"It's a tourist who thinks the world revolves around him and doesn't have any common sense and creates hazards for the rest of us. And hey, I gotta say, you gave a damn good impression." We both laughed at his razzing, though he much harder than I. That incident left an impression on me. I had fallen in love with northwest lower Michigan and wanted nothing more than to be one with the locals. To stick out like a, like a…Fudgie, well, that was unthinkable to me. From then on, I swore I would never deserve the moniker of Fudgie and would always stay conscious of Up North folkways.

✱

Now, many years later, when it comes to Fudgies, well, it's the same as it ever was, and perhaps ever will be. If not worse. The species is still easily recognizable, especially with the ever-increasing popularity of this special place thanks to *Good Morning America* designating Sleeping Bear Dunes National Lakeshore (which for all intents and purposes should include Traverse City) as "the most beautiful place in America" for a vacation destination in 2011. This designation has turned out to be an economic windfall as well as a curse, trying the patience of the locals. It's like the phenomenon of Chreasters: those guilt-ridden visitors to Catholic churches twice annually—on Christmas and Easter—whom the regulars must tolerate, if only for a while. Only this infestation of these outsiders lasts from Memorial Day Weekend through Labor Day Weekend. The real surge is most noticeable the weekend before the July 4th holiday, when they start pouring into Grand Traverse and Leelanau counties.

In June 2017, I had just spent more than two weeks at our Cedar retreat, one week alone, trying to recover from two hellacious years in the field of management that involved saving the school I worked for from the brink of financial ruin. Now, all was well fiscally with the organization, but it had taken a lot out of me. It was time for a sabbatical, but a nearly three-week stay would have to do.

I was driving my Honda Ridgeline truck with my mountain bike on the back-end rack, anticipating one of my favorite rides around Lake Leelanau, a 16-mile ride that provides stunning views of the lake while pedaling through cherry and apple orchard country and past lakefront homes. About a mile south of Leland, on M-22, I came around a bend near the entrance to the Whaleback Hill hiking trail. Suddenly, in front of my truck, a pudgy woman of perhaps 60 years materialized, calmly walking her bike across the road. It was a perfect spot for manslaughter, womanslaughter, or Fudgieslaughter, whatever the local criminal code. When she realized I was about to paste her to my grill, she froze—right in the middle of M-22. I hit the brake pedal, and the truck stopped, a mere five feet from the careless woman. Her trainee biking buddies, in a pack of four with their "sponsored" riding shirts and all the cyclist trimmings, were following her across the road like ducklings behind their mama. I slowly crept up next to the woman (no traffic was behind me or southbound). She looked at me in surprise then dumbly grinned as if she had been caught doing something wrong but easily forgivable. "Lady, do you realize I could have killed you?" I said in a voice just below a shout.

"Yah," she agreed while nodding her head, grinning still.

I took a deep breath and continued, summoning my inner Buddha to reduce my blood pressure and prevent me from getting out of the truck and making a scene. "You need to be careful on this road. You picked a really bad place to cross—right next to the curve where drivers have little warning. You know, vacations are best enjoyed and remembered if you survive them."

"Thank you, sir," she said to me, waving dismissively and resumed chattering with her homies. Then she slowly raised her rotund behind onto the bike saddle, and peddled her wobbly way across the road.

"God help them," I muttered. "And protect the rest of us from their kind."

This was only the beginning of such interactions with and observations of the invaders. My previous two weeks had been blissful among the locals. Now the company we were expecting had arrived. Our patience would be sorely tested.

When I finished my ride around Lake Leelanau, a successful attempt at exorcising my demons, I stopped by Carlson's Fishery in Fishtown to pick up some lake trout; Janet was returning for the week and I knew she would enjoy a fresh Lake Michigan-caught fish dinner. The college-aged woman working the counter was patiently waiting with a smile for two elderly couples to complete their tour of the small shop. Obviously, they were new to these parts and decision-making wasn't on the agenda. She eventually turned to me and asked cheerily, "Can I help you, sir?"

"Go ahead and take care of these folks first," I responded. She pursed her lips, shook her head from side to side, and rolled her eyes. Got it.

As the visitors—not customers—sauntered slowly out the swinging screen door, I shared my frustration at my near-death experience—somebody else's, that is—on M-22 earlier in the morning. "The invasion has begun," I concluded, speaking as if I were from around these parts, which I have been in training to be for 25 years.

"I know," she said sympathetically. "I bike all the time and it just freaks me out how careless some visitors are. It's like they think they're indestructible." Then she chuckled in resignation. There will be blood, and we all know it; it's just a matter of when.

I bought a nice piece of filleted trout, about a pound-and-a-half, as well as some smoked salmon to nibble on for the inevitable drive back to Indy. I tipped the "College Fund" jar placed prominently near the cash register. She smiled at me like a comrade and said, "Have a good day. And be careful out there—*they're here*."

❉

On Saturday, my wife texted me about her impending arrival. She had left for Indy a week and a half earlier, now hitching a return ride with our son's family, as they would be vacationing in Northport the week of July 4th. "We're a half hour away. Your son is fried from the drive. Why don't you meet us at Good Harbor Bay with a few beers and the kids can see the beach?" It was a capital spur-of-the-moment plan for 3 p.m. on a gorgeous Saturday afternoon.

When I pulled up at the National Park Service beach parking area, there were just a handful of vehicles, none of them my people's. In fact, the lot was practically deserted. The Fudgie horde had yet to make landfall. I walked over to a sandy trail and spotted contrails from the USAF Thunderbirds aerial acrobatics team as they screamed back from a loop toward the Cherry Festival in Traverse City. Although I couldn't be in town for the main event, I was privy to an equally enthralling airshow: American redstarts were zipping in and out of the thickets in the dunes just a few feet away from me. I must have struck the black, blaze orange, and white warblers as a friendly, as they continued their pursuit of bugs unimpeded by my proximity. My birdwatching trance was broken when the familiar white Honda Odyssey pulled up. Hugs. Beers distributed to mom and dad. Beach walk with the boys, ages 4 and 18 months. Then I introduced the youngest to Lake Michigan, picking him up from behind and gently placing him bottom-first on the tideline. His apprehension instantly melted away once the water proved as harmless and as fascinating to him as Lake Michigan has been to me since my first introduction.

After the 30-minute respite and recharge, we turned to walk back to the beach entrance, about an eighth of a mile away. And then we saw it: Fudgie beachhead. Where moments ago there was clear beach with just a handful of humans, the entrance was now teeming with approximately 50 tourists who ventured no farther than the trailhead at the beach, clogging the whole area. As predicted, D-Day had arrived. The locals would endure the onslaught for the next two months or so, working hard to sustain a smile—whether artificial or genuine—and be as patient as possible. All in the interest of making a living, ensuring that they would make it through the leaner days of winter.

Our kids and grandkids would be staying a comfortable distance away in Northport: good for everybody. Of course, they needed Mom and Dad to pick up a few things for our July 4th cookout there: like charcoal, lighter fluid, wine opener, beer, ground beef, hot dogs, bratwurst, potato salad, chips… So we stopped at Tom's Food Market in downtown Northport, just beyond the harbor. Inside, I was marveling at a Chinese-made baseball cap with the Great Lakes logo design, trying to find the missing price tag. I picked an orange cap with a navy-blue logo, and as I was walking away from the merchandise stand I nearly took a charge from a young mop-headed blonde twentysomething who braked hard, missing me by inches. I stood my ground, saying nothing, saying everything. He mumbled, "Go ahead," to me. I did. Whatever happened to "excuse me" or "sorry" or even the fingernail-on-chalkboard-to-my-ears "my bad"? I headed for the beer section to relieve my renewed lack of faith in society and those who will eventually inherit the Earth.

So the title of yet another book I will most likely never write came to me on the spot: *We Were Fudgies—Once.* I shared the working title with Janet after recounting the experience at the hat stand. She laughed. We left the store, cautiously looking both ways as we made our way through the parking lot to the truck. Fudgie season was on.

CRITTERS

For years, rumors have abounded about cougars being present in Sleeping Bear Dunes National Lakeshore. At one time the National Park Service posted instructions at trailheads as to what to do should you see one of the big cats (adults can be well over 200 pounds and reach speeds of nearly 50 miles per hour). Like stay calm and don't run (in my case, I will do precisely the very opposite), and if the carnivorous *Puma concolor* begins to approach, wave your arms to appear bigger than you are. It's suggested that such antics should do the trick; so, not to worry. (Um, ri-ight.) Still, the first time I saw the trailhead posting about the chance of crossing paths with a cougar a few years ago, it put an extra zip into my step as my survival radar went up and my reptilian brain awareness took over. Before entering the woods, though, I returned to my truck and fetched a sturdy walking stick for extra measure—as a predator basher.

Each summer, with visitors flocking to the National Lakeshore, alleged cougar sightings surge. Yet, to date, there is no evidence—nothing has been caught on video, and no paw prints or big cat scat has been discovered. However, my guess is, like UFOs, they're out there (i.e., *if you believe*). And I have to admit, I do like the idea of large predatory mammals like cougars returning to where they once roamed for thousands and thousands of years, and where they still belong. America's "progress" has specialized in moving the native locals out and away for far too long.

Black bears certainly inhabit Leelanau County, and the Michigan Department of Natural Resources has a fall hunting season for them. Last

October, while traveling through beautiful downtown Cedar (about a 60-second ride; it's a one four-way-stop town), Janet and I noticed a sign near the hardware store stating, "Bear Crossing." We thought it was a joke. When I ran it by our Cedar neighbor Paul, he straightened me out. "That's no joke, my friend. A mother and two cubs have been seen around here for several months. *In Cedar!*" he emphasized, as if the risen Christ had been seen and my name was Thomas.

Several years ago, in the wee hours of one summer morning, I was awakened by a racket outside that sounded like something metallic was getting knocked around. Despite the noise, my curiosity quickly surrendered to the spell of a dark, starry summer night's slumber in the woods. At sunup, I went out to the shed behind the house to fetch my mountain bike for a ride around Lime and Little Traverse lakes. There was our Weber charcoal grill on its side, the cover about five feet from the upended kettle. The grill grate, the cooking surface that had been used the night before for burgers and a nice ribeye steak from Burritt's Fresh Markets in Traverse City, was removed, and remnant charcoal briquets were scattered about. Interestingly, the grill cover had a new pronounced dent in it. Had we been visited by a bear? Well, since then, that imaginary possibility has been conveniently converted to fact, due to the recent bear sightings in Cedar, and now is part of our ongoing Up North family lore. The chance that it could have been some rowdy raccoons will never be mentioned in the telling and retelling of this tale. My storytelling integrity is at stake, you know.

Years ago, when our son, Matt, was 18, he, my Michigander buddy Craig and I sailed out to South Manitou Island on Craig's Flying Scot in early August for a four-day extended weekend on the isle. On our only overcast day, we hiked near the Old Cemetery and came across some raspberry and blackberry patches, ripe for the picking, as they say. The blackberries were the largest I had ever seen, and we didn't hesitate to begin relieving the canes of their succulent fruit. As we harvested and grazed, Craig said to us in a grave voice, "Fellas, be sure to keep an eye out for a black bear in the area. They love berry patches, you know." Matt and I froze. "Say what?" I asked in my Hoosier tongue.

"The National Park Rangers told me that a black bear has been seen here on the island this summer," Craig responded. "It decided not to take the ferry out of Leland and swam over from the mainland. But seriously, just stay alert." Then he resumed his bearlike preoccupation. "Man, checkout these monster blackberries—and they're mine, all mine!" Despite his ecstatic berry picking, this unexpected news put the kibosh on the feasting Matt and I had been deliriously engaged in; we hustled to fill our plastic bags with the berry bounty and be on our way. Never did see the bear, a natural thrill we were okay with missing. Craig, however, was disappointed. "I was really hoping to see that great big ball of black fur," he said, as we hiked back to our campground. "Oh well. Let's try our luck again tomorrow, then maybe—"

"We're good," I said while Matt eyed me with concern for our well-being and pleading for fatherly intervention. Our tour guide just laughed at us greenhorns.

❋

Not ever having the pleasure of sighting cougars or black bears on the loose in northern Michigan, we have certainly enjoyed seeing abundant animal life out and about. Whenever I'm driving with Craig, he spots deer in fields along the highway—every time—with his instinctive deer hunter's eyes. Having developed a decent sixth sense of wild game spotting, Janet and I now see whitetails on most of our drives in Leelanau County. As common as deer sightings are, we always enjoy them as if it's the first time. (Not too fond of the mysterious deer statues in some of the locals' front yards, though. I'm quite unsure whether they're teasing the tourists or find the oversized tchotchke somehow adorable.) But we've experienced other sightings of mammalian critters that are a bit more exotic than the everyday whitetail variety.

Back in the early 2000s we decided to attempt what every visitor to Traverse City and the greater area dreams of: having a slice of land to call one's own. So we set off on what would be more than a yearlong search for a modest vacation property. We traveled hither and yon with our cheery and ever-optimistic realtor, Sam Abood. Like every dreamy-eyed downstater and out-of-stater, we were looking for something on the water. Having champagne taste on a beer budget, we partnered then with another couple so we could have greater purchasing power. Getting husband and wife on the same page is hard enough in a real estate search; as Janet and I discovered, inviting another couple to share in the deliberations exponentially compounds such difficulty. Nonetheless, we worked with Sam to find listings that appealed to the four of us, at least potentially. One of many was located along the Boardman River, outside Traverse City. As things would turn out, it would be the first and last riverfront property we visited. It featured a modest-sized two-bedroom home on several acres with plenty of river frontage. Upon pulling into the driveway in Sam's Chevy Suburban, I could tell that my partners, including my wife, weren't impressed. Of course, I loved it. Northern Michigan rivers—clear, cold, sparkling trout streams—enthrall me. As they stood with Sam assessing the property and showing no inclination to go inside the house, I ventured down to the river itself—the real draw in my mind. I stood on the rickety seen-better-days cedar dock and watched for signs of trout in the rippling water. Suddenly, a small, elongated, entirely black furry critter slinked from the grass onto the dock: a mink. Then another. I stood still, amused, as the two chased one another over and under the dock. I called Janet to come join me. "Wow, so cute!" she exclaimed. But neither their cuteness nor the river's attraction were enough to convince Janet and company to seriously consider the property.

While biking around Little Traverse Lake one fine summer afternoon in July 2017, as I veered away from the lake and approached M-22 for my return home, two river otters loped across the road about 20 feet in front of me. I skidded to a stop and watched as they made their way to the marsh on the north side of the road. I remember watching an episode of the *Magical World of Disney* as a child during the 1960s in which otters starred and, of course, anthropomorphism reigned. Although the program captivated me back then and instilled a longing in me to see these lithe, playful creatures in real life, the otters wanted nothing to do with me. Which made it more of a *Mutual of Omaha's Wild Kingdom* moment—thankfully.

❉

For three months in 2005, I lived in a cottage on Spider Lake that we formerly co-owned with another Indianapolis couple. I had landed a job at

Mercy Hospital in Grayling (now Grayling Hospital), a relocation experiment that didn't take. As a result, my wife and I discovered a few things about ourselves: 1) she is a Hoosier with sycamore tree-like roots and will never permanently leave Indianapolis; and 2) we really can't live apart from one another.

During my short stay on Spider Lake, my evenings and weekends were always spent outside. Hiking, biking, walking, fishing, or just sitting on the dock watching the lake's wildlife. Early one pleasant Sunday morning in late May, I was riding my mountain bike on Rennie Lake Road near Ranch Rudolph. I came wheeling around a turn when I saw, crossing the road—*I swear*—a gray wolf, who quickly disappeared into the roadside brush then into the woods. I had skipped Mass for a visit to the Lord's cathedral instead (which I trust the Creator prefers we do anyway) and was rewarded with this startling sighting. When I returned home, I called Craig immediately on my trusty flip phone. (This was the pre-smartphone era, and I had not yet developed the unfortunate habit of carrying a phone with me wherever I went.) "I think I just saw a wolf, bro!" I exclaimed.

"You might have," he responded carefully, not wanting to dim my enthusiasm. "Wouldn't be the first time someone's reported one in the area, but it's pretty rare. Sure it wasn't a coyote?" Too big, and the head was broader, I shared. "Did you check for tracks?" Of course my outdoorsman friend would ask that; and of course, in my elevated state, I didn't even think about it. "That would be telling." I didn't bother to pedal back and search for paw print evidence. I simply wanted to believe my eyes and not ruin a good story.

Two years ago, Janet came home from a quick trip to Cedar for some groceries and couldn't contain her excitement. "Tim! Tim! You won't believe what I just saw: a bobcat crossing the road near Paul and Marie's house. Just about scared me! I slowed down to watch it. It was amazing—so cool!" All shook up and thrilled, she was. And lucky. Paul had told me about the bobcat he and Marie see from time to time down near Victoria Creek, which runs below their hillside home and tracks along South Good Harbor Trail. Days earlier, Paul stood on his deck enjoying the sunrise and a cup of joe. He happened to look down the hill eastward toward the creek and saw the bobcat leap from a cedar tree limb to the ground then scamper into the woods. "Right where you were fishing for brookies the other day," he related. "Spooky, eh?" he said, laughing. "Not to worry. They stay away from humans—especially Hoosiers. Something about the smell and the tough meat."

✳

Traditionally, our last stay at Cedar for the season is the first week in October. As is my custom, I like to drive out to Shalda Creek to see if the salmon are still running. While driving along the dirt road before arriving at the creek last October, I spotted a large cat, perhaps feral, I thought. But as I slowed to a stop about 50 yards from the animal, it became obvious that that was no kitty, at least by the usual standards I was accustomed to. "What is that?" Janet said, reacting as I braked the truck.

"I think it's a young bobcat," I replied. The wildcat didn't seem concerned by our presence and padded along the road, occasionally quickening its pace to satisfy its curiosity, kitten-like. I let my foot off the brake and crept slowly toward it. The critter then leapt into the woods and I thought I lost it. But no: there it was, sitting about 10 feet off the road, watching me from a more protected vantage in the shin-tangle. I got out and stood near the truck; it then went about its youthful business of investigating its surroundings, yet didn't put a safe distance between the two of us. "I bet momma is in the vicinity," I suggested to Janet, "because that youngster is acting like it hasn't a care in the world."

I took a few photos, but couldn't get a clear visual, as the underbrush obscured a full view. "Good enough," I said as I got back in the truck.

"Didn't expect that, did we," Janet commented. Another prize animal sighting for the memory book we share.

✳

All of these creatures belong here as much, if not more so, than we humans. Although the thought of sharing the woods with cougars and bears and wolves and bobcats can make me a bit skittish for a moment, I am so glad they are among us; it's reassuring. Haven't seen a bear in Indy—ever;

not even at the zoo. River otters are nowhere near the farm-runoff-clouded White River that courses through Indiana's capital city. Wolf Run was a private golf course for the well-to-do in Zionsville, just northwest of Indianapolis; the members would have frowned on gray wolves adding a dimension of reality to the links (probably not crazy about the coyotes that *are* there either). *Where the Wild Things Aren't* should be Indiana's license plate tagline.

Someday I hope to see the elk that inhabit the Pigeon River Country State Forest near Gaylord. To lay eyes on moose in the Upper Peninsula wilderness. To unquestionably spot a gray wolf on Isle Royale. But until then, I'll keep my imagination stoked and be on the lookout for the wild things that inhabit Leelanau County and roam the backroads of my mind.

BROWN BRIDGE POND

On a storybook northern Michigan summer day in August 1989, Janet and I were paddling canoes on the Boardman River, about to conclude our several hours recreating on the water. She had teamed with our friend Craig's wife at the time, Connie, and Craig and I were in the other aluminum canoe. This allowed them to do their thing and us to fish for trout at our pace. Everybody happy. "Put a spinner bait on your line and get ready to troll," Craig shouted to me from behind. "We're about to enter Brown Bridge Pond."

I did as told. Within minutes, I hooked a smallmouth bass. "There you go!" Craig trumpeted, both of us laughing at my quick success as I unhooked the one-pounder from the Mepps lure. We traversed the pond in about 10 minutes and landed the canoes, which would be picked up by the Ranch Rudolph crew who would transport us back to our vehicles as we sat in the bed of the canoe-hauling truck, content with another great day spent in nature. The pond was lovely—one among what seems to be countless bodies of translucent water in northern Michigan. Years later, Janet and I would get to know the pond better, if not intimately, and its surrounding hiking trails.

In 2000, we went in with another couple to purchase a cabin on Spider Lake. We would become regulars at the Brown Bridge Quiet Area, just two miles south from our vacation digs. Every time we spent a long Memorial Day or Labor Day Weekend as well as our vacation weeks there during the summer, we made it a point to hike the Quiet Area trails almost daily, and would be sure to get our tandem Wilderness Systems kayak out on the pond at least once before making the return trip to Indy.

Hiking the ridge trail above the pond was a favorite activity of ours during those Spider Lake days. Some mornings I would jog the two-mile gradual uphill grade of South Hobbs Highway to the trail, then run about a mile on the woodland paths and return. Sometimes Janet and I would hike that same route and then do the trails. Usually, we would just drive up and park there so we would have more time and energy to spend on the trails themselves.

Back then, by habit, we would step down each of the four long wooden stairways to the water's edge. Before climbing back up the stairs, we took a long moment to regard the view of the pond and check for animal sightings: fish, reptiles, amphibians, birds, or any of the mammals that lived in and around the pond. Then a deep breath, and one of us would whisper a reluctant, "Okay," signaling it was time for the ascent. In our late forties then, we were in good shape, our joints not yet creaking, and we hustled back up, legs powering us upward, reveling in the heart-pounding workout. We'd stop midway to lower our heart rates a bit, and to appreciate where we were, then resume. Reaching the top of the ridge, sweating profusely, breathing hard, we'd smile at the small accomplishment, sip some water, then head toward the next staircase. This may not be everyone's idea of a good time, but it was ours.

❋

During my time at the Spider Lake cabin in the spring of 2005, one Friday afternoon after work in late April, I hiked down the east staircase of the Brown Bridge Quiet Area and walked the narrow wooden-planked path above the bog to a small cedar-surrounded opening on the pond. The sun canted to the west, dappling the trees around me. Out on the water were hundreds of migrating ducks—common and hooded mergansers, buffleheads, goldeneyes, and my favorite, wood ducks, as well as several pairs of mute swans. Other than birdcalls, including the chickadees sounding the warning that a human was in the area, it was completely quiet. No buzz or whine of machinery or traffic, and other than me, no evidence of people, which was a welcome timeout after a long week of work at the hospital. I waited until the sun started to drop below the tree line then made the 20-minute hike back to my SUV. Didn't see another soul the whole way. After this, I couldn't imagine heading to a bar or restaurant for Friday night festivities. Reset by solitude.

It was a Saturday in early June, during the waning days of my soon-to-be-dashed hopes of becoming an official northern Michigander. I had just returned from Traverse City, making a run for supplies at Target. About 3 p.m. a thunderstorm rolled in and out in a matter of minutes. I went down the path to our dock on Spider Lake to check out the fish activity: smallmouth and largemouth bass, bluegill, pumpkinseed, and the occasional northern pike hung out in our cove. As the storm moved on, I spotted a rare double rainbow forming to the southeast, a vivid spectrum of color bands arcing across the sky. It dawned on me that I would probably get a better view from Brown Bridge Quiet Area. So I jumped in my Honda Element and hurried up the road.

After parking in the wooden-fenced gravel lot, I jog-walked down to the southwest staircase to go out on the earthen causeway leading to the Brown Bridge Dam. As I hustled down the steps, I spotted a large common snapping turtle resting on the last one. I gave the *Chelydra serpentina* a wide berth, marveling at the hard-shelled critter that had "no fear" written all over its prehistoric face. The storm clouds were retreating to the east and the double rainbow loomed more dramatically from the less obscured lakeside view. As I stood near the pond's shoreline, I noticed movement around me. To my amazement, about a dozen full-grown snapping turtles were in my immediate vicinity. Some were swimming toward the bank; several had emerged from the water and were clambering up the pond's embankment; while others had arrived at the moment's certainty: both on the water-facing side and top of the earthen causeway, these females were clawing birthing holes in the sand and depositing eggs. It seemed as if some barometric signal went off with the storm, and the turtle mothers knew it was the right time for their egg-laying to begin. I gave the ladies their space, standing no closer than 10 feet as they went about their labor. So intent with their mission, they didn't seem to mind my presence at all. Just me and the snappers under a rainbow sky.

Two days later I returned to check on the turtle nursery. My heart sank. The nesting grounds had been disturbed, dug up by some varmints—most likely a family of skunks or raccoons. Cracked open and licked dry snapping turtle eggs littered the nests; not an intact one could be seen. Nature had taken its course. Hopefully, some of the nests went undetected by the opportunistic predators. In approximately three months, the surviving hatchlings would instinctively crawl to the water, and once their shells formed and hardened, they would be virtually predator free.

❊

During our five years at Spider Lake, we hiked the ridge line trail at Brown Bridge Quiet Area many times. The hikes were walking meditations, with only the sounds of the wind through the trees and birdcalls accompanying our footsteps. Sometimes, though, we would talk, usually with me processing some work-related issue and Janet playing counselor and coach during such walking therapy sessions. But mostly, we went in quietude. We have been married long enough that being in one another's company is an ongoing act of communication. Through our three-and-a-half decades together, Janet and I have settled into our own skins, and we understand implicitly that many times words don't add value to our sense of communion.

One rainy morning on a Memorial Day weekend, I got Janet out of the house for a hike at the Quiet Area. She tends to sadden if the sun isn't cooperating with her outdoor plans, especially during our vacation time, when the pressure can be on for hard-earned perfect experiences. But hiking can be just the tonic for such mildly depressive states, even a wet walk in the woods.

As we were coming back up one of the staircases, we stopped midway for a breather. And unexpectedly, we entered a birder's paradise. "Tim, look at all the warblers," Janet called to my attention. There seemed to be hundreds of chestnut-sided and blackburnian warblers flitting impatiently, as is their way, in the surrounding trees. Waves of these colorful spring migrants moved through the woods, traveling to their mating destinations in the U.P. (Upper Peninsula) and farther on in Canada, with some to stay and nest locally. We stood still in the steady rain, capitalizing on this rare sight.

"We're getting pretty wet," Janet noted, the downpour sliding off our waterproof jackets in rivulets. "Best move on, like our feathery friends." She was beaming now, the oppression of the cloudy day lifted by the tiny trilling birds and their spectacular color.

"Hard to leave this," I said, as she reached for my hand to resume our climb. We haven't had such a dense, intense warbler sighting since. But it's good to know one can.

On a late June afternoon, while walking along the Brown Bridge Pond causeway and enjoying the tree swallows darting and swooping over the water while feeding on flying insects and alighting on and entering the nesting boxes facing the water, Janet stopped suddenly and uttered, "Oh my God" as if she meant it. She did. She raised her Nikon binoculars and aimed at something at the top of the stand of white birch trees down below us to the west. "Tim, Tim—what kind of bird is that?" she asked urgently, but refused to hand me the binoculars. For this sighting, I really didn't need them.

"Well, that's no cardinal," I declared, as the brilliant red bird perched atop the tallest birch appeared to glow, its striking color standing out against the green-leaved background. She finally handed me the binoculars...and I, too, registered my first sighting of a male scarlet tanager, evidenced by its black wings. I've had the rare pleasure of seeing a male several times since, always in northern Michigan, though never a sure thing every summer.

One of my favorite things to do at the Quiet Area was stopping at the two observation decks that overlooked the pond. On picturesque summer days we would pause there on our way down to the causeway and again on our way back. The view had an endless summer quality to it. Occasional cottony cumulous clouds slowly drifted over the surrounding woods, the pond, and us, their shadows softly animating the scene. Janet would inhale deeply and exhale a huge sigh of contentment. If I were to pick a soundtrack for this experience (and showing my age), it would be the B-52's lyric-less track "Follow Your Bliss" from *Cosmic Thing*. A synthesizer monopolized melody that simply takes you away—just like the view from the scenic overlook. On more than one occasion we saw bald eagles perched in tall trees along the pond as well as soaring above it. True, the pond was manmade, a result of the damming of the Boardman River in 1922 to help generate electricity for Traverse City. But the wildlife it attracted and the serenity it provided made our time there all the better; it felt and appeared natural because nature always adapts to mankind's whims. But all good things must come to an end. Sometimes, even a better end.

After years of public meetings and arguments pro and con, the Brown Bridge Dam was removed in 2012. However, the much-anticipated engineering project didn't get off to a stellar start. The controversial draining of Brown Bridge Pond so that the Boardman River could resume its natural course became a deluge of rushing water when the temporary dam built adjacent to the original one failed. Downstream property owners experienced a surprise flood. Though fortunately there were no injuries, there was some structural damage and a resulting legal settlement with the general contractor. For nature lovers like us who prized the pond for its wildlife and scenic beauty, we opposed the dam removal. Repairing the aging structure, though, proved to be cost-prohibitive. Yet as disappointed as we were in the project because of our attachment to the area as returning visitors who unrealistically expect things to always remain the same, returning the river to its natural run was an admirable approach. The only problem for us was, we would lose the pond. And so we did.

We sold our interest in our Spider Lake property to the couple who co-owned it with us since buying it in 2000, well before the legal decision to remove the dam and restore the river was concluded. Years later, in July 2016, we returned to the Brown Bridge Quiet Area for a look at what had transpired.

Janet and I hiked down the long flight of stairs that used to lead to the causeway and dam, and made our way to the area that was once underwater. Farther below, about 75 yards from us, the Boardman River snaked its way through wild grasslands. It will be many years from now until the trees overtake the surrounding meadow, but it will happen. We watched several groups of kayakers paddle by—a few too many for our more secluded tastes. "It's just not how I like to remember the area," Janet said wistfully. But as the kayakers moved downstream, I saw greater possibilities. On the other side of the river a fly fisherman approached the stream. He made several casts and caught a brook trout on the third. I smiled. Brook trout used to struggle here, most likely because of the dam's presence. Now perhaps they were rallying. A few years from now, this awakened stretch of the Boardman could well become a prime trout fishery. This exciting prospect got my motor humming.

"Next time we come this way, I'm bringing my trout fishing gear," I informed Janet. I do miss the pond. I can't turn back the clock. But I can keep my happy memories of precious days spent on the pond in a kayak or hiking around it and watching the gathering migratory waterfowl and all of the other times we revisited this small slice of heaven. As for another trout fishing spot…well, I think I can handle that.

"Sounds good, honey," she said. "Maybe I'll come with you," fisherwoman that she isn't. "The river is pretty, you know."

The Boardman would be fine. And so would we.

EMPIRE

Early one summer day during our vacation in Leland in 1995, my good friend Craig, then a self-described "lot lizard"—car salesman, that is—called from work and suggested a new venue for us: Empire. "It's the beginning of the month and I can be out of here by noon," he offered, not one to miss out on an opportunity for merrymaking.

I always trust his recommendations for entertainment, and so I committed us to the outing before anyone else had stirred in the quiet of a vacation morning. Once the troops were fully conscious, I would give them their marching orders. There would be no arguments. Not because I lord over them, but because they loved adventuring with "Uncle Craig."

Empire was sleepy back then. There were summer visitors, but not the numbers seen today. Empire's public beach now features a dressed-up park, plenty of paved and paid parking, an aluminum dock stretching out into South Bar Lake, and well-appointed public restrooms. Back then, there was none of that. And we were perfectly fine with the spartan arrangements.

As usual, we marveled at this new perspective of Lake Michigan as seen from Empire Village Park. In those years before the word on the area got out nationally—before *Good Morning America* convinced the rest of the country that Sleeping Bear Dunes National Lakeshore and the immediate surrounding areas had to be on everyone's bucket list—the beach at Empire was quieter, easier to navigate. There was no competition for parking on that sunshiny early August day. Our contingent unloaded coolers and beach towels—those were also the days before beachgoers tended to bring their entire households with them—and headed south from the parking lot, Craig guiding us along the way.

We padded along the shoreline for about 75 yards when my wife, Janet, and her youngest sister decided that was far enough—and it was. There was no one around from that point south. Dune grass and gradually rising dunes behind, lake as far as the eye could see in front, and an infinite blue sky above. "Nice spot. You Hoosiers are really starting to come along," our local guide complimented us. "Now fellas, I got something else in mind for you. Ladies, we'll be back in about an hour or so."

"Take your time," Janet quipped. "We'll be fine—believe me." And the two laughed at the thought of them being deprived of our company.

Following Craig expectantly, we headed farther south. My son, Matt, and his best friend, Cory, were sprinting ahead on their 12-year-old rubber-band-like legs, dashing into the surf, splashing one another, heeding the call of the wild, inspired by our stunning outdoor location.

About a half mile from the girls' beachhead we suddenly halted. "Here we are," Craig announced, nodding upward. Above was a dune with a large vertical gash of open sand. The incline towered more than 300 feet high. "Up we go, men." Like Mount Everest climber George Leigh Mallory's famous utterance before his failed and deadly ascent of the world's highest peak in 1924—"because it's there"—we accepted Craig's order without protest or question because it clearly was our mission.

Unlike the popular Dune Climb overlooking Glen Lake on the National Lakeshore property, there were no signs posted for this dune climb. More importantly, there were no signs saying not to climb.

Matt and Cory were live wires. Once Craig gave the go-ahead, they began sprinting up the sandy expanse before we even took our first steps. My brother-in-law Vince, Craig, and I began to scale the dune at a more measured pace. Within minutes I was climbing on all fours, bare feet pushing off of the warm sand that gave beneath me with every step, seemingly inching our way up. Sweat poured out of us as our hearts threatened to burst from our ribcages. Every 30 or 40 steps I would stop for a minute, chest heaving, chuckling to myself as I caught my breath, checking my progress by looking down at the beach. It was a labor of love. Craig paused more frequently, his smoking habit causing him to suck harder for O2.

Before we were halfway up, the boys had already made the summit, panting, smiling, gesturing excitedly at the spectacular ocean-like panorama below. "C'mon, guys, you can make it!" they implored us.

"It's hell getting old," my brother-in-law uttered between gasping breaths. About 30 feet from the top, several deep gullies with bordering dune grass offered some welcome handholds at standing height. And then we were there, at the summit, standing with the boys.

"Isn't this amazing, Dad?" Matt perfectly summarized. "Man, I wish Mom had come. She doesn't know what she's missing." I smiled while staring out at the horizon-reaching lake. She was busy with her own decompression process, basking in the sun, idly chatting, reading fiction, dozing off perhaps. Besides, she knew she would get a full report from the boys.

"Check it out," Craig said as he pointed downward toward the shoreline. "About 50 yards out in the water. Those are fish—probably giant lake carp." Five dark bodies undulated lazily in the shallows. They had to be sizable, given how far away from them we were, and how easily we could see them.

Impatience coursing through their adolescent veins, Matt and Cory couldn't wait to head back down the dune. They started long-jumping, their elastic bodies bounding into thin air, easily covering two times their body height, plunging into the sand and shoving off again with a rebel yell. By the time we made it to the beach, the two young soccer players were scrambling up the dune once more, courtesy of young hearts with a lot fewer miles on them. Before we elders started down, we paused to savor the view. The wildflowers, vetch and violets. The ruby-throated hummingbirds cavorting along the ridge. The dragonflies, mostly hand-sized darners, darting here and there. The swooping bank swallows feeding on flying insects. And the mysterious radome in the background, seemingly hovering just above the tree line. The huge golf ball-looking radar device was a leftover from the Cold War era, when nearly 300 Air Force servicemen were stationed in the area, as part of the United States air defense. "That was to identify any bogeys—most likely Russian warplanes—if they ever came down from the north," Craig said, providing the mini-history lesson. That notion seemed completely absurd on this idyllic summer afternoon. Different times.

Eventually, we followed the boys' lead, lurching like astronauts moon-walking, laughing like children. Unlike the ascent, we were down to the beach in no time, with far less exertion. We waded into the cool lake water and gazed in self-congratulatory awe at the dune we had just descended. "Good call, dude," I said to Craig. "What a blast," Vince echoed. "You liked, it, huh?" Craig said, beaming with the positive reviews. "Better without the girls. You know they would have been whining all the way up," he added, reaching for a victory smoke. We all laughed. Cowardly sexism in private for married males was still legal back then.

❋

For the next few years, making a day trip to Empire for relaxing on the beach and paying homage to the unmarked dune climb was always on our August vacation agenda. The giant freighter anchor, discovered more than 40 years ago offshore and now displayed near the beach, served as our welcome to the quaint lakeside town. And the summer resident kingbirds' aerobatics above South Bar Lake while dining on local flying insect cuisine always comes to mind whenever I think of summertime in Empire.

Eventually, the kids grew up, as they will, and now have young children of their own. In days to come, they, too, will make the trek to the unmarked dune in Empire when their offspring are capable, and climb toward a view that will recall a time when their dad/grandpa had the legs and the lungs to make it to the top. And I hope my kids will tell their children how much I enjoyed my prime time Up North, and how much they should cherish theirs too.

Eight years ago, at the ripe old age of 56, I visited Empire once again on a couple's outing, just me and my much better half. It was an unusually warm week in late March when I had spring break from my work as a school administrator in Indianapolis. Once I saw the forecast the week before, since we had no other recreational plans, we decided to make a run Up North. Predicted temps were in the high sixties to low seventies during the day and fifties at night—about perfect. Because this was a late decision, we had nothing planned for the week. Spontaneity would rule each day.

We strolled the beach listening to the lapping of the waves, the best non-pharmaceutical blood pressure-reducing medicine there is. Soon we were at the base of the unmarked dune climb I knew so well. I decided to take one more crack at it, though it had been years since I last made the attempt.

"Be careful, honey," Janet nervously instructed me. "You start feeling bad, you stop and come back down. You're not as young as you used to be, you know." Believe me, I knew. But, my increasingly irrational aging mind broadcast false positives of eternal youth. No doubt such faulty thinking means the cardiac care unit at Munson Medical Center in Traverse City is never hurting for patients.

As I began climbing, I dropped down into an all-fours approach sooner rather than later. My chest heaved. Sweat dripped like a leaky faucet. My lungs craved air. Several times I stopped and waved to Janet, not only to allay her concerns but to take much-needed timeouts. Her arms were now crossed, locked in that seriously concerned position for the remainder of my ascent. Once I made the deep troughs near the top and could stand again and steady myself atop the dune, I became elated. For just a preciously long moment, I had returned to days of yore.

I took it all in, just as I last did those many years ago. The humming-birds were long gone, migrating back to Latin America for the winter. Didn't see any dragonflies either. The radome, though, was still there; no Russians in sight.

This would be the last time I would ever climb the unmarked dune in Empire, and I knew it. After a few minutes, Janet waved me down. I leapfrogged my way back to her. "Nice work, old man—you made it!" she enthused complimentarily. "But let's not do that again, promise?"

I did. We hugged as we turned to make our way back to the parking lot. A run to Munson could wait.

On the Beach

When we discovered Leland 25 years ago, its beaches weren't nearly as crowded as they are today. "Crowded," as in Coney Island in Brooklyn with miles of people jammed together supposedly having a good time, Leland summertime beaches are not. In the mid-nineties, 30 people on the Reynolds Street beach on a glorious summer afternoon in July was a busy day. Now, it's double that or more. Still, as with all things human, it's a perception thing. My local Michigander friend Craig says we still haven't seen the real Michigan until we've spent time in the U.P. walking along the rockhound-bonanza shoreline and virtually people-free beaches of Lake Superior. Escaping from Indy's teeming masses and driving nearly 400 miles to get to a Lake Michigan beach in Leelanau County has been good enough for us. Maybe someday Janet and I will avoid the "crowds" at Leland and Good Harbor Bay and surrounding lakeside areas and drive another four hours north to immerse ourselves in the promise of such grand solitude. Someday.

In those early days of our ongoing relationship with Leelanau County, like most visitors and locals, we frequented the beaches during the summer. My wife and her sister, both of Syrian descent with skin more welcoming of the sun than my Irish genetic heritage permits, would stay out basking in the sunshine for hours upon hours. We husbands would do our best to hang with them, taking breaks in the water with the kids to cool off and summon more staying power. But it was no use. Eventually we would give in and drag ourselves back to the vacation rental house on Lake Street to munch on something and take a nap, reviving our sunbaked (and as we now realize today, health-compromised) bodies.

At the end of the long expanse of July daylight at the 45th Parallel, we would head down to the beach to watch the sunset, kids in tow. The kids would look for choice stones along the shore, and the adults would take photos with, of all things, dedicated cameras, back then being the pre-smartphone era. Everyone eventually had a classic vacation rite photo taken portraying the subject "holding" the sun before it disappeared "below the water" on the horizon. Then we'd go back to the rental house and wait a few hours before returning to lie on beach blankets, wearing sweatshirts to ward off the chill of our sunburned bodies and the cool evening temps, and watch the stars, planets, and satellites materialize. We would tell tall tales, recount the sillier moments of the just-ended day, giggle into contagious ripples of laughter, then become quiet as our smallness showed under starlight. Once we heard snoring—more often than not from an adult—we called it a night and went back to the house to collapse in our beds for some vacation activity-earned deep sleep.

During those laidback summer days in late July and into August, our pre-teen boys and I would body surf in Leland, waiting to catch good-sized waves, with our arms outstretched and leaping ahead like dolphins, to be propelled by the force of the rushing water. Sometimes a strong one would drive us right into the sandy bottom. Of course, this was child's play by Oahu standards—which was just fine by us. We would ride the waves until fatigue set in, then crawl out of the water to air dry while dozing on beach towels. Such are the demands of a northern Michigan summer vacation day spent by the Big Lake.

※

One late July afternoon in 1997, I was sitting on the beach in Leland with Janet. It was about 5 o'clock, the beach nearly deserted. Always is at day's end, as people retreat to prepare for dinner and the evening's activities. This is our favorite time to be at the beach during the summer, as not only are there fewer people, but the sun's intensity has backed off, and there's typically a cool, comfortable breeze, often out of the southwest. During those more ambitious days of mine, while on vacation I made sure to read leadership and management books to contribute to my career development. (Now it's a good novel or nonfiction read about the great outdoors, the fixation on ladder-climbing and professional accomplishment largely being the preoccupation of younger adults.) I recall reading one that late afternoon about W. Edwards Deming and Total Quality Management; Janet was into something far less taxing and much more entertaining. At that time I was working for an international insurance association in public affairs and had recently had a major disagreement with my supervisor over his less-than-encouraging sense of employee empowerment, a quarrel which came on the heels of a two-week all-staff training in James Kouzes and Barry Posner's Leadership Challenge program. I belatedly realized that this immersion in change management focused on engendering a more progressive workplace—which I was deeply drawn to—was no more than a passing fancy for the organization's plethora of vice presidents and not to be taken seriously. The Irish in me tends to get easily worked up, and I still couldn't let go of this conflict with my supervisor, even while away in Leland. I closed the book and dropped it into the sand, looked out at South Manitou Island and the sun-bejeweled water, and said to Janet, "I quit."

She responded by reaching out and patting my right arm while continuing to read and said, "Good, honey. Now you can enjoy your vacation." And so, having the only support that counted to be rid of this nagging burden, I did. That summer, Leland became a long cleansing breath.

❋

In early August 2003, Craig had his marriage reception on Good Harbor Bay Beach off Michigan Road, where it terminates to the west near the Good Harbor Bay trailhead. This was our first exposure to this stretch of Lake Michigan beach. There was a small tent set up for the guests, which was family only, other than Janet and me. Appetizers and lots of iced-down beer were on hand, as were plastic flute glasses filled with champagne. Just before sundown, two of Craig's brothers built a roaring bonfire. Craig had picked this spot for a special reason: his great-great grandpa Jan arrived by boat here, on this very beach, after traveling all the way from the former

Czechoslovakia, and farmed the nearby rolling hills with his wife, Marie, and a family that eventually reached 20 children. The more than 1,200 acres they homesteaded—that reached to the shoreline of Lake Michigan in Good Harbor Bay—were sold off long ago, yet the family's strong ties to Leelanau County remain. Ten years ago we bought our retreat in Cedar. Good Harbor Bay would get into our blood too.

Since then, we have driven down Good Harbor Trail and walked Good Harbor Bay Beach countless times. The National Park Service paved the road to the beach from M-22 shortly after our seasonal home purchase, connected water service for drinking and rinsing sand from beachgoers' feet, and installed well-kept restrooms for visitors' convenience (a special thank you, NPS, for the hand sanitizer). This paving of a slice of paradise resulted in easier access and thus more visitors. When the road was dirt, people were scarce; it was a locals' haunt. Now everyone has to share.

For years, Janet would go down to Good Harbor Bay Beach for solo evening walks along the water to catch the sunset. But during our weeklong stay in June 2019—just before the tourist rush was on—I made the unexpected suggestion to take a hike on the beach almost every evening. Marriage is funny. Sometimes naturally self-interested men like me have the occasional if ever-so-slight breakthrough and realize that making your gal happy is good for both parties.

That first night we picked up a mutual personal best number of Petoskey stones—petrified coral fossils from the sea that covered the area nearly 400 million years ago. The telltale pattern of a Petoskey stone mimics the sun and its rays, rays that were once tentacles and the center once the mouth of these long-extinct marine creatures. The first summer we spent in Traverse City on East Bay at a now defunct family hotel, I actually *purchased* a Petoskey stone from a roadside stand outside Acme, achieving true Fudgie status. Little did I know I would find thousands myself once my local friends laughed at my purchase and clued me in. Nonetheless, it was a beautiful keepsake. Still is.

We also found plenty of pieces of water-action-polished beach glass: emerald green, hazy white, and chocolate brown. Locals say the fragments are remnants from settlers on the Manitou Islands in the 1800s who dumped trash into the water, including glass. The glass pieces are smooth to the touch. Whatever the historical validity of the beach glass origin tale, the story only adds to the childlike fun of finding these wave-worked specimens.

Those evening beach walks had no set schedule. For a change on this trip, I left my smartphone and wristwatch behind—thanks to the loving prodding of Janet. I knew the approximate time from the position of the sun, which on an agenda-free vacation is all one ever really needs. And there wasn't anyone I wanted to talk to—other than Janet. We would slowly plod along the shoreline and sometimes stray into the water. Every now and then, when the spirit moved us, we would stop at beds of small stones that had been propelled out of the water by the waves, then sift through the rocks for anything that caught our eyes, including Petoskey stones and beach glass. I also favor the black basalt speckled with ivory-colored crinoid fossils. So many stones, so little time—that is, for those keeping time.

I became addicted to combing beach stones while on our first sailing excursion with Craig and his wife, Connie, in 1988. We had his father's sailboat and pushed off from the public launch in Leland. For a landlubber from Indianapolis, this inaugural exposure to the spectacular waters of the Manitou Passage and the wind-powered travel over water was exhilarating. Because it was a mile or so closer, and Janet and I were kids-on-Christmas-Eve excited about making landfall on an island for the first time in our lives, Craig steered the boat to North Manitou Island for a beach walk. While we sauntered barefoot on the warm white sand, Craig paused and picked up a palm-sized bleached-white crinoid fossil, and handed it to me. "Here, I want you to have this. Welcome to the Manitou Islands." I've kept it to this day.

I've even managed to resist the pleadings of my 7-year-old grandson, Brennan, a rock-and-fossil hound in the making, when asking me earnestly, "Can I have this?" Similar to the old Bud Light commercial from the nineties, I respond: *I love you, (little) man. But you can't have my 500-million-year-old fossil.* Yet.

✳

It had been a while since we hiked Pierce Stocking beach, one of Janet's favorites. In July 2018, we made it again.

Like so many of the beaches in Sleeping Bear Dunes National Lakeshore, the access to Pierce Stocking and North Bar Lake had been dramatically improved by asphalt roads replacing dirt roads. In recent years, we have experienced full parking lots at North Bar Lake, which never happened prior to the "improvements" to the area. On this day, Thursday, July 19, at 10 a.m., the lot is a quarter full, and would only be slightly more so when our two-hour walk on the beach ended. Odd. But no complaints from yours truly.

We walk north at a relaxed pace. The dunes at Pierce Stocking are high—more than 400 feet—and dramatically beautiful in sharp relief against the sky. The observation deck above is always full, it seems, during summertime. Visitors there get a magical view of Lake Michigan. They also get to watch the more daring tourists who decide to go down the dune—and have a gargantuan struggle climbing back up. I nicknamed this dune "Heart Attack Hill," and by today's evidence, have no doubt that the park rangers and Glen Lake Fire Department make frequent runs here during the height of summer tourist season.

Janet and I continue walking by, looking up at one massively obese man who has no business climbing this steep incline. A quarter of the way up he moves in slow motion, stopping frequently to catch his heaving breath. "Oh my, that man is not going to make it," Janet gravely says to me.

"Yeah, bad move. What was he thinking?" I wonder aloud. I say a silent Hail Mary for him, as I do by existential habit every time I hear and/or see an ambulance making a run. Hopefully, he made it up without a major medical event.

As we hike below the precipitous dunes, I imagine how I would react in the few seconds we may have should one of them give way in a landslide, which last happened in 1995 at Sleeping Bear Point. Without warning, a 1,600-foot stretch of beach and millions of cubic feet of sand from the bluff above slid into Lake Michigan one February day (fortunately, it occurred when the beach was uninhabited). Should such an unlikely calamitous event occur, I would seize Janet and rush us into the lake—which might not be good enough but would be our only lifesaving option. (And not much of an option at that, as I'm not the runner I used to be.) Why I'm thinking of emergency measures right now on a clear summer day without a care in sight is beyond me; perhaps it's the ominous plight of the overweight dune climber. Or just blame it on the monkey mind, as the Buddhists do.

On the way back, we marvel at the few small beach houses up on slight rises above the shore and how they have not been reclaimed yet—if some ever will—by the federal government per the land reclamation that began in 1961 when the federally designated Sleeping Bear Dunes National Lakeshore project was initiated. It's a jigsaw puzzle of land acquisition that only a lawyer could understand. However the homeowners' family members back then managed to pull it off, good for them. "Can you imagine what their sunsets and clear nights are like here?" Janet asks enviously.

"Yes, I can. At least somebody gets to enjoy it, right?" She nods, smiling. Nonetheless, it's okay to be a bit jealous—the ultimate form of flattery.

As we conclude our beach walk, climbing the short dune trail away from Lake Michigan and arriving at the apex of the hill, I tell Janet to "turn around and let's stop for a moment to say goodbye." She does. We do. Breathtaking.

A freighter that may have unloaded taconite (low-grade iron ore), perhaps in Green Bay, is sitting high on the water cruising northward through the Manitou Passage. "So pretty," Janet defines the moment, and we both sigh as we reluctantly turn to descend the slope, trying to walk on the wooden beams designed for slowing wind erosion of the sandy hill and making it easier to negotiate the rise. Kids are frolicking in the short channel between North Bar Lake and the Great Lake. Monarch butterflies sail about in the wind. When we get to the bottom, wordlessly we reach out to one another, holding hands as we return to our truck. Once again, we've spent some good hours on the beach, and we're better now.

PART III

Endless Summer...

DECK LIFE

Whenever we're at our seasonal home in Cedar, our days begin and end on our front porch deck. It's a natural draw. Our deck, coincidentally, is made from cedar—because our contractor recommended it. "The weather is hard on decks in northern Michigan," he spoke to a member of the choir—that being me—who power washed, sanded, and repainted the former deck as an annual rite-of-spring event. "Cedar is my decking material of choice." He also suggested that we not put any sealant on it, clear or otherwise. Being good out-of-staters, we heeded his advice. That first year, our new deck was gorgeous, with the natural wood's features popping so dramatically that every visitor offered an unsolicited compliment. However, when we drove up the following Memorial Day Weekend for opening ceremonies, an unwelcome surprise greeted us. "Oh, no! What happened?" my wife, Janet, exclaimed as she stepped onto the deck. As our Michigander contractor had forewarned—we thought nothing of it then, dazzled by the deck's newly constructed appearance—over the winter the planking had turned gray.

I got in touch with our housepainter, who knew just how to handle the situation. He power washed the deck and applied a lightly tinted sealant to accent the house's new pumpkin-orange exterior color. It looked great—for a season. Of course, it will need to be power washed and the tinted sealant will need to be reapplied, now an every-other-year drill. Beauty is always fleeting in this world, as my bathroom mirror reminds me every day. And everyone with an outdoor deck in northern Michigan should own a power washer. Or know a good housepainter or handyman who knows decks.

Ours is an open platform deck, approximately 18' x 12', with a two-foot rise above the ground. It looks out over our poor excuse for a front lawn—more like a dandelion farm with a bumper crop each May, though occasional wildflowers do manage to claim some territory, such as white trillium in the spring and orange hawkweed in late June. Still, the "lawn" needs to be cut. Throughout the summer I work my way around most of the wildflowers, using a non-motorized push mower, just like my dad did 60 years ago. I enjoy the singing of the spinning cylindrical blades, even though they cut at about 75% effectiveness compared to a power mower. The tradeoff is in not using an emissions-discharging, serenity-destroying combustion engine. Fair enough.

Our three-quarters-of-an-acre property features soaring sugar maple trees and a few giant fir trees, many of them 60-70 feet tall. Dawn and sunset highlight the treetops, always catching our attention. We enjoy that natural lighting display in the morning with hot tea. As sundown nears, libations are raised in tribute to the retreating, never-to-be-repeated day. Occasionally, in the evening, we'll play some music on our Bose Bluetooth speaker driven by our iPhones—usually something out of the seventies and eighties: America, the Ozark Mountain Daredevils, the Eagles; you get the picture. More often we simply sit in solitude and talk sparingly as the gloaming deepens. Younger couples seem allergic to any dead space in conversation and nervously fill in the gaps. Older folks need only the presence of one another, with long lapses of silence in between bits of conversation. I used to wonder about that whenever I was at a restaurant with my wife during our early days of marriage. We thought that older couples grew tired of one another, a concept that we found disturbing then. Now, we understand.

✳

In a wooded area, there is much bird life to delight those inclined to look up. We keep binoculars handy, often lying on the deck table within easy reach. Last May and into June, Baltimore orioles frequented the airspace above our yard as they mated and built their nests nearby; in previous years, we had been treated to infrequent flyovers. Janet always exclaims in delight whenever she spots an oriole—especially the "flying torch" males—as if it were a bird-sighting first for her. Indigo buntings in their shimmering deep blues are seen here regularly in the summer. Cedar waxwings congregate on high limbs in their habitual groupings, and flycatchers zip out from treetops to seize flying insects and return to their perches to await the next course of their meal. From before dawn and well into dusk we hear the call of the Eastern wood-pewee, a flycatcher, the sweet and unmistakable *pee-a-wee* telling us all is well. The area woodlands abound with woodpeckers: downy and hairy, flickers, and the grandest of all, the pileated. Our wood-sided house had drawn woodpecker attention for years in the spring, evidenced by the machine-gun burst-like holes in the siding, vandalism of the natural kind. As it turns out, the woodpeckers were only seeking bugs that might be inhabiting small cavities in the wood, or males were just amorously expressing themselves by jackhammering on our exterior walls while attempting to attract a mate. After I shared my distress at this undesirable bird behavior, our ever-resourceful local friend, Marie, brought over some "predator eyes"—reflectors to hang in the surrounding trees to dissuade members of the family *Picidae* from attacking the siding. To me, they looked like one-eyed aliens staring from the tree trunks. So I fastened them around the perimeter of the house. When I mentioned my reservations about the gismos' efficacy to Marie, she responded with her usual lovable bluntness, "You're not a woodpecker, correct?" She had me there. Combined with the insecticide paint additive used by the housepainter last spring on the exterior (a suggestion he made as he patched the woodpecker damage), admittedly the weird reflectors have apparently solved the problem. For now.

Of course, one of our favorite aerial visitors we admire from our deck in Cedar are the ruby-throated hummingbirds—seasonal northland migrants like we are. Last Memorial Day weekend, we placed a disk feeder at the northwest corner of the deck among the leaves of our emerging Asiatic lily and spiderwort patch. A female had been frequenting the feeder, and we instructed family members using the cabin over the summer to prepare nectar and keep the feeder filled. She skittishly yet persistently insisted that any humans on the deck take a seat in the Adirondack chairs before she would land on the plastic perch to feed. The male ruby-throats in the area aren't nearly as trusting and won't come near the feeder if anyone is on the deck. So I watched them from inside the house through the sliding glass doors: ground rules. The compromise was well worth it.

※

We've owned this property for a rapidly passed 10 years: traveling at the speed of enjoyment. The towering trees continue to grow without our permission, which I admire. The canopy above the driveway facing westward has closed the airspace considerably. It's cut down on the sunlight pouring in the cabin's large quarter-moon windows above the deck, which bleached out our once navy now mostly sky-blue couch before we had the good sense to cover it in our absence. *Live and learn*, per my mother's existential explanation for all human understanding. The sunshine-hungry trees have also diminished the night sky viewing area. *Que sera sera*—whatever will be, will be—an insightful acceptance that mom also taught me. The summer sun still drenches the deck for a full hour or so every afternoon, which is enough sunbathing time for any reasonable sort. And the Milky Way still shines through, and we're able to see shooting stars in the heavens when atmospheric and astronomical conditions permit. The unrestricted trees frame it all well.

Whenever friends come by, the deck is the magnetic draw for them, too, and where we all eventually end up. It's an ideal platform for hosting conversation in The Great Outdoors. In our neighborhood on the north side of Indianapolis, regardless of the time of year, The Great Indoors tends to be where it's at, with families mesmerized by their gigantic, ever-higher-resolution digital TV screens imitating life. Nonetheless, I keep a good thought: perhaps the kids are playing, quietly, on their backyard decks. Perhaps.

On our deck in Cedar, the conversation flows (as will the beer, on occasion). The laughter rises. The communion is holy in its messy, meandering, whatever kind of way. Our voices echo around the wooded neighborhood. But the neighbors are okay with it, as they take their turns too. There is plenty of breathing room here at our Up North retreat. And people are like-minded enough in loving the area, so that respect is mutual.

❋

One July afternoon, Janet drove into Traverse City to pick up Marie, as she had just traded in her aging Volkswagen Passat, which had been on life-support for some time, for a newer-used Subaru Forester, which wouldn't be ready for delivery until the following day. Alone at the house in Cedar, I walked out onto the deck about 1 p.m. It was as if I were being called to the Liturgy of the Hours. I gazed upward at the treetops; I deeply inhaled the fresh air. I watched the few cottony summer clouds slowly drift by in the foreground of the blue sky. Then I looked toward our lily garden: a single bloom, a rich scarlet, remained intact on its stem. The petals from the others had fallen, a scattering of blaze orange and bright lemon. On Friday, we would pack up and head back to Indy. With that in mind, I tried to stay with the moment. *Be here now,* I reminded myself, the sage if impossible advice written by spiritual teacher Ram Dass in the seventies. Someday, God willing, I will be here now a bit longer. In Leelanau County, in Cedar, that is. Taking in this unique and precious angle of the universe from right here on this very deck. Caretakers that we are. All we are meant to be.

Pyramid Point

Among the overflowing bookshelves and stacks of papers piled up on my desk and floor, my home office is a repository for stones and fossils discovered over decades while hiking in Michigan, Indiana, and Arizona. They keep me silent company as I read and write, an open invitation to solitude. They are also reminders of good times that have contributed to my formation, though nanoseconds in comparison to the geological processes of rock formation over millions of years.

When I first became a rockhound, I sprayed some of my Lake Michigan beach stone keepsakes with lacquer to give them the same shiny luster as when I reached for them in the water. I stopped doing this when it occurred to me that this was almost blasphemous, altering the original state of the stone to suit my fancy. Now I simply wash off the stones and place them in glass containers—pint beer glasses do nicely—filled with water. However, I have tampered with the natural appearance of one stone during the past decade: a smooth palm-sized triangular chunk of limestone. Every time I glance at it, it immediately reminds me of a certain Michigan summer day.

A few Saturdays ago, I was thinking about Pyramid Point for no specific reason; sometimes consciousness carries on with its own business, random and not fully disclosed. The daydream prompted me to look for the stone that memorializes that special day in 2010 when Craig, Janet, and I went out to visit Pyramid Point, not by the usual route—exiting M-22 and parking at the foot of the hill and hiking up to see the breathtaking vista of Lake Michigan and the Manitou Islands (as well as South Fox Island on a clear day)—but by making landfall via boat on the beach below the point. That day, I had taken a black Sharpie and made inscriptions on four of the five sides of the stone (leaving the base untouched): **PYRAMID POINT; GOOD HARBOR BAY; TIM, JANET, CRAIG; 7.12.10**. As I held the rock and reminisced, I was astonished that so many years had passed. It was yet another one of those "only yesterday" moments that happen increasingly when middle age has been forever left behind.

Over the years, we have filled our vacation time in northwest lower Michigan with seemingly endless numbers of adventures. Ultimately, the point of it all is to more deeply engage in what naturalist writer Loren Eisley referred to as *The Immense Journey* (the title of his collection of essays published in 1959) we are all on. And with my simpatico always-up-for-anything friend, anything is possible: an aspect of our friendship I will always treasure. At that time, Craig owned a used but well-maintained Boston Whaler Montauk, and I recall him wanting to take the 17-foot center-console multipurpose watercraft out on Lake Michigan to see how it would handle on the Big Water. That July day, the Great Lake's surface was playing out 1- to 2-foot waves, well within the unsinkable Whaler's capability and calm enough for a decent day trip. Craig had called me about 7 a.m. with an invitation to join him on this diversion. "Whaddya say we take the Whaler out on the lake," he suggested. "We'll put out of Leland. Bring your snorkel gear. And what the hell, might as well bring Janet," he said, jesting. "We'll motor over to the beach in Good Harbor Bay below Pyramid Point. I've never been there before. Why not." *Why not* is the only reason we ever needed to do anything adventurous together.

We launched the Whaler out of Leland Harbor, leaving the protection of its U.S. Army Corps of Engineers-constructed stone piling breakwater and entered open water, the ever-beckoning Manitou Islands to the west. The July day was splendid, with a light northerly breeze and plenty of sun sparkling the surface of the lake. We stayed within a quarter mile of the shoreline, passing Whaleback Hill as we made our way across Good Harbor Bay toward our destination: Pyramid Point.

✳

Janet and I have hiked the just-over-a-mile Sleeping Bear Dunes National Lakeshore Pyramid Point trail quite a few times over the years. It takes about 20 minutes to traverse the uphill path through the remnants of a spent orchard and into the beech-maple and pine woods the trail cuts through. Then almost suddenly, you've reached the top of the bluff. And below you are Lake Michigan's aquamarine waters stretching off into the horizon, off into imagination....

During one Pyramid Point hike about five years ago, Janet and I made the ascent and emerged into the small clearing that opens up to the dramatic Lake Michigan panorama. As happens during the summer in such precious havens of tranquility, they become more "public": we were not alone. Already there—we were the intruders this time—was a group of Mennonites taking in the view. It appeared to be a family: a mother, father, grandparents, and five girls, ranging in age from perhaps 8 to 16.

As is their way, the Mennonite girls were wearing plainly beautiful pastel-colored summer dresses in yellow, green, blue, violet, and pink with white bonnets. Unlike the usual tourists and their other-people-be-damned white noise chatter, the girls were politely reserved as they gazed at the islands in the distance, pointing at features on the Manitou and out in the water: the navigational Crib in the Manitou Channel, several sailboats, seagulls and cormorants winging by. This was a Norman Rockwell painting come to life. Their serene appreciation for the moment enhanced that of our own. If only all tourists would leave this type of impression: loving it all while disturbing nothing.

✳

The Whaler and its crew of three were about 50 yards offshore when Craig cut the motor. "There are some huge boulders around here. With all this chop, the water is too murky to see them and we risk bashing the hull. So we're going to have to swim in." It was a direct order with zero options.

I hurled out the fore anchor; Craig tossed the aft. They easily found purchase in the sandy bottom. Flippers, masks, and snorkels on, we slipped into the opaque, turbulent water, careful not to be knocked about by the bobbing boat. Just a few feet from the Whaler I felt a giant rock underneath me, as big as my body. The water was shallow, perhaps five feet deep, as we propelled our way in, hands searching blindly for large rocks immediately below. Within minutes, we were standing on the beach, pulling off our snorkeling gear. Several hundred feet above us was Pyramid Point. This stretch of hard-to-get-to beach below saw few visitors.

"Made it," I announced under my breath as I pulled myself up to standing position, in one piece and quite glad of it.

Placing our snorkeling gear out of reach of the clawing waves at the shoreline, we took a short walk scanning the beach for stones that merited closer inspection. Near our landfall, a large tree limb that had washed ashore from the Manitous or Wisconsin or who-knows-where rested half submerged in the sand. "This is a fine place to chill for a while and take it all in," Craig announced as he did just that. I joined him while Janet kept to her walking meditation, slowly moving away from us.

"You know, I said a few prayers as we swam in," Craig confided.

"They worked," I said with relief.

"I'm surprised none of us got hurt," he added. "Those waves could have driven us into one of those boulders and really messed things up. You know, an orthopedic surgeon's dream," he noted, with his proprietary got-away-with-it-again laugh of victory I was so familiar with. "And just to give you a preview of coming attractions, it's gonna be just as much fun, if not more, going back out against those waves."

Dammit, I thought. "Did you have to bring that up just yet?" I asked.

"Let's keep it between you and me," he said, mercifully wanting to avoid the topic with Janet. With Craig, no outing would score as a major success if there weren't an element of risk if not outright danger involved.

But I didn't agonize over the prospect of making our return swim to the Whaler. Here, for the moment, was serenity, so precious and rare to Janet and me, suburbanites out on liberty. Getting to here, though, is a laborious and involved process. Earning our release time to get away and restore our sanity. The tantalizing run-up to summer vacation with all the preparations and the lovely anticipation. The long yet awakening drive north from Indy. And then there's the long-awaited moment when we realize that we finally made it to our ultimate destination, made the summit to peace, and an overpowering sense of grace sets in. The effort—including this somewhat perilous yet certainly thrilling swim—is always a fair exchange.

It took a few minutes longer going against the beachward-insistent waves, but we made it back to the Whaler unscathed. Back across Good Harbor Bay, past Whaleback Hill and into Leland Harbor. Back up the boat launch with the Whaler, securing it to the trailer. Back into Craig's Chevy truck to retrace the seven miles down M-22 to South Good Harbor Bay Trail. Back to saying goodbye—and trusting not for long—then climbing the short-and-steep driveway hill to our seasonal home. We made it all the way back. Accomplished and pleasantly fatigued once again.

Perhaps someday we'll have another opportunity to motor over to the beach below Pyramid Point, though I doubt it. The degree of difficulty in getting there is beyond my comfort zone now that I'm well into my sixties and more risk averse as a result of having made it this far. But I can look back fondly on that day, that very short chapter in my own Immense Journey, whenever I glance at the Pyramid Point rock on my desk. And that will do just fine.

KAYAKING

In 2001, Janet and I joined forces with another couple to share a 600-square-foot cabin on Spider Lake. After years of dreaming about getting a foothold in northwest lower Michigan, we had made landfall.

The main attraction of our humble abode (humble indeed; e.g., my knees would touch the wall in front of me when I sat on the toilet in the closet-sized one-and-only bathroom; definitely not for the claustrophobic) was having 100 feet of lake frontage. Janet and I had never owned a boat and never had the urge. We had heard too many stories from recreational boat owner friends and acquaintances about seldom getting out on the water due to having to work to make the monthly boat payments. That boats were little more than money pits. That boat maintenance took too much precious time away from hard-earned vacations. All of that. Nevertheless, someone else thought otherwise. My Up North buddy Craig saw our boat-less status as lakeside property owners as a major deficit. "Need to get that fixed," he assessed.

Craig is a water baby and can't resist the magnetic attraction to snorkel, sail, or fish whenever an opportunity presents itself. His father had raced sailboats on Grand Traverse Bay for decades, and three of his five boys always crewed for him, including Craig. The boys also learned the ins and outs of marine engines and how to navigate many a small vessel out on the Big Water. Craig was also an expert canoeist, as I learned while out on fishing expeditions on the Boardman River; him guiding, me casting for trout.

"You just bought a lake cottage. You've gotta have a boat, dude," so his persuasion went. But I really didn't want to sign up for having something else to take care of. It was enough for me to open up the cabin in the spring, maintain it with our partners, then close it in the fall; the plumbing detail alone was enough for me. My resistance to the idea was clear. So Craig changed gears.

"Hmmm…well…how about a kayak? They're relatively inexpensive. The cool thing is, kayaks are pure stealth. You can glide right up on all kinds of waterfowl without disturbing them. You guys being birders will love it. What do you think?"

I was intrigued. And Janet was excited by the prospect. So we did our research. I came across a Wilderness Systems catalogue, and we immediately settled on a budget-friendly option: the Pamlico tandem.

I did some reading on kayaking technique, and it proved to be easy enough in actual practice. That is, easy enough when you're the only one paddling.

Janet was so captivated by the out-on-the-water experience that she would fail to hear me call out directional instructions (or else was conveniently tuning me out), and we would often end up not as happy with one another as we were at the start of the outing: two navigators too many. Sometimes I just gave up; when she noticed she was the only one paddling, she would stop. Then I would resume, and eventually she would do the same. And we would be right back to basically not complementing each other as a paddling crew of two. However, it wasn't always working against one another. There were times when we were in sync—kinda like being married.

Like so many new things with couples, the first time out on the Pamlico sold us. We did as Craig said, taking it out in the morning before most people were up, when nature presents best—without human interference. Once out of our cove, gliding through the thin mist, we entered the narrows, which is a no-wake zone, a rule easily honored in a kayak. We passed an elderly woman in her robe having coffee on her dock. She smiled and waved; no words exchanged: no talking in church. Moments later, a loon surfaced less than 10 feet from our port side. We both instantly ceased paddling. Janet whispered excitedly, "Oh my, it's so close!" The diving bird, with its black-and-white patterned feathers and red eyes (summer color) prominently set in its majestic black head and its long slim bill, entranced us. A second loon, no doubt its lifelong mate, surfaced about 20 yards from us, breaking the plane of the still morning water, sleekly announcing its presence. They were feeding. The one closest to the boat stayed near us for about 30 seconds: a lifetime for a birdwatcher graced by such a sighting. Then they were gone, swimming beneath the water for several minutes, having covered a remarkable distance between us and them.

All we could say was wow. Craig was right. We would be kayakers evermore.

Every stay at the cabin thereafter, we went out at least once a day on the Pamlico, weather permitting. Sometimes we headed out to the nearest island, about a 30-minute paddle trip. The island is so small, in fact, it's not easily shared by another party if you want any privacy at all. We would get out of the kayak and wade around the island, which took about five minutes. Then we'd hop back in for our open water return to the channel that led back to our cove. Other times we simply lolled about the lake. On one such no-agenda outing, Janet spotted a smallish heron near the public launch on the west side of Spider Lake. "Little green heron?" I inquired while paddling slowly toward a better view of the unusual bird.

"Don't think so," she responded. I slowed the kayak to a wind-driven drift about 30 yards away and peered through the binoculars. It wasn't a bird we had ever seen before. So we took a few photos as we crept closer while watching it hunt small fish and frogs in the shallows. We floated within 15 feet of the feeding waterbird; it never flinched. Once home, we got out our *Sibley Guide to Birds* and I identified the mystery bird as a tricolored heron. If I ascertained the species correctly, the bird was way off its range, more typically frequenting the Gulf Coast and much of Florida.

I emailed several photos of the apparently stray heron to the Michigan Department of Natural Resources. A wildlife biologist confirmed the sighting, saying that tricolored herons are extremely rare in northern Michigan but occasional sightings had been increasing. The one we spent time with on Spider Lake was a juvenile, noted by the distinct reddish-brown neck. "Great sighting," our DNR contact congratulated us. "Not your everyday variety of northern Michigan heron, to be sure."

❈

When we sold our interest in the Spider Lake property to our partners in 2006, we unloaded the Pamlico too. Craig would be traveling solo to Lake Superior for a week and mentioned he might buy a kayak. Didn't have to: we gave him ours. Though he protested what he thought was too grand a gift, he had been so good in opening up the great outdoors of northern Michigan to us. We would hear none of it.

I thought our time Up North as summer regulars was up. But Janet decided in 2009 that we weren't done just yet. While staying at a rental in mid-May on M-22 in Leland, owned by some fellow Hoosiers flying their IU (Indiana University) flag proudly on the front porch, she and her mother went seasonal house-hunting with good ol' Sam Abood, our realtor. Janet being fourth generation Syrian-American, and her mother knowing her way around a Middle Eastern kitchen, having prepared meat-stuffed grape leaves and Lebanese meat pies on special occasions, hit it off well with Sam, a Lebanese-American who loves to eat and fancies anyone with a heritage common to his own.

In one day they found a modest little A-frame home in Cedar near Sugar Loaf Mountain in the Manor Green housing addition. The price was right, and Janet insisted. She knew I wasn't yet ready to pull up stakes. And so we ended up buying it. Home again.

The house sat up on a small, heavily wooded hill nestled away in orchard and farm country, the glaciers having done a marvelous job in shaping the countryside with its kettle and moraine features. And there were plenty of outdoor diversions nearby, including Sleeping Bear Dunes National Lakeshore, but two miles from the house. What it didn't come with, however, was a lake and a boat. What all vacationers to the area dream of.

That July, when heading up for our first summer week in Cedar, Janet surprised me once we entered Traverse City heading north on U.S. 31 by blurting, "Let's stop at MC Sports and shop for some kayaks." Spontaneous spending gives me a serious allergic reaction. But this made sense.

Within minutes we picked out two individual kayaks that would do well: a 10-foot fluorescent green Perception boat for Janet, and a 12-foot Wilderness Systems Pungo in blaze orange for yours truly. And they have floated us into many close encounters with nature on oh-so-many summer and early autumn afternoons.

Since that fortuitous purchase, we have explored a number of local bodies of water from the near-surface cockpit view of our kayaks, including Little Traverse Lake, Lime Lake, and North Lake Leelanau. Our favorite trip, though, has always been on the Cedar River.

Just 10 minutes paddling in a winding east-northeasterly direction is about all it takes to lose the sound of vehicles driving on Cedar's Main Street. Then it's nothing but peace: the soft sound of paddles slipping through water and the wind rustling the cattails and the *conk-la-ree* call from male red-winged blackbirds who stake out territory all along the river, the females hopscotching the lily pads in search of insects, the males darting back and forth across the river while chirping bluntly to let the kayakers know they own the area; the warblers and their sweet trilling and impatient movement from branch to branch; the kingfisher making a racket as we disturb its preference for a human-less river; the kingbirds and cedar waxwings watching from shoreline tamaracks. We are so removed from any concern in this sweet liberating interlude. Time and again on this river—what we in Indiana would call a creek, given its modest breadth and depth—while cutting through the Solon Swamp, Janet and I will cease paddling to draw deep breaths and exhale with heavy sighs, entering a deeper communion with nature. Time stops. Or goes. It just is, as we are truly off the clock.

Our best moments on this river have been in late June when the sky is a vast summer blue and a few lazy cumulous clouds drift overhead. Hawks and eagles soar high above the swamp. When we put the glasses on them, we discover that the skies are much more trafficked than we realize, with even more predatory birds at higher altitudes outside the reach of the naked human eye. We make a game of passing by painted turtles sunning on semi-submerged ancient cedar trunks, trying not to alarm them so they don't slip into the water, a chain reaction when more than one is parked on a preferred perch. Sometimes we succeed, other times, not so much. This is the kind of tensionless therapy that reduces blood pressure better than the pharmaceutical I take each evening to calm the force in my veins. This reminds us of a better way to live, which seems tantalizingly almost within reach. Almost.

❋

Despite their ability to help us access the increasingly elusive state of tranquility, kayaks can also be unsafe, especially when one fails to respect Mother Nature. Diligence is always required when piloting a small boat that is easily tipped, whether by high waves or carelessness—or both.

In August 2000, when Craig, my then-18-year-old son, Matt, and I were camping out on South Manitou Island, early one morning we were hailed by bullhorn by a National Park Service Ranger patrolling slowly along the shore in a motorboat. He asked if we had seen a yellow oceangoing kayak during the past 24 hours; we had not. Minutes later, an orange and white Coast Guard Dolphin helicopter approached at low altitude across the Manitou Passage flying in a Z-pattern over the island then heading over to North Manitou Island, repeating the pattern, then back again. We learned a few days later that the solo kayaker had drowned in rough water. Going it alone on such a massive and temperamental body of water is never recommended.

This week, a neighbor up the street here on the north side of Indianapolis mentioned to Janet that she and her former college roommate from the University of Michigan would be kayaking from Leland Harbor to South Manitou, then camping for a few days. I shuddered. "Did you tell her that 16 miles of kayaking across the Manitou Passage isn't for the casual day kayaker?" I asked.

"Absolutely. I tried to talk her out of it. She said they would be fine." Don't they all. Yet fortunately, they were, living to tell about their bold crossing. I suppose flirting with death doth a great adventure make.

In the 19 years since we purchased that tandem Pamlico and began our love affair with kayaking, Janet and I have yet to put our kayaks in Lake Michigan. Perhaps we can do so one vacation day when the wind is down and the surface of the water is as smooth as glass. We'll stay close to shore, appreciating the view while not taking the kind of risks the youthful version of me might once have encouraged. And with no ambition to be boat owners of the inboard/outboard kind, we will simply stay in our lane. Slow and easy, quiet and calm, in no hurry to get anywhere, nonconformists we.

Dreams I'll Never See

For the past several years, I've been mulling over the idea of being a boat owner. Again.

About 15 years ago, Janet and I were part owners of a modest cabin on Spider Lake. Initially, Craig, our good friend and avid outdoorsman, encouraged us to buy kayaks to get out on the lake on the cheap, thus avoiding the steep cost of inboard/outboard motorized watercraft. And so we did. Once we initially launched the low-riding people-powered zero-emissions vessels, we were hooked for life. A few years later, with no input from us, Craig decided it was time for us to move to the next level of boating.

"You know what you need *now*," he began, as we had a beer while standing on our dock looking out on the water early one evening during Memorial Day Weekend. I gave him a *now-what* look of suspicion and we both started laughing in anticipation of what was coming. "You need a powerboat."

"I've got enough stuff to take care of around here," I responded dismissively, no longer laughing. "The kayaks are just fine."

"Dude. A powerboat gives you the ability to tool around the entire lake whenever you like. It's the genuine lakeside cabin Up North Michigander experience. Know what I'm sayin'? You only live once; what the hell are you waiting for? C'mon. I've got just the ticket for you." Craig is always impossible when it comes to insisting on what constitutes fun and how much one ought to have: and that is, lots.

Up to that time, I had never had any real interest in being a motorboat owner. Over the years I had been on plenty of fishing outings with friends in aluminum v-hull boats—theirs; no ownership required on my part. I had fished from my father-in-law's deluxe bass boat that could fly across a lake at 50 miles per hour. I had cruised on "party barges"—pontoon boats—with the sole purpose of laidback relaxation on the water. And I had used a friend's jet ski on multiple occasions on Morse Reservoir just north of Indianapolis, opening up the throttle for the simple thrill of it all. Fun in the moment, but hardly addicting. Such watercraft just didn't register on my must-have list.

Craig's "ticket" turned out to be a red and white powerboat that had to have been at least 30 years old and not much bigger than a dinghy. "Clean, isn't she?" he said, having taken it upon himself the following afternoon to drag the boat over to Spider Lake, put it in the water at the public launch, and motor over to our dock for a test drive. "The engine's been overhauled by a boat mechanic I know well and it should run forever, especially as seldom as you guys will use it. I got it—stole it—for two grand. If you don't want it, I'll keep it. That's how good this boat is. Nice, huh?" Craig, at that time a salesman in the auto industry, was making it hard for me to say no. As usual.

We took it out for spin. And it was nice. It had enough horsepower to get up and go and rode smoothly, at least on a relatively becalmed 250-acre residential lake. Janet joined us later, and the smile on her face as we cruised about Spider Lake with the wind in our hair and our cares nowhere near told me all I needed to know. Sold.

Our first solo outing without Captain Craig took place later that summer when we were staying at the cabin for a week. One of Janet's friends from work, a nurse at St. Vincent Hospital in Indy, had come up for a few days. To show her a good time one sunny afternoon, we decided to take her out for a boat ride.

We cruised out of the no-wake zone channel and into an open expanse of water. I was feeling pretty good about myself as a first-time skipper, when about 10 minutes into our excursion the engine suddenly quit. The unexpected pall of silence dampened my maritime enthusiasm. "What happened, honey?" Janet asked with mild concern. Her friend, who didn't get out on the water much, had a Titanic passenger-like look on her face.

"Not sure," I said, trying to hide my rising anxiety and acting like I was in control of the situation. "Shouldn't be a problem. Just give me a minute."

But try as I might, it wouldn't restart. I initially entreated the speedboat to live up to its purpose: no go. I then used some salty language to express my frustration and, irrationally, to attempt to inspire some cooperation. It apparently didn't care for that approach either.

Our guest became really concerned when the exchange between Janet and yours truly got rather heated: she angry with Craig about "the boat we didn't need or want"; me angry with her about the critical commentary I didn't need or want at such an inopportune time. Oddly but fortuitously, or so I initially thought, there was a single antique oar stowed on the boat. Although it was missing part of its blade, I thought we now had a sporting chance to get back to our cove. "Oh, good!" Janet exclaimed upon seeing my discovery. "It will be some work, but at least we'll get back to the dock." Easy for her to say.

And some work it was. The wind was up a bit, about 10-15 miles per hour, blowing right out of the southeast, which was our return heading, of course. Try as I might—and I did for about 20 minutes, straining against the incessant wind—we were going nowhere fast.

As defeat set in, I wondered what to do next. Cell phones had yet to reach the can't-live-without-it prevalence of today; vacation-brained, we left our for-emergencies-only flip phone back at the cabin. But our deliverance was at hand. A much larger, beautifully appointed powerboat approached us. On board were three teenage boys, perhaps 16 years old. The boat slowed. "Hey, do you need a tow?" one of the young mates perceptively offered. "We could see you guys were struggling."

Actually, we were transitioning from struggling to desperation. And mutiny wasn't far behind.

These good Samaritans may well have saved our marriage, let alone our vacation week. I caught the tow rope and secured it on a bow cleat. Ten minutes later, we entered our cove and the young skipper masterfully took us in toward the dock, slowing to release us with just enough speed to glide in for a soft landing. I made sure the boys waited while I hustled up to the house to get them a $20 bill for the kindness. "No thank you, sir," the skipper insisted while reversing his engine to resume their afternoon out on the water—in a trusty vessel. "Have a nice day."

My faith in young people had been completely restored. My faith in that little speedboat that couldn't, however, had sunk. There would be no mission to raise it either. "Tell Craig he can have the boat back," Janet ordered as she and her friend headed for the cabin to shake off the near-disaster and reorganize for a day of sunbathing and girl talk on the dock (and perhaps some understandable male bashing), admiring the view of the water from a safe distance. She got no argument from me; I had been traumatized by the whole ordeal. The Pamlico would do quite nicely, thank you very much.

A few weeks later, Craig came by with his pickup to remove our must-have boat from Spider Lake, and from our lives. After a diagnostic assessment and some trial and error, he managed to get it started. "Maybe some bad gas. Who knows. It's running now. Sounds healthy. You sure you want to part company with it?"

"I'm sure. I'm not mechanically inclined and I'm too much of a boating neophyte and that's a bad combination to own a boat that old. Besides, I don't think I could ever get Janet back on board again." We motored over to the public launch and secured it on the trailer.

"I'll throw a sign on it and get your money back," Craig offered. "I feel bad about this."

"Don't. You meant well. We're just a couple of landlubbers. It's best that the divorce is final. It just wasn't meant to be."

As it turns out, Craig wasn't a motivated seller, and we weren't hurting for cash. And so the fickle powerboat sat in his "boatyard" at home for the next two years, alongside a 16-foot sailboat and a dinghy and a few tired marine engines, along with two pickup trucks, one in need of mechanical attention. His wife is a saint—and a native Michigander, too, which probably explains her patience with yard clutter of the boating kind.

That third spring, though, he decided to gift the boat to a young couple that lived next door. "I didn't think you'd care, since you hadn't said boo about it in several years," he explained. "Those kids thought they hit the lottery. About every weekend throughout the summer they took it out on Grand Traverse Bay and motored over to Power Island. No mechanical issues whatsoever. I wish you guys would have kept it. You never really gave it a chance. But hey, at least it found a good home."

After our doomed outing, my bride was one and done. And like a well-trained husband should, I didn't miss the message. That boat had to go. I was just too fond of and invested in Janet to think otherwise.

✳

According to the National Marine Manufacturers Association, in 2018 Michigan ranked fifth in the nation for economic activity involving recreational boating, at $7.4 billion. At one time, there were more than one million recreational boats registered in the state of Michigan. That's probably about right: everywhere we travel in Leelanau County throughout the boating season—Memorial Day through Labor Day—there are boats out on the water, on trailers on the road, and in front yards for sale, especially in late summer. For the past several years, I've found myself window shopping online for a fishing boat and while out driving or on walks. I was recently reminded of this when I received an email from Lund informing me of the sports fishing boat manufacturer's annual season-ending sale. (I had visited the Lund website about this time a year earlier, requesting a print catalogue I never received—perhaps Janet intercepted it; but still they "remembered" me.) I have also taken photos of several boats sitting in yards or driveways that weren't for sale; they just looked like something that would work well for me: 14- or 16-foot aluminum V-hull; two casting seats; live well; outboard motor; trolling motor. Reference material for later use. Whether I will actually pull the trigger someday remains to be seen, such is my ruminating nature. Could be just a pipe dream.

We all have dreams we may never see. But dreaming can hold its own satisfaction.

One persistent and recurring daydream I have could well be a dream I'll never see. It's a fine summer day in Leelanau County. It's about 5 p.m. I hook up my gleaming fishing boat—a TRACKER, Alumacraft, Lund, or something similar. Newer used. Seaworthy. Dependable. I slide the boat off the trailer into the water at the public launch just south of the M-204 bridge over the Lake Leelanau narrows connecting the south lake to the north.

I'm sitting in the stern chair with my hand on the tiller of a purring Honda 30 HP outboard motor, guiding the boat; Janet is up front in a casting seat taking in the view. When we enter North Lake Leelanau, I put out a few fishing lines, trolling for smallmouth bass, a brown or rainbow trout, or whatever decides to strike my lures. I may sip a beer; maybe not. About 45 minutes later we head up the Carp River (a.k.a., the Leland River), perhaps the shortest river in America, joining Lake Leelanau to Lake Michigan and running less than a half mile, tie up the boat at the public launch across from the Leland Township Library, and walk to the nearby Bluebird Tavern, a favorite destination of ours for decades now. There I'll definitely have a beer. We'll share a basket of fried smelt and split a whitefish sandwich. We'll remember those summer days when the kids were young and Leland was new to us, and we were enchanted by Fishtown and knew we would return for years to come. Then we'll shove off from the dock for our return trip, trolling slowly down North Lake Leelanau. This dream doesn't feature me catching a lunker; catching anything, for that matter. It's a vision of what could be, out on Lake Leelanau with my soulmate on a summer evening. Forty short years ago I met Janet by chance, by fate, or by cosmic design. So I know that anything is possible. Seeing her in my mind's eye on that imaginary boat on a summer evening an hour or so before dusk remains but a wish, yet one I hold dear as a private joy. One should always be open to what the future might bring.

❋

When I was in my teens, I became a fan of the Allman Brothers Band. One of their early songs was "Dreams (I'll Never See)." Gregg Allman, playing his trademark Hammond B-3 organ, sang his smoky-voiced blues best on that one, with his brother, Duane, accompanying him with his soaring slide guitar work: *'Cause I'm hung up on dreams I'll never see....*

Although I appreciated the song as an anthem of hope against resignation, the dreams I may never see don't bother me. Perhaps I simply love the blues. Or am content with living a life not quite fulfilled. Another dream I may never see, but replay it on occasion just the same, is owning a lakefront home in Leelanau County.

Although throughout the county along its shorelines, the trend is to build spectacular multimillion-dollar homes that make a statement with their massive square footage, there remain some folks who prefer a smaller footprint, which is what we favor. This is a "when-we-hit-the-lottery" dream we entertain from time to time. Mine would be a modest abode on Lake Leelanau with plenty of elbow room: perhaps 200 feet of lake frontage; is that too much to ask? It would be an older cottage with all its yesteryear charm; nothing ostentatious; no "smart" home. Janet much prefers a Lake Michigan dream home. I suggest that if we hit the lottery, we get both. We can alternate weeks. Farfetched, but wouldn't that be something.

These dreams of a fully appointed fishing boat and a charming lakefront property may never materialize. Yet there is nothing to stop us from pursuing them, i.e., if we ratchet down our ambitions. A used boat with just the essentials; a simple cottage on a small residential lake. Both are within our means. Yet after so many years visiting the area, with so many days in, on, and near the majestic bodies of water in Leelanau County, well, perhaps maintaining our current inland cabin-owner status without the title (or the tax burden) of a waterfront property is close enough. Gratitude makes for a wonderful view.

SPOTS

Our dog, Benny, has finding a good spot for a long snooze down to a science. If he's on our bed, he'll begin circling as if hunting some unseen creature beneath the blankets then madly paw at the targeted area for his repose. Once the spot has been adequately prepped, he suddenly ceases his franticness and collapses, head resting on his front legs, eyes gradually closing for some quiet downtime. For humans, this habit or genetic predisposition of locating just the right spot for countless purposes goes way beyond just bedding down for the night. This is especially true of our family's time spent in northwest lower Michigan, particularly Leelanau County, and all of the destinations and diversions in the area that call to us as our "true north" homing device.

Whenever Janet and I arrive in Cedar after our just over six hour-drive north and the stops for essentials—beer, bait, and groceries, in that order—I inspect the property and the inside of the house for signs of concern or things out of place, unload our vehicle, drag our suitcase upstairs to our loft bedroom, quickly unpack and put every piece of clothing in its proper location in the dresser. Once that mission is accomplished, I open the window just above the head of our queen-sized bed and lie down for a nap. This ritual is one of my finer pleasures in life, especially as I grow older. Being at our seasonal retreat is the quintessential definition of home and relaxation for me. In that very room, on that bed, with the sounds of woodland nature just outside—birdsong, wind rustling the leaves—I'm confident that my blood pressure drops significantly as I nod out and leave my big-city cares behind.

Typically, I nap for about 20 minutes, and typically, I'm awakened by my own snoring. I take a few delicious minutes before rising from my supine position. Then I slowly sit up, take a deep breath, and sigh, marveling at my being here now in this special place: *home.*

※

As any fisherman knows, when it comes to fishing, it's all about the spots. Like real estate, it's location, location, location. Anglers spend much of their time seeking what looks, feels, and seems to be the right spot holding hungry fish. It's about using that uncanny sixth sense as a fish finder.

Each May or June, when I manage to get out on a Michigan river like the Jordan or the Boardman for a day of trout fishing, I revisit the spots that have been good to me in years past, as well as determine new ones I come across where the spring flooding from snowmelt has made its annual alterations in the river's structure and flow patterns. Scanning the water as I hike along the shore under the shadows of cedar and pine trees, I'll stop every now and then once the stream's conditions in certain places appeal to me as promising locations for trout awaiting their next meal to glide by with the current. "They're in there," Craig, my longtime Michigander fishing pal, will say in his low stealth voice. Can't be noisy around trout. This ultra-careful practice only heightens one's awareness—trout-fishing consciousness. We toss our lines upstream and let the current take the bait naturally downstream, ideally rolling toward a deep hole in front of a downed limb, where the clear water darkens with unseen promise. Sometimes we get what we came for: a sudden strong tug—*Got a hit!* And sometimes—more often the case—we don't. Cast, wait, retrieve, repeat. And repeat. And repeat.... Eventually, it's time to relocate, to go fish-finding elsewhere, i.e., to find another, and hopefully a better, spot.

When Craig and I fish our favorite trout streams, we start out by splitting up and going our parallel ways: He'll cross the stream and we'll track each other from opposite shores. After an hour or so, we'll reconnect. He'll return to my side of the river and we'll leapfrog our way upstream for another mile or so, then head back toward the truck, fishing all the way, not wanting to miss an opportunity for a strike. Once back at our parking spot—which is our usual parking spot, of course—around noon, we'll drop the tailgate and pull a couple of cold ones from the cooler. Craig will have a smoke. We'll have a "surprise-us" cold cuts and cheese sandwich kindly packed by one of our wives (who are both enjoying a day away from us; everybody is a winner) and get rejuvenated for an afternoon of pursuing the wily trout.

If we're making a day of it at the Jordan River, we'll sit at Pinney Bridge before heading out for our afternoon fishing. We adjust our tackle, making any changes that might bring us more, better, some luck: switch from leaf worms to a crawler or leech; add an extra split shot lead sinker; rig a crawler harness; use a wet fly setup that works with a spinning rod and reel; or tie on a Mepps Rooster Tail for the heck of it. Might even have a second beer while sitting on the riverside, the spring sun's welcome warmth giving us pause. "We're in no hurry," Craig says. "Just relaxing by the river. There's nothing I like better. Know what I'm sayin', Vern?" We laugh. Today is an entirely private matter, communing with nature and each other.

As we close out our fishing experience in the afternoon, heading downstream about 3 p.m. as the temperature climbs toward 70, we make our way to areas that are not tree covered, near the relics of what once may have been a wooden footbridge across the river. We end up shedding our jackets near several young tamaracks to get some sun-inspired color on our winter-paled faces and necks. Here, every year, we "pull up a chair," as Craig figuratively suggests, and "take a load off." Here, we experience what we're really after; a few nice trout on a stringer is a bonus. We would never come to this spot first; it takes a good half day or so of fishing to arrive at the proper mental state to fully appreciate it. Contentment. After 30 minutes or so we both know what comes next, and Craig, my good-time guide, will reluctantly offer it up: "Time to call it a day. Or do you want to keep pressing on? We can, you know." The invitation to continue fishing without end is an existential tease, as we both know it's not true, but what if it were....

And then it's most likely that Craig, the master of ceremonies, will announce, "I think we've hit all the good spots," the official nod to our outing's conclusion. "Another great day spent along the river, eh?"

"Amazing," I say, taking a long parting look, enraptured by it all. "Not sure I deserve this."

"Stop it," Craig corrects me. "Yes you do. We both do. God did this.

We're just taking advantage of His good graces. Just be thankful, that's all. Now let's go have that last beer. You feel me, man?" he asks in his hipster imitation voice. I do. I really do.

❋

Several times each year we drive the winding seven miles north on scenic M-22 to the village of Leland with one purpose in mind for me: to ride my bike around Lake Leelanau. We always park on the south side of Reynolds Street near the stone wall ringing the "old money" lakeshore property there, underneath the overhanging boughs of its grand trees. Janet walks down to South Beach with Benny for some quiet time on the shore of Lake Michigan. This is one of her favorite spots on the planet, sweet echoes of summers long past when the kids were young, when we were younger, and we rented a house on Lake Street for a number of two-week "endless" summer breaks.

I get ready to ride. Bandana wrapped around my head, helmet and gloves on, smartphone cradled, water bottles on board, PowerBar stowed in the seat pack for mid-ride energy renewal. But before pushing off on my Specialized 29er mountain bike, I take in my surroundings. I remember walking with our barefoot kids to the beach on sunny July and August afternoons, the boys prancing ahead burning off nervous energy, teenage daughter, Shawn, in no hurry, being more adult-like. Back then, after a full day wearing out the kids by land and sea, Janet and I would return to the then-vacant beach about 5 o'clock to enjoy the quietude. Then after supper—either grilled in the backyard or served at the Bluebird Restaurant a few blocks away—around 11 p.m., our clan would go to the beach and lie on beach towels watching the celestial light show in the clear, dark summer night sky. Meteors streaking. Satellites orbiting. Planes flying. And the occasional UFO, perhaps, doing its mysterious thing, or so we imagined. The following day, I would awake early to go for my morning four-mile run along Lake Leelanau on M-22 then conclude by veering down Reynolds Street and running on the yet cool sand toward Van's Beach. It all happened here. Well, time to ride.

Three years ago in late June, we came to South Beach for a few hours. Of course, it's not exactly the same as it was when we first visited 25 years ago. More people. More dredging has changed the contours of the beach. There's now a well-equipped water rescue booth. Trash cans provided by the village. And signage outlining rules for proper beach conduct, as well as identifying the beach. Before all this "progress" came about, the beach stayed a local secret (though shared with the occasional summer renter), remaining much as it has for thousands and thousands of years since the last ice age that formed the lake.

During this visit, as Janet and her girlfriend from Colorado made their way to the beach to find their special spot to catch some rays and catch up, I noticed a swarm of large dragonflies hovering above the dune-grassed hill. "Wow, check that out," I pointed out to the ladies. "Cool," Janet responded. Her girlfriend looked over as directed then looked away toward the water, not quite having the same visual experience as I. And they just kept walking. No natural phenomenon would interfere with their fixation upon finding their special spot. I stopped. There were hundreds of large dragonflies about 8 to 10 feet above the ground, facing the lake and into the breeze, the sunlight glinting off their translucent wings. This remarkable sighting prompted me to buy a field guide when we were back in Indy: *Dragonflies and Damselflies of the East* by Dennis Paulson—a dense scientific catalogue with everything about dragonflies one could ever imagine. Paulson's photos indicate that I witnessed a large gathering of common green darners (*Anax junius*). I stood there for at least 10 minutes marveling at the three-inch-long flying insects with helicopter navigational capabilities. Obviously, the darners liked this spot too. A summoning shout from Janet broke the spell, and I left the darners to their own ends. Apparently, a good spot for soaking up sun on the beach had been located.

❋

When it comes down to it, our seasonal visits to the area are really all about revisiting favorite haunts. We are drawn to them as if by migratory instinct. Returning to all of these special places—whether a long unused bed in our cabin loft or hiking the beach below Pierce Stocking Scenic Drive at Sleeping Bear Dunes National Lakeshore, one of Janet's favorites—resumes and enlivens our close relationship to such personally sacred spaces.

Why, I can see myself now walking the shoreline just north of North Bar Lake. Old pier pilings have emerged from the sand, revealed by storms, and we step around them. The waves continue toward us in their rhythmic manner, an offshore breeze taking the edge off the summer heat. Along the way, countless beach rocks are underfoot. Seagulls wheel in the sky and float in the surf, just being seagulls. We walk past the Pierce Stocking overlook, where tourists have congregated on the wooden observation deck on the apex of this massive dune. They're watching the happy fools gleefully hurry down the dune—and breathlessly trudging back up. (On more than one occasion, Janet and I have witnessed first responders coming to the aid of a poor judge of the degree of difficulty, as well as his cardio fitness—such flawed judgment typically the domain of men.) We pass them. Flame-orange wood lilies have bloomed sporadically across the surface of the dunes. Once well past the dune climb, we stop at our suddenly designated halfway point, undoubtedly receiving the same mysterious "just right" signal as Benny receives when bedding down. We gaze at the horizon. Hug. Listen to the waves as they announce their never-ending onshore arrival. Thoughts diminish. Talk ceases. We treasure this spot. Together. And it almost seems as if this moment could last forever. But we know better. Which is why it is so precious.

STONES

One day, when I was almost 4 years old, sometime in 1960, which is as far back as my memory permits, I accompanied my father on a visit to his workplace. At that time, he was employed by the Pennsylvania Department of Transportation, building and maintaining highways across the Keystone State. My family lived in Scranton, once the center of the anthracite coal-mining region of northeastern Pennsylvania, in the Wyoming Valley of the Appalachian Mountains.

What's most remarkable about this memory is that nothing remarkable occurred during its making, nothing especially worth remembering. Yet the recollection remains vivid, as if it happened just yesterday. That goes for a fair number of the "videos" contained in my memory bank. Certainly not highlight footage from my life, these recordings of random non-events perhaps are no more than demo tapes for the brain to show off its capacity for memory, or to kill time during a lag in the thought process. But these conclusions are drawn from the obvious. Maybe these unremarkable memories are kept for a greater hidden purpose, inviting me to think harder about them and their themes to detect an undercurrent of meaning. This one, having played moments ago without any apparent reason, somehow slipped into the foreground of my consciousness. And just as inexplicable as this memory clip seems to be, now seems to be the right time to hold onto it for a while for a closer examination.

There we are, Daddy and I, riding in the one-and-only family car, our big and beautiful two-tone, sky-blue and pearl-white 1955 Buick Special. We exit the highway, Daddy turning the large steering wheel hand over hand like a pilot at the helm of a tall ship changing course, and veer onto a bumpy dirt road and into a growling, dusty scene of heavy machinery and men at work, with manmade mountains of stones piled here and there. My little heart must have quickened at the prospect of it all.

Daddy brakes the car. His right arm protectively swings across me to prevent me from falling forward, seat belts a thing of the future in those days. He gets out of the car and comes around to my side to let me out, and I eagerly jump into his arms in this oft-repeated joyful drill back then. He carefully deposits me next to a dump-truckload-sized pile of gravel along with some toys, this thrilling diversion for me no doubt enabling him to talk with his coworkers without my youthful interruption (these were the days before OSHA regulations—Occupational Safety and Health Administration—a simpler if not more dangerous time). There I sit contentedly with a plastic pail and shovel and my metal Tonka trucks and construction vehicles, miniature replicas of the heavy equipment noisily going about their business around me. Dump trucks and front loaders and cranes with giant dredging maws—the big boys' toys—work on the periphery of my playscape. I babble along with the din, imitating the machinery's sounds while fancifully steering my fleet of toy vehicles, my imagination guiding me.

Who knows how long I sat in that pile of stones, digging my stubby, dirty hands into the disgorged heap of gravel, a film of dust coating me, playing among, as the late astronomer Carl Sagan could appreciate, "billions and billions" of little stones. In their quiet way, they seemed to have done nothing more than encourage me to be myself. I'm not at all sure why this memory persists, nor why it resurfaced once again. But whether by chance or design, the remembered experience does seem to foreshadow my fascination with stones that emerged decades later while visiting northern Michigan.

*

In 1988 Janet and I journeyed to northwest lower Michigan for our first sailing experience. Craig had invited us to sail with him and his wife out on

Lake Michigan across the Manitou Passage to the Manitou Islands, using his father's sailboat, a fine vessel that could sleep six and smoothly handle the inland ocean in sailing-friendly weather. We would cast off from Leland and sail westward nearly 16 miles to South Manitou Island, part of the Sleeping Bear Dunes National Lakeshore, where we would camp for several days.

It was an idyllic early August day. The sky was a blissful forever-blue; the water an aquamarine so foreign and enthralling to Janet and me, landlocked Hoosiers. The cream-colored beaches of the islands stretched for miles as irregular giant rings, seldom-disturbed sand beckoning the more adventurous to cross over from the mainland to repair their state of mind. Janet and I had never been on a sailboat, had never been out on Lake Michigan, and had only traveled to an island once previously: Nassau, in the Bahamas. Other than it being our honeymoon, the trip to Nassau did little more than empty our pockets and make us long for home. These Michigan islands spoke to us on a much different level.

Craig sensed our impatience to hit the beach, so he steered the sailboat toward North Manitou, a few miles closer than our destination of the south island. We anchored the boat in three feet of water just off the beach. Janet and Connie, Craig's wife, eagerly abandoned ship then waded in with mild complaint, soft feet making hard contact with the stone bed lining the beach. They scampered up onto the warm sand and headed north for a get-better-acquainted chat, the two wives having just met. Craig secured the boat with bow and stern anchors, and we headed south, padding barefoot along the vacant beach.

My mind was on hyperdrive, scanning everything, the surroundings so alien and wonderful. I watched Craig search for things in the sand while trying to pay attention myself, though quite unsure of what I was supposed to be looking for. I was a trainee in the natural world, not having been brought up in a family that appreciated the great outdoors. I had tried Cub Scouts, but quit soon after my first Pinewood Derby, my meticulously sculpted and painted but non-competitively engineered race car losing miserably in the first heat (a father and son team effort), the disappointment of the loss moving me to drop Scouting, and as a result, I missed out on camping with my pack. Our family once rented a cabin for a weeklong vacation on a lake in northeastern Pennsylvania, but all I remember is Dad struggling to figure out what Creepy Crawler-like plastic artificial baits to use and how to use them, having mail-ordered a fisherman's starter kit from the back of an outdoor magazine. He fished impatiently with us from the bank, as we threw everything we had at 'em into the lake, hoping for a fish, or even a bite. We didn't catch a thing, and our family packed up and evacuated prematurely, not allowing the vacation to run its course, not so much due to the poor fishing as the strained relationship between our parents. So, not knowing any better, we continued to invest ourselves wholly into the urban kids' milieu of television and sports, and became increasingly removed from the wonders of nature. But here on the peaceful beach of North Manitou Island on a perfect summer day—our party the only humans in sight—I began reconnecting with the inheritance all of us share: we are born to love the planet.

I was having fun there on the beach with my buddy, but was unsettled, unsure of myself, overthinking the experience, seeking technique and reassurance. I kept respectfully quiet as we walked the North Manitou shore. Craig would occasionally stop, pick up something, examine it with his keen artist's eye, then either pocket it or, more frequently, toss it aside. I'm sure that he noticed my unbalance, that I didn't get out much. "Here, I want you to have this," he said, handing me a stone that seemed quite indistinct in its features and unremarkable in color, a rusty brown and black mottled rock. I was puzzled. Seconds later he reached out a hand to me, wanting to look more closely at the stone. I returned it to him, anxiously awaiting his geological verdict, when suddenly he pitched the rock toward the water and laughed hysterically at my confusion. "Definitely not a keeper," he said. "That was one ugly rock. I can see you're going to need a lot of help getting this down." I laughed at myself; my intensity began to ease. I knew then that I wouldn't be graded on my ability to discover beach treasures and to present a convincing argument on the merits of my finds. I could let my guard down, for I was among friends, which, I would soon discover, included stones.

A few minutes later, Craig handed me a palm-sized artifact. Now becalmed but ready for his unpredictable sense of humor, I mustered all my aesthetic faculties so that I might be attuned to the proper appreciation of this primitive art form. The fossilized stone was an oval-shaped opalescent piece of ancient coral worked by the action of the waves over eons, Craig explained. One side of the piece was worn smooth, the other looked like a spider web, the tiny, irregular rectangular crevices mostly pockets of caked sand. I shook out as much sand as I could, and as the fossil emptied it took on greater definition. I found it curious, this primeval, silent story of former life in my hand by chance. Although I was hoping for an opinion to confirm my own, I knew that I liked it, and that counted. But of course, that wasn't enough. When I had sufficient visual data to make my fragile personal determination of artistic merit, I looked up at Craig, hopefully searching his face for a sign of approval. He took the fossil, turned it over in his well-practiced hands, his examination underway. An agonizingly long moment passed before he gave his verdict: "This, my friend, is a keeper," and gestured for me to take it.

As a rookie rock hound my stone greed surged, the natural first stage of this pursuit, when the inner child is released, when you begin to ever so slightly comprehend the concept of infinity through the endless number of beautiful stones there are to pick and choose from, and when all you can think is *mine*. "You sure you want me to have this?" I asked.

"Hell yes," he said. "If you like it, keep it. If not, throw it away. There are plenty to go around." He glanced at my bulging pockets, where I was storing my rapidly accumulating finds. "I can see you don't buy that."

We were amused and content on this island, away from it all. And with Craig's unique guidance—Scoutmaster one minute, trickster the next—my appreciation for stones was rapidly growing. Never again would I stroll a beach without prefacing my footsteps searching the sands for geological objets d'art. I was a convert, once lost in the sedimentary indifference adulthood can bring over the years, now found through the recovery of my childlike sight. I had entered my very own Stone Age.

❋

For a decade we vacationed in Leland, renting a local's house just a block and a half from the beach. Janet and I became aware that vacation consciousness set in when we were going for frequent spontaneous walks along the water-line, looking for treasure revealed by the lake: stones, beach glass, fossils, driftwood. The image that best depicts summer vacation for me is sitting on the public beach in Leland, the Manitous prominent on the western horizon. It's about 5 p.m., and the sun is still high in the sky. There are but a handful of people left on the beach, the rest having retreated inland for supper or happy hour. The waves roll on inexorably in their never-ending quest for the shore, and climb the beach with approximate regularity as if God's timepiece. Below the surface the waves encourage the stones, slowly nudging them toward the beach and into the sunlight. The seagulls pace along the edge of the water, anxious for a handout, somehow knowing tourists when they see them. Janet is walking along the rim of the wave's furthest reach through fields of small stones, recent offerings churned up from Lake Michigan's depths. She walks slowly, her mind watchful and serene. Every so often she will pause, stoop gracefully, carrying herself with a hint of the little girl she once was, and reach toward something that calls to her. The operating procedure of this exercise is simple: if it delights, it's worth keeping and showing others. And if by her lights it is, she'll place the object in her fanny pack. She'll stroll south toward Whaleback Hill, nearly a mile away, until I can barely make out her form, slowly disappearing into the distance. Eventually my wife reappears. She patrolling for stones of particular interest, and I cherishing the view.

When they strike my fancy—when they call to me—during my own beach strolls, I pocket stones and take them to Janet, seeking an audience, which is always granted, and we focus on the natural beauty of stone. She'll put aside her reading, remove her sunglasses, and join me in the moment. We remark at the stones' qualities, fascinated by the individual expressions of each one, a joy that mounts as the sharing continues and we work our way through the pile. Once back at the house, we put the stones in bowls of water and regard them throughout our vacation week. The water vivifies them. Some weeks later, back in the daily grind, the vacation glow gradually dimming, we take time to fill jars with the stones, fossils, and beach glass then again add water to bring out their glistening sheen and definition, their "original" state when we first discovered them. I have but one container of collected stones on my office desk (not bad for an addict). It's an Arizona Iced Tea bottle, the label removed. It's filled to the brim with small Lake Michigan stones of manifold color, pattern, and shape; translucent white, emerald green, and beer-bottle brown smooth-edged beach glass pieces are blended in. When I need a breather from my white-collar work, I reach for the bottle. I slowly rotate it, treating myself to the endless visual delight the contents offer and the warm memories they prompt. I never tire of the sight.

❋

During my first few years of stone gathering, I had a habit of collecting large specimens, weighing anywhere from 1-10 pounds, and loading up our van with what Janet accused me of: unnecessary tonnage, if not evidence of committing an act of theft. "You need to put them back," she would gently scold me about the more sizable stones. "They don't belong at our house in Indiana; they belong here, near the lake. They are the property of the state of Michigan."

"Sorry, honey, but God owns them and He gave them to me," I retorted. But even that didn't stop her.

"You have enough stones. Now put them back," she ordered, her left index finger now pointing menacingly at me as if a drawn gun about to be fired. But I've seen that gun before, and it only fires blanks. And so her wifely commands fell on deaf ears, as I would surreptitiously hide my geological acquisitions beneath our luggage for the trip home as if stowaways. By the time she discovered them—when we were unloading the van in Indy—it would be too late. I gladly suffered her protestations, knowing there was nothing she could do but reluctantly accept the new members to the collection—rather, to the gathering, to the assembly of stones. As our northern Michigan summer vacations began to add up over the years, the stones began to overrun our Indiana home as if promiscuous life forms, appearing on coffee tables, bookshelves, desks, nightstands, dressers, atop toilet tanks and bathroom sinks, and eventually spreading outdoors onto patio tables and into perennial garden beds. After five or six years, I, too, became aware of the magnitude of the invasion I had triggered.

Eventually, I complied with Janet's request and gradually began to downsize my stone selections, both in individual size and quantity. I now hunt for quarter-sized or smaller stones (for the most part). This is partly due to my wife's insistence, but mostly to my fatigue with hauling large rocks back and forth: from the beach to the car to the vacation house yard back to the car to Indianapolis and then about the house, positioning the stones here and there according to my own wave-like effect.

❋

The first year we traveled to northern Michigan on a family vacation, in 1990, we teamed up with my sister-in-law and her family, two young couples each with a small child. We were happily crammed into an overpriced vacation hotel, The Bayside Something-or-Other, the mom-and-pop kind of operation that's all but extinct along Grand Traverse Bay due to the corporate hotel chains buying up all the available frontage. The Bayside Something-or-Other (now history) was little more than a compound of white-washed cracker-box cottages, the cottages snug against one another so as to maximize tourist dollars per square foot. We spent lots of hours sunbathing and frolicking in the water along the hotel's grounds with lots of other blissfully ignorant people easily satisfied by the stereotypical vacation experience, the exploration of the greater area limited by unfamiliarity or lack of an adventurous spirit. That year, although we never bought the stuff in any of Traverse City's confectionary shops, we qualified as Fudgies. (Cash, all major credit cards, PayPal, and Apple Pay welcome, however.) Proof of my quite unintentional fudgie-ness was my purchase of a polished, clear lacquer-sprayed Petoskey stone at a roadside Michigan cherry stand, which we stopped by on the return trip to Indy. I just had to have one to bring back for show-and-tell at work, for none could be had along the Bayside Something-or-Other's well-combed beach. The next year, our first in Leland, I felt like a complete fool: Petoskey stones were widespread along the beach. Retail quality too.

Geologists say that Petoskey stones are remnants of ancient coral colonies that lived in a sea that covered Michigan during the Devonian Period, some 350 million years ago. Each "stone" is actually a gray cake of fossils. The compacted masses of early life are round or oblong, and smooth—

courtesy of eons of wave action and the influence of glacial movement. In Leland, and northward to Leelanau State Park, Petoskey stones are commonly found along Lake Michigan. The area is a rock-hound's paradise. During the summer, people of all ages are attracted to scouring the edge of the water for pretty rocks—a prime indicator of a Michigan shore vacation working its magic—Petoskey stones high on the list. Up North, many are easily and willingly transformed into seekers of stones.

❋

From behind my sunglasses and the lazy perch of my beach chair settled in the sand in Leland, I notice that stone hunting seems to be a largely female pastime. Generally, my male counterparts entertain themselves in the water or up on dry land, and tend to avoid the margins of the shoreline, leaving it to the province of women. I suppose this behavior is only natural, given women's love affair with precious stones, a proclivity since the beginning of human time. The most dialed-in stone seekers, though, appear to be older women. Unlike most of the rest of us, they know what they are looking for. These stone aesthetes usually appear either during the early morning hours when the beach is vacant or later in the day, after 4 p.m. or so, when the summer sun is not so intense and people are fewer. Quietly they materialize, as if wraiths rising from the sand, unobtrusive in their routine, blending in with the beach activity. These old pros have net bags to secure their treasures, and often carry scooping and sifting equipment to pry potential prizes loose from the sand. Sometimes they're equipped with homemade or purchased sifters or scoops with long handles that reduce the need to bend over and are therefore easy on stiff joints. They wear wide-brimmed sun hats and protect as much of their skin as comfortably possible, attired in white or light-colored clothing to reflect the sun's rays and mitigate the heat. I love my brief encounters with these venerable beachcombers. When closing on me as I approach from the opposite direction along the shoreline, they typically slowly lift their heads and allow their well-trained eyes a moment to break off from their search pattern, acknowledging my presence with a cheerful hello or a friendly nod in recognition of our shared love of rockhounding. In their twilight years, rid of the distractions of commercial life—of making a living—and finished with most of the demands of child-drearing (most, that is, for Mother is always Mother), they are fully focused upon *what really matters now.* Their contentment radiates angelically, and I feel as if I am in the presence of celestial beings.

The beach in Leland, as elsewhere along Lake Michigan, gives up its stony treasure every second, and in its own order, unimpressed by human time, desire, or imperatives. White quartz, brown jasper, speckled granite, banded agates, fossil-rich dolomite, sandstone, limestone, "Leland Blues" (slag cast off from an iron smelter in the late 1800s), and countless varieties this amateur will never be able to identify, are rearranged constantly as if by a mighty hidden hand guiding the force of the water. *Look! Look here! And there!* the joyous voice of the Creator seems to whisper to all his children at the water's edge. *Take a peek at eternity through stones and waves, sky and stars…it is my gift to you, for you are my beloved. Isn't it grand?*

Ah, so many stones, so little vacation time. On the beach, here and now and then again in the village of Leland at high summer, along Grand Traverse Bay, on any shoreline along which you may find yourself near open water, all is precious and divine.

❋

Several summers ago, while enjoying a welcome-to-Michigan vacation-launching beer with Craig in his flat on Front Street, Traverse City's main drag, as we planned a week full of diversions on, in, and near the water, I noticed some rock forms basking on his kitchen windowsill. There were a half-dozen palm-sized, flat, smooth, charcoal-colored stones. I picked one up. Holding the stone, I marveled at its contours, its density, heft, and permanence. This stone and its brethren in the window possessed untold patience, calm, contentment. They inherently knew their place in this world. "You like that, huh?" Craig said, regarding me regarding the stone. He took a long pull on a Harp Lager, then on a Marlboro Light. He exhaled, then confided in me. "That's basalt. They are my friends. They understand me. They know, man, they just know. They know everything there is to know, and that even knowing that much, it's all still a gigantic mystery just the same." He winked and laughed. It was absurdly funny; perhaps possible, even true.

Then Craig told me what he's been doing with this particular size, shape, and hue of this species of rock. For years he's been collecting them along Lake Michigan's northern beaches. As he talked, I remembered beach walks with him and being recruited to be on the lookout for basalt that was rounded and flat. I accepted the assignment without question. We found scads of them at the beach at Petersen Park, out on the tip of the Leelanau Peninsula, the edge of the universe, Craig maintains. Back then, when his daughters Leigh and Molly were of middle-school age, on a quiet Saturday night during Lent, Craig and the girls would search his apartment and round up the dark gray stones. They gathered them from the bathroom floor, under the coffee table, beside and under their dad's bed, from inside the closets, atop the refrigerator...and deposited them onto the kitchen table. There, with glossy white paint and thin brushes, Craig and his girls painted one side of each of the stones with the Christian sign of the fish. On Sunday morning after Mass, or later in the day around sunset, when the Grand Traverse Bay beaches are devoid of people, Craig carefully placed the stones in one of his Army-issue duffle bags, and he and the girls would cross Front Street to the West Bay beach near the mouth of the Boardman River. The three disciples stationed the duffle bag at a central location, fanned out along the beach, and sent the stones sailing over the water one by one, to break the surface and settle to the lake bottom. I'm sure this was a momentous activity for these ancient sentinels of time, specially selected for this sacred work. It certainly was for Craig, fully investing himself in this moment on the verge of doing something that really, really matters to him, a gesture of great faith and love. And the girls, how they must have marveled at the depth of their daddy's soul and his giant heart, as he ignited their spirit with understanding that goes beyond words.

During those summers back then, while indulging in an evening swim, and when the spirit moved him, Craig would take several of his hand-painted stones and wade into Grand Traverse Bay. When the water was chest high, he would dive in and swim out until satisfied with his distance from shore. Then he'd execute a series of surface dives and place the stones one by one on the sandy lake bottom. Some of them would be set Christian sign up, others symbol-side down; a beckoning, a hiding. As with all things, this arrangement is only temporary, for storms did with them what they would, and the stones would gradually creep shoreward.

Someday, beachgoers will begin finding these stones. They will fancy them, remark upon them, speculate. Some discoverers will be captivated by the mystery behind them and what the stones represent, each one deemed a miraculous find. More likely, most others will be puzzled, perhaps laugh a bit nervously in their unknowing—or worse yet, snicker from their unbelief—then hurl the stones back into the lake, a fitting return. Once gravity overtakes the stony medallions and they disappear beneath the surface of the water, the accidental discoverers will resume attending to their Bud Light and Mountain Dew, Fritos and Cheetos, and their general public brand of fun in the sun. No matter. Other than between you and me and Craig and his girls, the origin of the painted rocks will remain secret; their effect on each person who happens upon them impossible to gauge. Which is what's so wonderful about this minimalist art form…simple articles of faith, a quiet evangelization, waiting to be found, there for the taking.

Craig has long appreciated stones as faithful companions with an inanimate intelligence that belies their appearance. He says they understand his joie de vivre, his loneliness, his range of hope and despair. The stones listen, refrain from judgment, accept, and are unbound by time. And because of this, they do seem to know what really matters: being. Just being.

❋

In her essay "Teaching a Stone to Talk," in her book of essays by the same name, Annie Dillard tells of a neighbor who keeps a stone that is special to him. Several times each day he holds private language lessons in an effort to teach the stone to talk. Dillard calls it "noble work, and beats, from any angle, selling shoes." Respectfully, I believe Dillard's friend is missing the mark. Like all things in nature, I would argue that stones speak their own language, on a frequency which is accessible to people, but only if they are attuned to it. It can take a while to connect, and there are no guarantees, for a certain state of mind, of receptivity, is required. For some people, like me, it can be an apprenticeship of a lifetime. Stones, however, have all the time in the world.

ONE HELLUVA SAIL

An unusual multimedia wall hanging is on display just above my home office computer monitor; my wife won't allow it anywhere else in the house. She says it's too rustic, and well, rather creepy.

A copper wire ring scavenged from North Manitou Island by my intrepid friend, Craig, one Labor Day Weekend, holds seven items:

- Two orange sailing telltales (pieces of yarn attached to sails to indicate wind direction)
- Two small pieces of driftwood—smooth, flat and elongated, each approximately four-inches long, with words written in black Sharpie: "A FRAYED KNOT" on one, with "AFRAID NOT" on the backside; on the other are the words "BIG LAKE SAILOR" then "MULHERIN" on the flip side. (That be me.)
- The centerpiece item is a round slice of driftwood, about two inches in diameter and roughly three-quarters of an inch in width, that's been shellacked, the words "BEAVER ISLAND • SAIL 96" inscribed on one side. In the middle, the tiny heart of a sacrificial northern pike is affixed. An actual frayed knot dangles from this personally precious keepsake.

It's the preserved fish heart—a talisman, according to Craig—that banished his artistic gift from sight in any of the "public" spaces in our home where a guest might happen upon it. When my dear wife first set eyes on the wall hanging, she asked what was that "thing stuck on the circle." When told, her face contorted and she proclaimed, "That's disgusting." Whatever. It's mine. So are the memories. I earned the award—and lived to tell about it. So on the wall in my office it will stay.

I can't recall how the idea for this adventure germinated. Most likely, it developed during one of those Saturday afternoon phone calls Craig and I would have about once a month, just checking in on each other. Probably sometime in April or May, when we shake off the rust from winter and begin planning time outdoors together. No doubt I was standing on my backyard deck in Indianapolis enjoying the late afternoon sun, and Craig was in his garage on Old Mission Peninsula in Traverse City, door open, cigarette in hand, and the conversation went something like this:

"Do you think Janet would let you break away for a few days in August?"

"Well, maybe. We'll be up for the first two weeks of August in Leland. What's up?"

"I want to sail to Beaver Island from Charlevoix."

"Cool. How far is that?"

"About 40 nautical miles. (Immediately followed by a sudden gale of laughter—on his end of the line.) Not to worry: God will be with us. And if He's not, then hey, the worst that can happen is we drown. This world is overrated, you know."

(Now hysterical laughter—on the other end of the line. Then a pregnant pause.)

"Hey—you still there?"

"Yeah, yeah. Just wondering if this outing will get me killed."

"Something will get you eventually, you know," he said, so casually and omnisciently. "Why not something worthwhile?"

"Can your sailboat handle a trip like this—on open water on Lake Michigan?"

"Handle it? You kiddin' me? With me as skipper? And with The Big Guy watching out for us? C'mon, dude: ya gotta have faith!"

"Hmmm…I'll think about it."

"Think all you want. But let's plan on it anyway. You're goin', matey." And then the incorrigible captain of the 19-foot Flying Scot open-cockpit single-class racer, never designed for such an extensive and ambitious open-water trip, raved for the remainder of the phone call about the memorable fun we were going to have on his beloved *la Orana Maria* (Tahitian for "Hail Mary"—in reference to the Paul Gauguin painting of that name—of which there would be many said by this first mate, as things would turn out).

Craig has often pushed me beyond my comfort zone. This trip back in August 1996 was the one that just about sent me overboard, both figuratively and literally.

✸

Sunday morning, August 4, 1996. Our family arrived in Leland the day before for our annual two weeks of R&R. Permission to crew the *la Orana Maria* as first mate for a three-day trip was graciously granted by my wife, who wouldn't mind some time away from yours truly as part of her vacation package. So Craig and I left early in the morning to drive up to Charlevoix. The forecast called for a postcard-perfect northern Michigan summer day: sunny sky and a high in the low eighties, with a trace of wind.

Craig picked me up at our vacation rental in Leland, the Flying Scott dragging behind his pickup truck, making for a much longer drive than necessary for him, as we would be doubling back to get on U.S. 31 North for Charlevoix, where we would set sail. He just wanted to reassure Janet that all would be well.

"I trust you, you know," Janet said to Craig—not me—as we stood in the front yard saying goodbye.

"Why would you do something like that?" Craig answered—getting a weak punch in the chest from her for his flippant response. "Hey, I'll bring him back in one piece. You know I will." Then he gave Janet a bearhug, I gave her a kiss, we jumped in the truck and skedaddled toward our adventure on the high seas of Lake Michigan. I trusted Craig like a brother. Still, I had my misgivings about this outing: it was way beyond our usual escapades. Before I jumped in the truck, I took a long look at the Flying Scot, with its baby-blue trim and white hull looking so, so…small. Oh me of little faith.

As we drove toward Charlevoix, I reminded him that we were skipping an essential practice: Sunday Mass.

"I know," he said in a low, serious voice. "But," his voice rising, "we have special dispensation from our Dear Lord; I put in a good word, you know. He would rather we be out on Lake Michigan enjoying his creation today than sitting in a pew and simulating worship. This—this is the real thing. You know what I mean?" I did indeed.

We launched the boat, then motored through the channel—the incredibly short Pine River—connecting Lake Charlevoix to Lake Michigan, passed under the open drawbridge—the mast too tall to clear it when closed—then headed out to open sea. Since the water was as smooth as glass, we didn't put the sails up until later in the day, traveling by marine engine power for many miles, the trusty 4hp Nissan outboard motor propelling the Flying Scot while the wind was down. And of course, we enjoyed a few beers. Craig also pulled out a flask of Remy Martin VSOP Cognac for sipping. "Just a wee skosh, laddie," he insisted. "It's a pirate thing," he said as he handed it to me, chuckling conspiratorially in his raspy voice.

"Want to cool off for a bit?" he asked, a few hours into the voyage. And with that invitation, he killed the Nissan and jumped in. Like a little brother, I followed without question. The water was cold but refreshing.

"How deep is it here?" I asked while treading water, not much of a swimmer.

"Oh, about 450 feet," he responded calmly. I immediately free-styled my way back to the boat and rocketed up the ladder. Craig guffawed. That's the way the whole trip went. Captain Courageous as my mentor, testing my limits in survival experiments, while enjoying my anxious engagement in such manly challenges.

We went under sail late in the afternoon, and made slow but steady progress, averaging just under four knots, arriving at Beaver Island's St. James Harbor a few hours before nightfall. (Beaver Island is the largest island in Lake Michigan, approximately 55 square miles, with a year-round population just over 600.) We ended up sleeping on board, which was a version of torture I no doubt deserved, so I took it as a penance. It was warm and muggy, the unwanted mosquitoes kept us company, and the bench seats were hard and about half as wide as my body. Although exhausted in the morning, we were excited to be heading out and over to Garden Island, one of the 14 islands in the Beaver Island Archipelago. "I could use a visit to a chiropractor," I groused upon awakening. Craig was already up and about and handed me a cup of coffee. "Here, this is a better adjustment for ya. Cheaper, too."

As we approached Garden Island, which is just a few miles from St. James, the water became choppy, and gigantic hull-crushing boulders broke the surface as we neared the shore. "Get up on the bow and help me navigate through these monsters!" Craig shouted through the wind. I thought he was kidding. He wasn't, as he waved me on. There was no railing to grab for the final five feet or so to the bow. So I crab-walked out there and planted my posterior to the deck as if it had a magnet in it. As the boat rose and fell, I managed to point out all the rocks to avoid, and we safely made our way into Northcutt Bay.

The bay waters were calm because it was afforded natural protection from the wind. As we motored up to shore near our eventual campsite, we spotted a large sailboat anchored across the bay. During the entire two days we were there, we never saw any other human activity, which was strange. "Ghost ship," Craig commented as he saw me eyeing the boat repeatedly. "We'll just stay clear of her. Who knows what the hell is going on over there. You ain't in Traverse City anymore, matey."

That afternoon after setting up camp, I drifted into a short nap on the stern of the beached boat while Craig took his speargun out for some snorkeling. Fifteen minutes later I was awakened from my doze by the sound of swimmer kicks as Craig swam toward me, his masked eyes now above the waterline and wide with excitement. He soon revealed why: a five-pound northern pike impaled by the projectile, still wriggling with life. He released the snorkel and pantingly announced, "That pike was deranged and tried to kill me. It was self-defense. But hey, fresh fish on the barbie. Doesn't get any better than this."

We camped out on Garden Island for two nights. The first morning there we explored the area, but not extensively. Like me, Craig had concerns about the mystery vessel sharing the bay with us. "We need to stay close to the camp. If they raid it while we're gone, we're screwed." Adding to the spooky ambiance was the nearby Anishinaabe burial grounds. "We don't want to piss off the local spirits," Craig whispered as we hiked, "so we'll steer clear of that." He was deeply respectful of Native American culture. And, he was serious.

We really couldn't wander far anyway, as a squall line moved in early in the afternoon. We sat in the tent sipping coffee while Zeus-bolts stabbed at the island. The strong fire-brewed coffee was exciting enough, but the meteorological phenomena gave it extra zip.

On our last night on the island, over a campfire dinner of kielbasa and canned baked beans, he let me know that our return sail tomorrow would be "something of an adrenaline rush."

"What?" I asked, startled by the news.

"The waves are going to be interesting, thanks to the storms this afternoon," he said, as he ate with gusto.

"What does that mean?" his nervous rookie first mate inquired.

He laughed wickedly. "It means get ready to hold onto your ass, bro. Could be rough. But we have no choice, because I gotta get back to work Tuesday morning." He looked at me, a picture of concern. "It'll be okay. Have I ever let you down before?"

True. But there was always a first time.

❋

Early that morning, we headed out of the safe cover of the bay and were soon in the relentless grip of thrashing 7- to 10-foot waves—speaking of firsts for yours truly. Our tiny boat wasn't made for these conditions. But our captain was.

"Yee-ha!" he shouted gleefully. "Let's find out what we're made of!" He wisely instructed me to bail water, both to keep me busy and to keep my anxiety at a manageable level, a preoccupation that would last for nearly 12 hours as we battled our way back to Charlevoix. Water was indeed coming over the side, so the activity was not just a distraction but a necessity. The boat topped and bottomed in the gut-wrenching swells. A couple of hours into our Voyage of the Damned, a schooner from Traverse City hailed us and came alongside, asking if we were okay. Craig maniacally shouted thanks, grinning from ear to ear, and waved them off. But he wasn't speaking for me—far from being exhilarated, I was overwhelmed and held captive by the conditions. Unfortunately, the schooner cut us off from the wind and put us in irons for a few anxious minutes. Craig scrambled to turn the boat back into the wind to fill the suddenly limp sails. It was the most terrifying moment of our voyage, he would later confess, once we were back on terra firma and reliving the event days later with beery bravado. For now, I just did what I was told.

The captain and the *la Orana Maria* did the job, and aside from bailing, I did mine: repeating a mental rosary for hours on end, saying a record number of "Hail Marys," especially befitting our vessel's name.

Somehow, we managed to time our return perfectly. The drawbridge allowing us entry into the Pine River and then to Lake Charlevoix went up just as we approached, our tall mast clearing the opening. "Made it!" Craig shouted in utter glory. I was too exhausted to celebrate our victory, though certainly glad to still be among the living.

Just before we reached the drawbridge, folks along the river walk below the Weathervane Terrace Inn stopped and stared at the small boat coming in from an angry sea, the bedraggled, exhausted crew returning from an adventure that very few would classify as fun, and more like an episode of *Survivor.* Eight inches of water sloshing about the cockpit; the mainsail jammed and crimped into the mast; soaking wet gear, lines, and sheets in total disarray. The *la Orana Maria* had chaos written all over it. Yet still, she floated.

When we got back to Leland about 8 p.m., Craig gushed about the trip to Janet and our young teenagers, Shawn, Matt, and C.J., as well as to Janet's sister's family who was vacationing with us. They all smiled for about 30 seconds, and as the details came spilling out of Craig's mouth, they soon were astonished by the danger we were exposed to. Craig drove off, deliriously happy, and we promised to see each other on Friday night to relive our hair-raising adventure over cocktails. I walked quickly to the Mercantile in Leland and bought a six-pack of Miller Lite beer. I downed them all in an hour, sitting out on the backyard deck by myself, pondering what happened, what we accomplished, and what might have been. "You okay, honey?" Janet asked with concern, leaning over me, her hand on my shoulder.

"I'll be fine—in the morning. It was one helluva sail, Jan; a trip I won't forget. And the best part is, I never puked." This is how men evaluate success in such matters. Janet just shook her head in puzzled sympathy.

I couldn't put the experience into words then; it was just too fresh. So after a few quiet minutes together, Janet, realizing that this event had got-

ten my full mortal attention like no other to date, gave me some space and
went inside.

※

I went to bed just before the northern Michigan summer sunset called it a
day. Twelve hours later, I stirred from my sleep of the dead. The sun was up.
The sky was blue. And for a blurry, unsure morning moment, I wondered if
the three days before had been just a dream.

Years later, my commemorative wall-hanging artifact featuring the
preserved northern pike heart talisman attests that our *one helluva sail* was
entirely—if not all too—real. Whenever we recount our maritime adventure
of long ago with others, Captain Craig always concludes the tale with something to this effect: "Despite the angry seas battering our brave little boat
for hours and hours on end on our return trip, for the record: my first mate
never did puke. And I'm still damn proud of him for that." Me too. Especially because I lived to tell about it.

LAKE ANONYMOUS

There is a small residential all-sports lake near our cottage in Cedar that we've gotten to know and love over the past 10 years. Every spring, summer, and fall, we eventually end up on what I'll call "Lake Anonymous." I am not disclosing the name, as the tranquility it offers us two crazed Hoosiers from Indianapolis is precious. Perhaps you think I'm overreacting in my protectiveness. Perhaps some of you already understand. And perhaps the rest of you will a few pages from now.

Even with the waves of tourists that have descended on Grand Traverse and Leelanau counties in the past decade, and even during peak vacation season in July, being on the water or in the woods with few other humans to disturb the peace is easy to come by in these parts, as there are plenty of getaway places where semi-antisocial solitude-favoring folks like me can be left alone. Still, I'd rather not chance it. Throughout this essay and in perpetuity by my lights, Lake Anonymous it will remain.

We discovered this 650-acre gem while exploring the area during our first year in Cedar. I first found it while riding my mountain bike through the rolling hills of Leelanau County. Back then I was more powerful on a bike, and I sought hills to climb, caring neither about my redlining heart rate nor the physical strain. Now I seek flatter, less challenging roads to pedal, as arthritis is having its way with me, and I'm beginning to act my age. So just off M-22 sits Lake Anonymous, and the roughly five miles of surrounding roadways are pretty level and infrequently traveled by vehicles. A perfect playground for an aging cyclist.

❋

The north side of the road abuts federal parkland—Sleeping Bear Dunes National Lakeshore. There are several hiking path trailheads accessible from the road, and much to my satisfaction, none of them are marked. One is only discoverable by a keen eye, as the woods keep it mostly shielded from view—a slight parting in the leafy cover the only hint that this could be a trailhead. The other is wide enough for a truck, but a large tree trunk has been laid across it by park rangers, dissuading any attempt to traverse the path by four-wheeler. Janet and I have hiked them both, as the trails connect to an "official" park trail that wends its way to Lake Michigan. You can make it directly to the Big Lake in 30 minutes or take the trail in roundabout fashion for an hour or so, eventually getting to the beach. The heavily wooded trail was temporarily closed due to the furious August 2015 windstorm. Although the park rangers and tree removal contractors cleared the paths, a massive job that took months to accomplish, there remain many downed trees and tree-caught "leaners," some 60 feet high or more, mostly maples, their root balls ripped from the earth as if by Paul Bunyan when an angry child. In the spring, the haunting song of the wood thrush adds to the children's storybook ambiance of these woods. And leopard frogs abound near creeks and seeps that cut through the area; we spook them into jumping away to escape human intrusion. For us, it is a magical place.

On the northwest side of Lake Anonymous is a public park with a launch that never sees any real competition. Of the many times I've been on this body of water, I've never seen more than a handful of watercraft out on the lake. Usually there's a kayaker or two, a pontoon boat, and a fishing boat with some locals trying their luck at the yellow perch the lake is known for. A jet ski will sometimes charge out onto the water, but its pilot will keep a respectful distance from kayakers like us. The jet skiers usually whip about the lake for no more than 20 minutes or so, no doubt releasing some citified tension, and so the annoying high-pitched engine's whine is short-lived. Nature is intent on returning to its own equilibrium; it has infinite patience. It can wait us all out; even jet ski-riding thrill seekers.

Each summer, Janet and I are asked by one of her best friends, whom she attended North Central High School with in the seventies, to join her and her husband on Geist Reservoir just northeast of Indianapolis to relax on their boat at a popular area there called Cocktail Cove. As my mother would say of such a repugnant suggestion (though admittedly a generous-in-spirit invitation), that will be the day. I know that turning down an opportunity to be cavorting among an armada of drunken sunburned boaters who don't get out much, idly floating on a muddy lake, is the chance of a lifetime, but hey, call me crazy.

When I was in high school at Lawrence Central (Class of '74) during my senior year, I rode my canary-yellow Schwinn Varsity 10-speed around the reservoir, formerly owned by Indianapolis Water Company, which provides water to thousands of central Indiana residents. At that time, there were two buildings on the entire lake: an abandoned dilapidated bait shop and one that remained open. My high school buddies and I would drive out and fish almost anywhere along the reservoir, catching crappie, bluegill, catfish (channel and bullhead), and the occasional largemouth bass. Now, it seems that every square inch of lakefront has been sold and developed, the shoreline jam-packed with homes of the upper-middle class and distinctly upper class, their expansive residences a testament to their impressive financial success: the "winners." Yet their taste in water quality remains questionable: the lake was murky back in the early seventies and remains the same today—an oversized Indiana mud puddle. Since we've been heading to northwest lower Michigan for the past 30 years, I've become a water quality snob. Give me the clear, cool waters of the north with rivers clean enough to support trout. Cocktail Cove? Please.

✳

In the summer of 2017, I spent three weeks from June into July at our Cedar seasonal home, a very short and much cherished sabbatical. The day of the summer solstice, June 21, I went for a bike ride at about 2 p.m. It takes me about a half hour to get to Lake Anonymous by bike. I pedaled around another local lake (whose name quite intentionally escapes me), then got out onto M-22 for a couple miles before accessing the road that encircles my destination. June was remarkably cool that year, with daytime highs sometimes not even hitting the seventies. But that day, it reached the low seventies, making for optimum biking weather. I stopped at the modest park for a moment (which is actually little more than a boat launch and a field for parking pickup trucks and boat trailers), retrieving a piece of gum from my seat pack. Looking upward into the ever-captivating blue sky, I saw a bald eagle soaring in the thermals rising above M-22. I had nothing pressing chasing me—no juggling of multiple assignments or other spur-of-the-moment workplace demands for my immediate attention; no phone calls to make or return; no I'd-rather-be-somewhere-else/anywhere-else appointments to keep. I stood straddling my bike and gazing up at the eagle until the great bird soared out of view. Then I pedaled off, happy—just happy—my mind no longer terrorized by trivial pursuits. Vacation consciousness was setting in.

Back on the road, I passed an older woman strolling the opposite direction, and another walking to her mailbox. Both of them waved, as did I. It's just what you do when life is moving at the perfect speed, which it was for me that day, for a change.

One reason this writing will not reveal the name of Lake Anonymous is because of troubling recent developments there—as well as on many lakes in this increasingly high-demand summer vacation area. Lake houses used to be places where you went to get away from the anxiety-inducing daily grind. You would leave all the complications behind and indulge in simpler things offered by a rustic waterfront cabin. Like swimming. Fishing. Napping on a dock, paperback book splayed against your chest, a cool breeze lullaby as dragonflies flitted about. Now, Lake Anonymous is showing signs of gradually succumbing to a threatening invasive species called New Money. A handful of palatial summer homes have been built during the past several years that are monuments to capitalism and excess (if not insecurity). Some of them are nearly zero lot in scope, eating up the surrounding land of modest homes knocked down to make way for the new tenants and their infatuation with impressive square footage. One, constructed of logs, with a pretentious look more in keeping with the Colorado snow-skiing gentry, has a guest house that dwarfs our own retreat in Cedar. But hope remains. An adjacent property has a vinyl-sided modular home that's at least 40 years old. It's a nondescript tan with chocolate brown trim; nothing special. Which is exactly why it's so special. The owners use it for old-fashioned lakeside cottage R&R. The new "show home" next door will most likely take another year to finish, as it's already been a year in the making. Someday, the modular home will disappear, surrendering to some privileged fat cat's checkbook. Meanwhile, I salute the resistance and send best wishes for the traditionalists to hold out as long as they can.

*

Enchantment matters. In late May and early June, at one area of the lake, near where I saw the otters dashing in front of my bike one lucky day three years earlier, showy lady's slippers bloom near a roadside bog. The magenta and white wild orchid is stunning to those who treasure such things. Each late spring I stop and take photos of them; they recur each year in the same area, which I've only disclosed to my wife. They invite a closer look and almost beg to be touched, but I always simply enjoy the view, as the wildflowers are protected by the state of Michigan, and thankfully so. Excited by my botanical discovery, I send pics of the orchids to relatives, who seem not quite as taken by them as we are. And I'm fine with that. Best not to draw too much attention and have people love these wildflowers to death, as we tend to do with so many things in the natural world.

And then there's the lake itself....

*

In early October, when we return "home" for a week prior to closing the cabin down for the season, Janet and I kayak on this undisclosed lake. There we quietly pursue more proximate looks at the migrating ducks; kayaking affords such otherwise rare closeups. Although it is difficult to close in on many water birds—due to their natural skittishness perhaps aggravated by duck hunter buckshot zinging by—we've spotted mergansers (hooded, common, and red-breasted), as well as buffleheads, wood ducks, northern pintails, canvasbacks, green- and blue-winged teals, and more. One sunny day last October, Janet and I paddled about 50 feet parallel to the shore, slowly closing in on a half-dozen mallards. The sun glinted off their emerald necks, so that even these most common of ducks were magnificently otherworldly in the canting autumn light. On a quiet northern lake on a glorious fall afternoon, all things otherwise unnoticed attain a natural splendor.

That day, once we were through with our two-hour meandering about the lake, we landed back at the area we fondly call "our spot." There's a sparsely gravel-covered pull-off from the road, enough room to park two or three vehicles. We put in the kayaks from there. I've snorkeled the reed bed about 30 feet out, watching yellow perch and "smallies" swim almost within my reach. We've taken nephews and nieces and grandkids there to wade in the warm summer lake water. I've caught smallmouth bass from my kayak and by simply wading in up to my waist—best times being just before or after a cold front has moved in when the bass get hyperactive and hungry, or during the nesting period in June. Janet always likes to stow a couple of beach chairs in the truck just in case we'd like to sit for a bit by whatever body of water we happen to be near when out and about. That day, we decided to do just that once we returned to shore. Like a dear insistent host, the sunshine on the lake wouldn't let us leave the party just yet.

After we secured the kayaks in the truck bed, we set the beach chairs along the shoreline, our feet resting in the water as we faced the westward sun approaching evening. Sunshine poured across the surface of the lake, its reflection dazzling. Janet was reading intently. I just couldn't open my book, for I had found my happy place once again at Lake Anonymous. And as much as I'd like to, dear reader, provide you with further details or clues about that precious location, it's simply out of the question. Forgive me. But do keep looking. You'll find that special lake spot of your very own someday. A place where you, too, will want to keep it all to yourself. Trust me.

Up North Armageddon

I should have been there. Been there to witness the eerie world's-end squall line menacingly rolling in over Lake Michigan from the west, fast approaching the mainland, come to lay waste to whatever might be in its path.

I've lived in Indiana since 1966. When we first moved here from Scranton, we took heed of storm and tornado watches in ways that the locals didn't seem to. Whenever we saw muscular black-and-blue clouds darken the horizon and the local TV weather forecasters instructing us to take cover, we paid attention. Northeastern Pennsylvania's skies tended to dump nothing more sinister than snow, and lots of it. Here, the weather seemed like it was out to kill you.

As years passed, we gradually became full-fledged Hoosiers: less concerned with threatening weather, slower to respond to tornado watches and warnings. Although I was never a storm-chaser (that's just plain insane), I have developed a habit of going outside at work or at home to watch the angry skies and check for cloud rotation—a funnel cloud or even a twister— just to experience for myself the immense power of Mother Nature. Whenever such conditions arise, I'm usually not alone. Curiosity just gets the best of some of us.

Nearly 30 years ago, I worked for SEMA: the Indiana State Emergency Management Agency (now the Indiana Department of Homeland Security). It was a Friday evening in June, about 8:30 p.m. I was already in bed after a brutal week. My pager was within reach on the nightstand beside my bed. I was reading, and the beeper, as they were also known back then in the Digital Stone Age, was going off intermittently, as it had been for several hours. Two of my colleagues in the Emergency Operations Center (EOC) downtown in the belly of the vast southern Indiana limestone-walled Indiana Government Center were issuing a steady stream of weather updates. There were numerous severe weather watches across the state, with several warnings here and there for tornadoes and straight-line winds. Despite my increasing annoyance, I begrudgingly admitted our SEMA weather watchers were just doing their job. So I went back to my book, trying to ignore the weather alerts. Bad idea.

I was dreading the possibility of being called back into the office over the weekend. I worked in External Affairs, meaning media and public relations. If a newsworthy weather-related incident would occur, chances were high that one of us in the External Affairs Department would need to report to the EOC. "Boy, your pager is overheating," Janet said, just before turning out her reading light and calling it a day. It had grown darker prematurely that evening due to the wave of storms. It was summer. Our windows were open; the rain pattering then coming down in dense sheets.

Just after 9 p.m., I noticed that the heavy rain had abruptly ceased and a weird calm had set in. Instantly, I had a sobering realization and my emergency management instincts kicked in. I leaped out of bed and looked out the bedroom window. The neighbors' home to the north was separated from ours by a driveway and a thin strip of grass. As I peered outside the air suddenly exploded, with ferocious winds and debris completely obscuring my view. "Janet, get up!" I yelled, grabbing her by the arm. "Get to the basement—quick!" She did as told—once she was sure that I was rescuing Matt, our then 7-year-old son. I lifted our groggy, dead-weighted boy out of his bed and hurried us toward the basement doorway, which involved making our way down a fairly long U-shaped path from our bedroom. I heard limbs cracking outside and our home being pelted by debris. I don't know just how long we waited in the safety of the flashlight-illuminated basement; maybe 10 minutes. Then I ventured outside. There were power lines down all over the neighborhood. As I checked things out, I heard a sickening crash at the major intersection of College Avenue and 86th Street, just around the corner. The stoplight was out, as were the streetlights. I joined several good

Samaritans in seeing to the injured drivers and assisted the Indianapolis Fire Department's responding unit with traffic management until the victims were transported by ambulance to St. Vincent Hospital just a few miles west of here. Wondering about the storm's aftermath, I took an early morning drive to scout the area and survey the damage. There were some downed trees, and the ones left standing had been ravaged by the high winds, their broken limbs and branches scattered about. I drove up to nearby Northview Middle School's campus about a mile east of our home. On the large practice soccer field in front of the school, three venerable oak trees had been corkscrewed from their moorings, now storm victims in repose. To me, the evidence of a tornado appeared to be abundantly clear. Yet on Monday, my SEMA colleagues informed me that the National Weather Service ruled the damage was caused by straight-line winds. *No way,* I thought, upon hearing the official verdict. But I was an emergency management novice back then whose conclusions were easily dismissed. Now I'm a weather buff. And major storms captivate me.

※

The first I heard of the violent storm to hit Leelanau County and surrounding areas was in the evening on Sunday, August 2, 2015, the day of this unforgettable weather event. Janet's Uncle Tom and his family, residents of Louisville, Kentucky, were heading to our seasonal Cedar home for a week of vacation. They had never been north of Indy, and Janet's you-haven't-lived-until-you've-been-here tourism-encouraging review about Leelanau County had convinced them to come. Once in Traverse City, Tom had texted Janet with a flurry of messages telling her that a "crazy scary storm" had struck the area. They had a difficult time getting around downed trees to get to the house, having been rerouted through Maple City by first responders, and had to drive in "the back way." The power was out and countless trees had been knocked down, cutting off roads and damaging homes. Once a determined Tom made it to our property, dodging debris strewn on the roadways, he phoned in a report that prompted a sigh of relief: "Your house is fine; praise the Lord. But the neighbors' houses ain't. It's like a war zone up here. You wouldn't believe it." The properties to the north and south of us and directly across the street had suffered significant damage from toppled trees. Ours, inexplicably, was untouched. All of the tall sugar maples surrounding the house and spread throughout the property had held their ground against the savage wind. Tom and his family stayed the night in the cabin. But disturbed by what they had unwittingly driven into—total mayhem—they fled early the following morning, as the power was still down and recovery efforts were underway, and would be for days. Despite our offer for them to give it another shot, Uncle Tom and company haven't been back across the Michigan state line since.

Our Cedar neighbors Paul and Marie, who live about a half mile away from our Manor Green subdivision, hurried over just after the storm passed to check on our seasonal dwelling. Marie had seen the ominous squall line coming from atop the hill they live on just off County Road 651 North (a.k.a., Good Harbor Trail). She had taken cover in their modular home, and, as she related dramatically on the phone, "I said my prayers.

"Every house around you got hit by falling trees," she continued. "Yours? Not a scratch. We get windstorms up here, but man, this was just incredible." Before surveying our property, they checked on a pair of neighbors across the street, whom they saw sitting in their SUV in their driveway "in a state of shock," Marie reported. "They could barely talk when I asked them to roll down their windows to see how they were. Their house had been hit by several giant maples pushed over by the wind. The trees were leaning against the house and had knocked some holes in the roof and walls. But hey, the good thing is, though they were pretty shaken up, the couple was safe." Marie apparently says some mighty influential prayers.

Paul's older brother, Craig, my best friend who lives out on Old Mission Peninsula just north of Bowers Harbor on West Grand Traverse Bay, got to experience the maelstrom from home. I sent him a text about the "helluva storm" out in Cedar. He texted me back late that Sunday night: "Power's been out for hours. Three different storms rolled in back to back. We're not goin' anywhere—Peninsula Drive is blocked in both directions. Debris everywhere. Very violent wind, hail, lightning. Total madness. A real hair-raising tempest. Gotta love it!" As is his nature, Craig gets amped up by hazardous weather events.

The photos I saw a day later in the *Record Eagle* and on UpNorthLive.

com showed a large gray-white then blue-black then creepy green cloud band that looked like an irradiated invasive species arising from Lake Michigan, Japanese monster movie-like, with lightning erupting over the surface of the water. Weather officials determined it was a rare bow-echo storm, seldom seen in Michigan but more common in "Tornado Alley" states such as Oklahoma and Kansas, with winds topping 100 miles per hour. To the onlooker, it might have felt like the Second Coming. I wished I had been there with Craig out on Old Mission Peninsula when this weather event of a lifetime occurred; maybe that's what a death wish feels like. You see malevolence coming toward you, perhaps for you, you know it could be curtains, and you *want* to be there for the experience, assuming it's survivable. Doors singer Jim Morrison nailed it: *People are strange…*

The following spring Janet and I drove to Alligator Hill in the Sleeping Bear Dunes National Lakeshore, near the historic village of Glen Haven. We have hiked there numerous times, one of our favorite trails on the federal property. But things had changed from when we last visited—dramatically. The hilly hike on an old lumber two-track dirt road used to be through heavy tree canopy. Now, sunlight poured in. Countless trees had been blown over by the straight-line winds—for miles. It was as if a giant bowling ball had been rolled through the forest. "This is heartbreaking," Janet said. "I don't like it at all. Let's go back." However, the scene of woodland carnage didn't strike me the same way; I had more exploring to do. Mother Nature has a temper, and I was drawn to the awesome aftermath of this particular tantrum.

"Just give me a few more minutes," I pleaded. She shrugged and turned, walking downhill to return to the truck. Meanwhile, I hiked farther uphill, checking out the devastation. On the bright side, the view of Lake Michigan from the trail was now opened up. And even many of the uprooted trees still put out leaves, as they remained tenuously anchored to the sandy soil. Nonetheless, it will take more years than I have left for the forest to recover from this blow.

In the fall of 2016, I was in Horizon Bookstore on Front Street in Traverse City, a favorite haunt of mine on rainy days. I picked up a copy of *Storm Struck: When Supercharged Winds Slammed Northwest Michigan*. I had to laugh. "I knew someone would write the book on that storm," I said to Janet as I got out my credit card. The photos of the devastation, taken by locals and visitors, told the story. Downed trees and power lines, crushed vehicles and homes and outbuildings, and seemingly not-of-this-Earth hostile skies said it all.

While hiking trails at Sleeping Bear Dunes—all of which bear some signs of The Great Windstorm of 2015—I've tried to imagine what it must have been like when the storm arrived. The sight and sound in the forest made by majestic healthy trees being knocked over and broken by a massively powerful unseen force, with one-ton-plus limbs snapping like twigs while the wind howled like a screaming banshee, must have been enough to make an atheist hiker an instant convert to God-fearing believer. Although I am already a disciple in my own unique way and feel the presence of the Creator most profoundly in nature, I'll take the vicarious experience of this once-in-a-lifetime weather event through *Storm Struck* and first-person accounts through friends and family as the next best thing to being there. No courage or foolishness required.

PART IV

Autumn

DISAPPOINTMENT

All countries, religions, and families have their treasured traditions. One of our favorites is traveling to northwest lower Michigan to spend the Labor Day Weekend, a 15-years-and-counting habit. This is so ingrained that doing otherwise is unthinkable, at least for me. This year, in 2018, however, we broke our streak. Which broke my heart. So I had to put it back together again. Somehow.

As is my habit before heading north, the weekend before I started checking the National Weather Service for the Cedar forecast. At that time, it was looking good for the coming weekend: partly cloudy, with highs in the low 80s. Eminently doable. I begin to daydream intermittently at work about the perfect Labor Day Experience: early morning walks; biking around Lime and Little Traverse lakes, to return on M-22 to South Good Harbor Trail then home; piddling about the house and yard, seeing to minor repairs—trimming low tree branches, patching ruts in the gravel driveway, tidying up the shed and its ever-increasing contents; sitting on the deck with Janet, Benny contentedly dozing in her lap, a good book, and maybe a good beer; grilling out with our neighbors Paul and Marie. The usual great American laidback good time honoring the end of summer. But as the week went on, the forecast deteriorated. The little image boxes on weather.gov indicating the daily weather for the week gradually went from heartening sky blue and white clouds to depressing gray sheets of rain and lightning. By Thursday, the prognosis was for abundant rain and thunderstorms daily from Friday through Tuesday: our window for the trip.

My heart sank; my mood darkened. I became irritable. Irrationally, I blamed the turning weather on my wife, who had been reporting the worsening forecast each day to me. I also tracked it myself, but somehow, her echo seemed more irritating than my own research. "It's just some rain," I scowled, unwilling to miss out on escaping Indy for a timeout from my labor as a school administrator. Good work, but it tires me so, especially the older I get, and reinvigoration is essential to performing well in such a demanding environment. "Well, you like to do things outside when it's raining; I don't," Janet reminded me. She was right. I will do things in the rain—like walk the beach, hike in the woods, and go fishing. Sometimes, rain even enhances these experiences.

"I'll just go myself," I threatened, which didn't go over well.

"Okay, I'll go with you then," she countered, which was an even worse idea. Janet is a sunshine girl who suffers from Seasonal Affective Disorder in the long gray Indiana winter months. And it shows hints of reappearing whenever cloud cover lingers for more than 48 hours, regardless of the season. This would be no mini-vacation for me with all of that sadness going on. Arriving at home from work on Thursday evening, I was met by Janet on the front porch, saying, "The forecast looks bad. But I'll still go if you want to."

Having given up earlier in the day, with my head down, mildly despondent, if that's possible, I responded, "No, we'll just stay home. Now I'm going for a long bike ride on the Monon Trail to help me get over it." I would just talk to myself and keep peddling on the urban trail for 20 miles or more until the disheartened voice inside became still. Rivaling a cold one, it's the best therapeutic intervention I know.

When I returned home about 8:30 p.m., it was dusk. I grabbed a pint can of Labatt Blue Light, realizing that would be as close to Michigan as I would get this weekend. Drank it while in the shower, and called it a night.

❋

On Saturday, I decided to get crazy and venture to Cabela's in Noblesville, just north of Indy. Going anywhere near a supersized store like that is just not in my DNA. After one visit to Costco with my wife, I now stay in the truck and wait for her, trying to avoid looking at those oversized grocery carts overflowing with stuff most Americans just can't seem to live without. Kegs of ketchup. Theater-sized TVs. Crates of toilet paper. Same with IKEA: wandering the entirety of the acres and acres of Scandinavian-designed household items while desperately trying to find the exit was enough for this guy. Never again. These monstrous warehouse retail giants send a message loud and clear to paranoid me that there are too many humans consuming the planet. But if you're a card-carrying capitalist, just look the other way and shop; I hear it's patriotic.

My always-up-for-adventure friend Dan joined me for the Cabela's outing. He had never been there either. I fooled him into it when he texted me: "Do they serve beer?" I texted back that they had everything. *Everything.* Everything but a liquor license, that is. Kept that small detail to myself.

Once inside the outdoorsman's superstore, we were overwhelmed immediately, akin to stepping into the ocean and getting knocked flat by a rogue wave. "Oh my God," Dan uttered, awestruck as we tried to determine where to go first. I was on a three-pronged mission: salmon bank-fishing gear for early October, a rod to match up with an ultralight reel to take my grandsons fishing this weekend, and window-shopping for a fishing boat I'll never own. "I'm already over-stimulated, and I just walked inside the store," he confessed. "So where's the bar?"

Despite having to patiently steer Dan away from countless apparently irresistible distractions—as if rowing Ulysses away from the Sirens—I was finally able to get us to the fishing equipment area. As I tested the action of several ultralight rods, Dan plopped into an outdoor portable recliner for a test ride. "This is actually pretty damn nice!" he marveled, giving it two thumbs-up. I took his photo for posterity; with smartphones, one is compelled to document everything (rarely to revisit the pic again). Once he extracted himself from the chair, he paused at the Yeti drinkware stand. "Hey, these are pretty cool," he noted, handling and inspecting each model of the trendy, overpriced, everybody's-got-to-have-one tumblers and cups. Watching Dan and listening to his consumer report, I soon succumbed to the seduction as well. We both found ourselves handling Yeti Rambler 20 oz. Tumblers, which fit neatly in a driver's cupholder and keeps drinks hot or cold all day long. (From a merchandizing standpoint, America is already great and never lost it, I'll have you know.) Then I began debating colors, moving to the stage of visualizing me having my very own Yeti thing while suffering that great American malady of indecisiveness owing to an epidemic of choices: black, gray, maroon, green.... Black it was, my conversion experience complete.

The Yeti spell was broken when I espied a rack of Shakespeare Ugly Stik GX2 ultralight rod and reel combos. "Check this out," Dan beckoned me, interrupting my new train of thought. "These are totally cool," he reported as he toyed with the electronic fish-finder display. "What an age we find ourselves in." Dan's marveling was hitting dizzying philosophical heights, scaring me away from him, while I was also afraid that we would forget our mission under such shopping duress. "Hey, I'll be wandering over this way; take your time," he said as he maneuvered toward Cabela's Bargain Cave. But Dan wasn't about to lose me. Unlike when I shop with my wife, he didn't just suddenly disappear, but left me with a precise location for rendezvous. Furthermore, he would actually be there. Every time I go into a superstore like this, my wife vanishes as if performing some magic trick, despite agreeing not to; she just can't help herself. With her being a mere 5'2" and therefore easily dwarfed by clothes racks and displays, I've been tempted to dial 911 and report a missing person rather than track her down myself in these unsettling retail jungles; it would be faster.

Prior to our Cabela's expedition, I spent the morning researching salmon riverbank fishing gear online, visiting outfitters' websites (Gander, Amazon, and yes, Cabela's, in a pre-flight check) and watching YouTube videos. One takeaway was to be sure to pick up some highly recommended Gamakatsu Octopus hooks. Last year while salmon fishing in a creek in the Sleeping Bear Dunes National Lakeshore, I lost four approximately 15- to 20-pound spawning kings due to not fully setting the hook. I discovered the hard way that razor-sharp hooks are requisite for penetrating hard salmonid jaws. Cabela's had fishhooks galore, of course. So many, in fact, that confusion set in, as did mental paralysis. I shook it off, grabbed a packet each of 1/0 and 2/0 Gamakatsu hooks, turned to Dan and cracked, "Let's get the hell out of here while we still can."

But there was no decent escape route. Dan ended up veering off into the men's clothing section and just had to show me the Columbia lightweight nylon ripstop pants that convert to shorts. "You familiar with these?" he asked, holding them against his waist and pondering their potential look on him. "My older brother loves them." Then over to the baseball-styled T-shirts. Then the sweaters, table after table of them. "Fall is coming, you know." He really fancied one in particular, a salmon-colored wool sweater, thematic for our outing. But, he wouldn't buy it. He wouldn't buy anything. He just delighted in the experience of appreciating the beauty of all these manmade things (largely produced overseas with American labels). Yet he wouldn't pull out his credit card to make any of them his. When asked why, he explained, "Don't really need any of this stuff. Just admiring it. For me, that's the joy. After all, you can only wear one sweater at a time, right?" Dan, as lapsed a Catholic as you will come across, and who has little regard for spending time—wasting time, as he would put it—in a church, would certainly make a fine Buddhist, for he had just put on a clinic in non-attachment. My content friend constantly encourages increasingly curmudgeonly me to not be so judgmental of all the foolish behavior on display in public, but to "go with the flow and just laugh at the absurdity of it all." He's right. But that particular Buddhist mindset is just beyond me. I'd rather be an easily upset Catholic in the here and now and work on my karma in my next incarnation.

※

Back at my house around 6 p.m., I interest Dan in a beer. We retreat to the front porch. He likes it there. It's peaceful to him, even though we can hear the constant stream of traffic on 86th Street, just a long block away, a main east-west thoroughfare on the north side of Indianapolis. Our lantana is in full bloom, the orange and red florets ablaze, and the purple and white Japanese anemones are just opening. Gigantic limelight hydrangeas tower nearby. Ruby-throated hummingbirds are vying for seats on the feeder as their appetites become more ravenous in preparation for the migration south in a few weeks. And tiger and spicebush swallowtail butterflies float throughout the garden, dipping eloquently every now and then before alighting on a flower to draw nectar. "It really is pleasant here," Dan says emphatically, as if reading poetry, taking it all in. The day's 90-degree heat is dying off, the humidity is low, and there's a gentle breeze wafting through the plant life.

"Here? You mean here as in Indiana?" I ask incredulously, questioning his judgment.

"I mean right here, right now," he answers. "You two have worked hard on your gardens over the years. Look at all of this. Well done, Mr. Mulherin." That we have, so much so that in my early sixties, I wonder if it's time to move on or relinquish some of the gardening to hired hands. "It's just nice to sit with no agenda for a change, isn't it?" His mindfulness puts me in my place. The sun is peeking through the maple trees across the street, glinting at us, as if teaming up with Dan to encourage me to just settle down. For the past few days I had been stuck in my gear of regret and disappointment. Regret that I hadn't just jumped in the truck and headed north by my lonesome. Disappointment that I was still in central Indiana on Labor Day Weekend. But we would be Up North in a month for a beautiful early autumn week, just short of the color tour, but close enough. Plainly, I was just spoiled and given an opportunity to realize it. As the Rolling Stones song says, *You can't always get what you want,* and that can be good for the soul. Really good.

We quietly drain our beers. Time for another round.

SALMON RUN

We are "returning home" as if by instinct to Leelanau County, to Cedar, in early October. We are driving on U.S. 131 North just past Big Rapids. Janet and I have been cruising at 76 miles per hour (ever-so-slightly and politely above the speed limit of 75 miles per hour) in loving silence since going through Grand Rapids. Breaking our driving meditation, I announce: "We'll be stopping by the Boardman once we're in Traverse City, you know, like we do every October."

"I know, honey," Janet replies, eyes forward.

"Got to see the salmon run."

"We will, honey, we will."

It's Saturday afternoon, about 3 o'clock. We park in the public lot where the Sara Hardy Farmers Market is located, between M-72 and the Boardman River. The air is clear and crisp, jacket weather. On the foot-bridge above the Boardman, I take a few minutes to adjust my eyes. The water is high and so darker than usual and moving fast; the sun is hazy and the glare troubles my view. But then—there they are: salmon. Coho and Chinook. Some of the kings—another name for Chinook—look to be in the 20-pound-plus range. To a central Indiana occasional angler like me, a crappie, bluegill, bass kinda guy, the kings are monstrously huge.

I am mesmerized. Enchanted. Having an interlude of little-boyish-ness. The *Salmonidae* face upstream. They are impatient in their spawning run. Sporadically, powerful tail fins kick and the salmon glide like missiles through the water, sometimes curling back with the current and repositioning themselves for another upstream launch. A female prepares a nest—a redd—fanning a gravel bed. She lets loose with eggs and a male, alongside, fertilizes them. Smaller steelhead dart in for a feast. I have seen what I need to see. Salmon spawning season is on: Autumn in northern Michigan is now official. We can resume our drive to Cedar.

✳

The first time I was introduced to salmon occurred in late September 2006. Back then we co-owned a cottage on Spider Lake with another Indianapolis couple. The men in the deal drove up on a Friday evening to close the cottage for the winter. But first, we stopped by my friend Craig's second floor flat on Front Street, back when he was a bachelor, for a couple of "welcome home" White Russians and a ridiculous amount of reunion belly laughs, then a visit to a local establishment for a nightcap.

We closed the U and I Lounge—with me and two other revelers dancing to "Georgy Porgy" by Toto and receiving a wild standing ovation from all three patrons at the bar, including my friends—then headed outside for a walk back to Craig's truck. We were crossing the Union Street Bridge when Craig stopped suddenly, putting a hand to my chest. "Look over the side. I want you to stare at the water for a minute or so then tell me what you see."

"Is this a joke?" I responded, knowing Craig's penchant for playing tricks on gullible friends.

"No, no; it's no joke," he said earnestly in a conspiratorial whisper. "Go ahead. Keep looking; let your eyes adjust." A minute or so went by. "See anything?"

"Nothing," I replied.

"Hmmm," he murmured. Then after a pregnant pause, he said, "Okay. How about now?"

Then, as if on command, flashes of silver-white materialized. "Oh my God—what are those? They're freakin' huge!" First contact.

"Salmon, bro," Craig revealed. "Those are kings—the big boys and girls. If you can imagine, the state record is 40-something pounds (46, according to the Michigan Department of Natural Resources). It's the annual spawning run." As my eyes adjusted I saw more and more of the long, dark, animated shapes facing upstream. I don't know how many minutes went by before Craig laughed and pulled me away. I was charmed by the salmon—for good.

The following autumn, when I was up again to close the cottage, I called Craig to ask about going fishing for salmon late Sunday afternoon. "I don't have the right equipment; do you?" he inquired. I wasn't sure what was needed. "Well, a noodle rod would be best. They run about nine or 10 feet long. You bein' a corn-fed flatlander, you're probably carryin' a bass rod and reel setup." He was right. A six-foot Shakespeare Ugly Stik rod and mid-sized spinning reel filled with 8-pound test. "Hell, no need to spend any money," he declared. "We'll just go with what you got."

When we got down to the north bank of the Boardman, well away from the weir so as not to generate interest by the "fish cops," as Craig and his family of "Don't Tread on Me" outdoorsmen refer to the DNR conservation officers, there were fishermen every 10 feet or so on both sides, wherever there were openings along the banks. We baited our hooks with orange spawn bags and tossed them in, letting the bait flow naturally with the current. There were plenty of salmon in this stretch of the river, their dorsal fins frequently cutting the surface, the spawning fish occasionally breaching in dramatic fashion. I was one amazed Hoosier. Within a few minutes of our arrival, a king was spooked by a cast landing nearby and suddenly sprang to the surface and thrashed ashore. Two fishermen dropped their poles and grabbed it. "That's one way to do it," Craig observed, shaking his head at the absurd scene. "But let's see if we can hook one."

Minutes later, the gent to our right called out, "Fish on!" We retrieved our lines out of courtesy to give him space to work the fighting fish. It took about five minutes before our neighbor landed a nice steelhead. Craig waded in and netted it for him. "Looks like that one's nearly 10 pounds," Craig admired. "What kind of bait are you using?" he asked. Our neighbor had a silver-white-colored soft plastic worm used for bass fishing that he cut into pieces, fixing one on the hook. He handed several whole ones to Craig, in thanks for netting his steelhead.

"Here, put one of these on and see what happens," Craig instructed. My first cast attracted a murderous strike. The line suddenly went taut, the pole bent nearly in half, and the drag whined as the fish ran. "Fish on!" Craig called for me. In an instant I was transformed into a salmon fisherman with no idea how to work a fish that size. After what seemed an eternity, but was really no more than perhaps 10 seconds, the line snapped and rebounded limply back at me. "Oh, shit! You had one, you crazy bastard!" Craig roared. I was nearly shaking, half glad to have lost the beast. "That must have been at least a 15-pound king," he said in support. "You had one on, bro! Now here, bait up again and get your line back in the water."

Wham!—fish on again, just minutes after I lost the first one. And, with the same unfortunate result. "Okay, that's enough," Craig announced, surrendering to the futility of my overwhelmed equipment. "Your baptism in salmon fishing madness has concluded. You're official now. Let's go get a beer and celebrate." Although coming away empty-handed, I was certainly hooked.

❈

Three years ago during Labor Day Weekend, we took two friends to the lower Platte River to kayak out to Lake Michigan. Bad call. Make that *very bad call.* Although the river is gorgeous and the route delightful—paddling the river, then traversing Loon Lake, then finishing at the mouth of the river at Lake Michigan—on Labor Day Weekend, the river trip is far from a quiet immersion in nature. We encountered dozens and dozens of partiers guzzling beer and passing bottles of higher-octane joy juice. We had to weave our way through flotillas of tubing young people who had lost interest in traveling the river from start to finish but were intent on getting a serious buzz on. Our friends from Florida, no strangers to happy hour, were delighted by the festive atmosphere. Cindy, Janet's high school friend who never met a stranger, asked for beers as we negotiated openings in the inner tube blockade. Intoxication tends to make people generous, and Cindy's thirst was slaked the entire way. Aside from my disappointment in the company we were forced to keep (my wife often refers to me as Good Ol' Mr. Wilson, the crotchety retired neighbor in *Dennis the Menace*), one positive memory of the relatively disappointing river trip for yours truly occurred at the lower Platte River weir. Janet, Cindy, and her husband got out and portaged around it, as the fence was submerged to prevent the salmon from running upriver. There must have been something about me that spoke to the DNR worker who was unclogging parts of the weir grid, something kindred that communicated my love of all things fish, including salmon. As if a mind reader, he looked directly at me and said, "Here's a jack king salmon," pointing directly in front of him on the other side of the weir. "Wanna look?" I immediately beached my kayak and walked onto the weir. "Pretty, ain't it," he said.

"That it is," I answered, nodding in complete agreement. I waved my party of kayakers over to have a look themselves. "Huh," they said collectively, watching the early run young male salmon, devoid of my enthusiasm. Then Janet commanded, "Okay, back to the boats." As they quit the weir, the worker said to me in a hushed voice, "They don't get it, do they?"

"No, they don't. But that's okay; we do." He laughed, nodded, and bade me good day and "good luck."

❋

Over a bottle of cabernet a few nights later with Craig's younger brother, Paul, I turn the conversation to the salmon run. Paul smiles knowingly; we speak the same language when it comes to fishing. I show him my iPhone video of salmon and steelhead gathered at a culvert at nearby Shalda Creek the day before. His eyes twinkle. "Want to try our hand at some whatever-fishin' tomorrow?" I look to my mate for permission. "I like Paul. Permission granted," she says, as if she's in charge—ha! Marriage is funny like that.

"Thanks, honey," I say, hugging the boss lady.

About 10 a.m., we drive down a dirt road and over the creek's culvert, then park a few feet away. Nobody's fishing but us. Across the road and up over a cedar-populated ridge lies Lake Michigan. We get out of my truck and walk over to stand above the culvert. Here Shalda Creek averages about two feet deep. "There they are," Paul notes reverently. There they are indeed. About a half-dozen salmon are holding in the middle of the current. We return to the truck, attach the reels to our rods, run line through the guides, tie on hooks, affix the floating spawn bags, then toss our lines toward hope: prayers, hooks, and all.

First cast, and I calmly call over my shoulder to Paul, who's fishing behind me on the other side of the culvert, "Fish on."

"What? You're kidding!" he reacts. My rod is dancing as the water roils with a hooked salmon. The tugs are hard and the line peeling as it heads downstream. I adjust the drag with my right thumb, tightening it just a hair. Line continues to give, the drag whining. The fish thrashes madly...and my hook comes loose. "Dammit—it's gone," I say to Paul, who's watching. We both laugh, because you just gotta laugh. At my age, I'm over severe disappointments like this, like losing my potential first salmon. I've been there before; my ego is still intact.

Minutes later, I've hooked another. I quickly work my way down the embankment, hoping to cut the distance between me and the fish and horse it up on shore, as I don't have a net. But again, after 30 seconds or so of adrenaline-rushing man versus fish combat, the hook works its way out and the thrill is gone—for the time being. Over the course of the next two hours, I have a dozen solid hits and lose four salmon, all in the 10- to 15-pound range.

Paul, one of the nicest guys on the planet, refuses to join me where all the action is happening, working his way farther south along the creek. "You drove all the way up here, so you need to catch one. I can get out anytime. I'm smart enough to live here." He winks. Despite my gentleman friend's best wishes, I call it quits after a few hours. "Time to head, Paul. I've had my fun. It's been a good day."

"Fishin' today, catchin' tomorrow, eh?" he says, a good sport. "Praise God." Paul is a devout Catholic; I'm just an everyday member of the church. He is beyond good luck to have around. Today just wasn't my day. Or was it?

As we're breaking down our gear, an old-timer pulls up in a sparkling new gold metallic-colored Lincoln MKX. Like his ride, he is dressed to impress—fishermen, that is. He's wearing hip waders, pulls out a noodle rod and reel setup, and has a big game landing net. His deep tan suggests snowbird status. "How did you guys do?" he asks politely.

"Had four on—with all the wrong gear," I confess. "But I had a great time. They're in there. Only had one break my line. The rest got off the hook after a decent fight. Pretty strange."

He smiles with wisdom accrued over many years of fishing, of frequenting brooks and streams and lakes in quest of that you've-got-to-experience-it-for-yourself sensation of having fish on, catching and releasing, catching and keeping—story upon story accumulating over a lifetime. "Watched some guys in a boat on the Leland River near the dam yesterday. They must have had a half-dozen salmon on, and lost every darn one of them. Same drill as you, it seems. The secret is, they weren't setting the hook. When it comes to spawning salmon, their jaws harden at this time of year. So when you go to set the hook, really whale on it. That should do the trick."

As the veteran salmon angler trudges off, Paul says, "I never knew that. Huh."

Meanwhile, I am energized by the tip. I am already envisioning us back here a year from now, at this very same spot. Early October. Nothing on the agenda except pursuit of spawn-running salmon, fishing pole in hand. First hit, I will jerk that noodle rod like I mean it—having rehearsed my visualization of salmon fishing success throughout the year leading up to it. After a 10-minute match with a worthy king or coho, Paul will help me land it. I will breathlessly marvel at my accomplishment. Of course, now that I have the hang of it we will catch several more. Photos will be taken for posterity, smiling without asking, for the camera. Then one by one, we will place the fish in the cooler on a bed of ice and eventually head home with our catch. Paul will do the cleaning honors (otherwise, my unpracticed hands filleting a fish of this magnitude would turn things into a crime scene). He will say grace before we eat the freshly caught and grilled fish, thanking the good Lord for the bounty taken from Shalda Creek, the salmon's ancestral birthplace, having returned home for their inevitable death and contribution to the lifecycle. Paul will be sure to remind me that Christ was a fisherman. And my mind will be carried down a stream of consciousness to a year from then and, God willing, another divine day such as the one I'm imagining— or even the one I just had.

SEARCHING FOR JIM HARRISON

In the late-nineties, Craig was intent on meeting the famed Leelanau County writer Jim Harrison. At that time, other than Craig's ever-ready sense of adventure, I wasn't sure why. But it would eventually come to me.

Those were the years when we began taking family vacations in Leland, renting a home on Lake Street. Every trip, I would stop by the Leelanau Bookstore, always drawn to browsing the Michigan books section. There I would peruse and occasionally purchase field guides on Lake Michigan rocks and the state's birds and wildflowers, as well as books on local history, especially those covering Great Lakes shipwrecks like the Edmund Fitzgerald. (Almost every Michigander knows the tale of the sinking of the doomed iron-ore freighter during a storm on Lake Superior on November 10, 1975, as do many more of a certain venerable age thanks to the Gordon Lightfoot ballad of 1976 commemorating the wreck.) Yet the best-stocked sub-section would be that of Jim Harrison's works: fiction, nonfiction, and poetry. Back then, I never bothered to skim even one page of any of his titles. When something is popular with the general public, I tend to look the other way; it's just my counterculturist nature. Little did I know that Harrison's readers are a special breed: lovers of Michigan's outdoors who can appreciate a drinking man's take on life put to wonderful words.

I wasn't completely ignorant of Harrison's work. I had read his column on food in *Esquire* magazine, "The Raw and the Cooked," years earlier, when I was a young married man who enjoyed reading fine nonfiction and, of course, paging to the photographic works of art found in this men's magazine—the only one of its kind allowed into our house. Although Harrison's *Esquire* columns really popped—not only was he a wild game gourmand but an exquisite wordsmith—the topics just weren't of much interest to me. Harrison, a glutton for the good life, notably had (by my budget) prohibitively expensive tastes in vintage wine. At that time, I was a bar manager in my late twenties and going to school full time, majoring in English, of all things, and a young family man with a working and college-going wife and two young children. (How we did revel in a challenge in those days, the best of times. No parental safety net offered nor requested; just our own gumption driving us toward a better future.) After finishing my Saturday night closing shifts, I would party with my fellow bartenders, quaffing Coors Light and indulging in Kamikaze and Lemon Drop shots. Harrison would have found me quite the trainee, I'm sure.

❋

Janet and I began visiting Naples, Florida, during my school's spring break in 2012. Her idea. Although I dreaded going anywhere near throngs of hard-partying college students, my fears were put to rest in Naples: it's just too expensive for these young folks to handle—the ultimate spring break buffer. For some mysterious reason, that was the appointed time for me to find out what all the Michigander literary infatuation with Jim Harrison was all about. The Naples Barnes & Noble happened to have a paperback copy of his 2009 novel *The English Major.* Being one of those myself and not knowing what I was in for, I immediately found the writing hilarious, insightful, and master crafted, with Harrison's keen wit for the absurd and his appreciation for wine and women unabashedly stated through his characterization of Cliff, the novel's protagonist. From then on, I began inhaling his fiction and poetry, amazed I had ignored his work for so long.

A few years ago, while at my favorite bookstore on the planet, Horizon Books on Front Street in Traverse City, I reported directly to the "H" area of the store's fiction collection. Of course, Horizon was well stocked with Jim Harrison's work, with multiple copies of almost all of his titles. In particular, I was looking for *Legends of the Fall.* When the film came out in 1994, starring Brad Pitt and Anthony Hopkins, little did I know that it was based upon the book of the same title by Harrison. I had been working my way through all things Harrison, and this was one of the remaining titles I had yet to read. Surprisingly, it wasn't on the shelf. *Julip*, however, was in stock, a collection of three novellas, one of which featured his lovable somewhat low-life character Brown Dog, a Michigan Chippewa Indian (Anishinaabe, to be precise, as Harrison likes to point out). As any reader of Harrison knows, his strong suit was the novella.

It was early October and Horizon was relatively quiet, the tourists gone for the year, the locals at peace once again until Memorial Day weekend would roll around for the next seasonal invasion. As I placed my purchase on the counter, I revealed to the cheerful book-smart cashier, which Horizon is renowned for, that I had read just about all of Harrison's work. She kindly congratulated me. I made conversation by providing, in hindsight, a somewhat awkward editorial comment: "Although he's a bit of a sexist, he apologizes somewhat for it, which gives him permission, I suppose. Besides, he's pretty darn funny." The sixty-ish woman, who could have easily passed for a retired teacher, rang up the transaction. While presenting me the credit card receipt to sign and bagging the paperback, she smiled and said, "I didn't care much for his work for quite a while; I found him to be rather rough around the edges. But as he's gotten older he's softened, and I do enjoy the novels and novellas he's written during the past 10 years. I especially liked *The English Professor*."

"You mean *The English Major?*" I gently corrected her, laughing politely, for I confuse book and movie titles all the time, to the same amusing joke's-on-me effect.

"Oh yes," she giggled. "*Major*. Lord, there I go again," she confessed while tucking a bookmark in between the pages of my new read and handing it to me. "Thank you, sir. Come back and see us." And of course I would, as I do every time I'm in the neighborhood.

✳

My friend Craig reminds me of Harrison. He reminds me of Ernest Hemingway too (as does Harrison). Craig is almost a dead ringer for Harrison—as the sixty-something version—with the exception of having both eyes intact (Harrison lost his left eye in a childhood accident). Burly and barrel-chested, low to the ground, with a weathered and mustached face, straight and thinning hair, he is uncommonly intelligent, unbearably funny, artistically brilliant, with a sharp eye for beauty—especially for the opposite sex—one to enjoy a good drink whenever an opportunity presents itself, has a fondness for fish, fowl, and other game cooked over an open fire, and is ever insistent upon life lived to the extreme and, as often as possible, in the outdoors. There is certainly just cause to suggest that Craig is Jim Harrison's doppelgänger.

Early one summer Sunday morning—like 3 a.m. early—while I was vacationing with my family in Leland in the late-nineties, Craig and I were closing the Bluebird Tavern. We had spent a few years tending bar together when we first met in the early eighties and enjoyed bellying up on special occasions on the other side. Craig was proud of his time behind bars—the serving kind—and didn't hesitate to let the Bluebird barkeep know that we plied his trade once upon a time. We hit it off with him, and so we were allowed to linger after last call and continue drinking with our newfound friend. We sipped vodka martinis while the bartender had an endless draft beer and an occasional shot of bourbon as he wiped down the bar and re-stocked bottled beer. Of course, we tipped our way into extended time.

During our laughter-saturated conversation with the barkeep, Craig commented, "Say, I heard Jim Harrison comes in here once in a while."

"He does indeed," the bartender confirmed. "Usually it's on a Sunday evening. He likes to sit at the bar and relax with some of his local buddies." I could sense an adventure coming on.

"Well, I'll be damned," Craig said, turning to me. "Perhaps it's time I make his acquaintance. Maybe he could get me connected with someone who might take an interest in my painting. Maybe I could get a sponsor. Then I could quit my day job selling freaking cars and make art all the time—like I was meant to. Whoa!" With eyes playfully wide, he killed his martini.

"Hmmm," I murmured.

Given my underwhelming response, Craig asked, "Hey, do you even know who Jim Harrison is?" I decided not to tell him that I had avoided reading any of his works because of his popularity in the area and my suspicion of such things.

"Should I?"

"Jeez, everybody Up North knows who Jim Harrison is. You keep coming up here as much as you have been and you'll soon be an honorary local. So you need to read some Harrison and get on board, bro. He's a hoot, a rascal—like me. You gotta love that, right?" he said, elbowing me in jest. "Now drink up—we gotta beat feet. Before we know it, the sun will be saying good morning. That would be bad form."

Turning to the bartender, he said, "Great talkin' with ya. And thanks for the intel on our friend Mr. Harrison." We pushed off, leaving plenty of cash on the bar as a gratuity, now properly mentally adjusted, and walked the four blocks home under cover of darkness, our laughter slicing the still summer night.

"Looks like we did it again," Craig said, as I unlocked the door to the sleeping house, trying yet failing to suppress his laughter. "Well done." I tried to get him to spend the remainder of the evening here and sleep it off, but as usual back then, he would have none of it. "I'd best skedaddle. Great night for a drive. Give me a call this week. There is more mischief to be had before your vacation is done."

It took me long enough, but eventually I would heed his advice and become well acquainted with Jim Harrison's extensive body of work—and wonder what took me so long.

❋

Later that fall, when the regular firearm (rifle and shotgun) deer hunting season was past and the land of the 45th Parallel grew darker earlier and life slowed down to a near-hibernation state, Craig made his pilgrimage to the Bluebird on several late Sunday afternoons, driving the 25 miles from his home on Old Mission Peninsula, hoping to catch Leelanau County's prized writer and strike up a possible life-changing conversation. But alas, Harrison never showed. On his last attempt, holding out hope, Craig composed a note and left it with the bartender to pass along next time he saw the elusive writer. The connection never occurred; I doubt if the message was even delivered. Throughout his career, Harrison must have been accosted by countless fans, especially aspiring writers, and apparently valued and protected his privacy, as a sign to unannounced visitors to his Leelanau County farm warned: DO NOT ENTER THIS DRIVEWAY UNLESS YOU HAVE CALLED FIRST. THIS MEANS YOU. If Craig had managed to hear from Harrison, I would have definitely heard about it.

In 2002, Harrison and his wife Linda moved to Montana, staying during the warmer months, and would winter in Patagonia, Arizona, forever leaving his beloved Leelanau County behind.

Years went by, and I forgot all about Craig's failed attempt to meet Jim Harrison; that is until word came of the writer's sudden death on March 26, 2016. (His writer friend Philip Caputo was one of the first on the scene at Harrison's winter home, recounting, "He'd died a poet's death, literally with a pen in his hand, while writing a new poem.") My wife first informed me of the sad news that evening, coming across his obituary online. She knew that I was fond of his work, that he reminded me so much of Craig, and so she shared the unwelcome news gently, as if I had lost a dear friend. I had. Indeed, I had come to treasure Harrison's writing and felt a kinship with him, as readers do with all their favorite authors.

I never asked Craig what he wrote to Harrison in that note that went nowhere. A private matter. I do applaud the attempt, for having the cojones to try. As for me, I met Harrison in his writing, the place where readers are always searching to make meaningful if not lasting connections. Like so many of Harrison's admirers, lucky me.

DEER CAMP

The first 10 years of my life were spent in deer hunting country in northeastern Pennsylvania. I remember one crisp autumn day when I was eight years old watching our neighbors on Muncie Avenue in Scranton clean a large buck they had brought down. For children, all new things are strange; wonder is a constant state. Blood and guts give youngsters pause, as the sight of such butchering carries a macabre fascination. Like the hunter's knife blade slicing through the dead deer that carved a visceral impression in my memory back then. And each November, once I hear from my hunting friends in northern Michigan inviting me to come up for the hunt, I recollect that long-ago day.

Our family moved to Indianapolis in 1966, and for years thereafter I never thought much about deer. That is, until early October 1995. A call came from Traverse City, inviting me to "come north, grasshopper, and join the clan in the woods to kill some innocent woodland creatures. It will do you some good."

When she learned of the invitation, my wife was hesitant. Very. She reveres life, and so abhors killing, guns—violence of any kind. She is sweet. And not male, and not a male friend of the most persuasive male friend a guy can have. Really, to remain friends with Craig (also known as the "Master Blaster," written in permanent black marker on the back of his orange hunting jacket), I have always had to be up to his latest challenge. Carrying a loaded rifle through miles of hilly woodlands and being prepared to shoot a deer was just another part of our program together. "It will be fine, Janet," I tried to assure her. "These guys are all former military."

"Will they be drinking and hunting?" she asked, naturally, as alcohol typically found a place in our friendship ritual. Craig and I were bartenders together. So this would be expected natural behavior.

"Yes, but no. No drinking before or while hunting," I explained. "But definitely some drinking afterward."

"You promise?" she asked demandingly. Of course I did. What I didn't tell her, is that "downstaters"—as the locals call folks visiting the area from all in-state points south of Grand Rapids (Detroit, namely)—who come up for deer season have a reputation as guys with soft hands who push paper for a living and don't get out much. And once in the woods they tend to cut loose and get careless, a few too many being under the influence while toting rifles. Accidents happen. (The hunters from the north like to blame the downstaters for hunting tragedies, which isn't always true. It's just an understood territorial practice of assessing blame and being derogatory—the habit of the American sportsman. American sportswomen, I daresay, are usually much more levelheaded.)

So Janet blessed the trip, which was an absolute requirement. I didn't own a rifle, even a shotgun for Indiana hunting (no rifle hunting is permitted in this state). "No problem, ace," Craig said. "Just be sure to get your gnarly ass up here. We'll get you outfitted. There's no shortage of weapons here. Heh-heh...."

It would be a quick nearly 800-mile roundtrip. I left Indy at 6 a.m. on Friday and would be returning late Sunday. The November drive was unremarkable—the farther north I went, the barer the trees, the cooler the temperatures—save having to stop on the bridge over the Manistee River on U.S. Highway 131 while a Wexford County sheriff's deputy tried, and eventually succeeded, in shooing a magnificent yet highly resistant to law enforcement trumpeter swan off the roadway. When I arrived Friday at deer camp, located in the Jordan River Valley, it was 1 p.m., overcast, with nearly a foot of snow on the ground. "Hey, goombah, you made it. And the good news is, there's time to get in a late afternoon hunt, if we hustle," Craig said in greeting. "But first, throw your shit on one of the bunks and have a beer to calm your nerves." Already I was feeling a bit guilty, as I was breaking a promise to Janet—no drinking before hunting—and I just got here. Craig sensed my hesitancy. "Hey, just one beer. We always hunt legal."

The cabin—the dacha, rather, as Craig's family fondly called it—was used twice annually: for deer camp in November and fish camp (trout camp, to be specific) at the end of April. It was the very definition of rustic. The wooden building, perhaps 600 square feet inside, was elevated off a hillside a story or so. An outhouse located nearby made for a chilly morning constitution, more sobering than a cup of strong coffee. Otherwise, the guys typically whizzed in the woods. Or when playing poker at night, just let it all hang out from the deck. Ah, the primitive joys of manhood.

There were banners strung about the unfinished walls from fish and deer camps over the past two decades, all of them featuring logos of various libations: Bud Light, Miller Lite, Coors Light, and, of course, the local light favorite, Labatt Blue Light. On the rectangular table that had seen better, more mannered days, was a fifth of Old Grand-Dad and a half gallon of Seagram's VO, family deer and fish camp traditions. A buck knife stuck upright in the tabletop next to a half-eaten pumpkin pie, the clear plastic top ajar. An unopened bottle of Baileys Irish Cream next to it. "Have some pie, bro," Craig invited as he cracked the Baileys and poured two generous glassfuls. "This is it, promise. Then we're outta here. Not much light left, but enough for a nice late afternoon hunt." A subtle buzz, and still legal.

A half hour later, we were at a favored spot near Deadman's Hill. Over the years with Craig, I learned that spots in the woods, along a river, or on a lake, matter—a lot. Picking the right ones takes instinct. The right angle. The right feel. Knowing the game you're after and where it/they will likely be. To the uninitiated, it's a complete mystery. To hunters and fishermen, it's everything.

Craig opened the trunk and handed me a rifle. He showed me how to load it, then we hiked up a modest hill to a grove of cedars on the crest, the swamp just below us. Downhill beaver slides ending at the den in the bog hinted at the amphibious rodent's sense of delight and innovation. Destructive, clever, funny creatures they are. Northeast of us, Craig said, were deer. "See the prints?" he noted as he pointed to the freshly imprinted snow. "Looks like three large deer went that way. I'm going to swing around and try to drive them toward you. Couple things: First, don't shoot in my direction, got it?" he said with a seriousness quite unlike him. "Second, make sure you see some horn before pulling the trigger. Now sit down, stay alert, and I'll see you in about 30 minutes."

I dusted the snow off a fallen cedar and sat facing northwest, as instructed, good Catholic boy that I am (Craig too). In my hands was a .30/06 Remington, locked and loaded. My senses were overloaded with nervous excitement. Time crawled. A chickadee alighted on a branch but inches from my face, snow powder trickling onto my nose, a St. Francis up-close-and-personal moment. I stayed completely still, enjoying the bird's curious company. After a few minutes, it moved on. And I waited.

About 20 minutes after Craig marched off, as I was watching the roughly 10-foot gap of opportunity spread between stands of cedars about 40 yards northwest of my position, a large white-tail suddenly appeared, walking through the target area. A second sizable deer immediately followed the first. "Holy shit," I whispered to myself, a strange phrase of excitement if ever there was one. Then a third adult deer trudged by, closing the column of three. Seconds later, I heard splashes in the swamp and the sound of what I would later learn was a buck on the make for some love. Minutes later, Craig trotted up to my makeshift blind.

"I didn't hear a shot, dude. Did you see those deer I tried to push your way?"

"Yeah!" I enthused. "They went right across the gap in the trees, exactly as you planned it. There were three of them." Craig looked puzzled.

"Did you see any horn?" he asked.

"Um...not sure."

"What do you mean *not sure?* Didn't you take a look at them?" Now I was puzzled. He pointed at my rifle. "Did you look through *the scope?*"

There are times in one's life when you wish you were elsewhere, at least momentarily. Pregnant pause.

"Oh my God, I didn't even think about it," I revealed in complete embarrassment.

"Oh my God is right," Craig uttered in big-brotherly disappointment. "You missed your chance. Shit." He was still panting from the exertion of hiking through the deep snow. Twilight was coming on. "Well, it's times like these that there's only one thing to do." He went to a flat spot about

20 feet from the cedar cover I was under, hollowed out a wide ring in the snow, gathered some firewood, and built a Boy-Scout-quality fire, the blaze burning away our mutual disappointment, then pulled out that bottle of Baileys from his Army-issue rucksack, kept from his days in the service. "Let's celebrate the one that got away." We passed the bottle back and forth for about 30 minutes until the flames flickered and died, and the stars began to emerge, and all was good again. "C'mon. Let's go make some supper."

❉

The following day was sunny and in the low thirties. Craig and I traversed hills all day, tracking deer prints in the snow. We saw one buck from high atop our perch on Deadman's Hill and pursued it for an hour. But it never was quite within range for us to get a shot off. Years later, I'm amazed by how much ground we covered back then. We were younger, more energetic, and our bodies had yet to betray us. Good times.

Craig's older brother, Fred, had nailed his buck earlier in the week, so he and the opening party—"Pa," as they affectionately called their father, and younger brother, Paul, and several cousins and uncles—were done, so Craig and I had the place to ourselves. On Sunday, we hung out at the dacha. It was sunny and much warmer, the snow melting. We hiked up the hillside and hunted on his dad's property for a few hours. Then we had lunch— a hunter's stew one of them had concocted, featuring quail shot by Fred, which was sublime—then had a few beers. That was then. Today, I would never dream of having a beer or two before a seven-hour drive. But, like Craig, I was squeezing out the last precious moments of a short but sweet trip, my first-time encounter with the world of deer hunting.

"Come back home soon, bro," Craig said, hugging me in a quick manly embrace, sunglasses on to prevent showing emotion; I had done the same. My throat ached. Little did I know that it would be several years before I returned to deer camp.

❉

In November 1998, I met Craig's mom at Larry's Bar on U.S. 131. Larry's is a revered local institution frequented by hunters, fishermen, and snow-mobilers. Joannie (a.k.a., "Ma") was the only woman in the place except for Larry's wife, who was helping Larry tend bar and wait on the patrons scattered about the lounge: all deer hunters in their camo and day-glow orange gear, knocking down some cold ones and yucking it up, a break in the action—or more likely, non-action. Joannie had raised five boys and so was comfortable in a man's world, in a masculine domain such as Larry's Bar.

Joannie and I had a cup of chili while we waited for Craig to drive over from camp to guide me in, as my memory was foggy about the last trip there three years earlier and Google Maps didn't exist yet. Craig's family members were all "pious Catholics," a classification my father esteemed. They tended to lean toward the rightward, more orthodox side of the church. Joannie took the opportunity of our first in-person meeting to provide me with the second edition of *The Catechism of the Catholic Church*, a revision undertaken under the authority of Pope John Paul II, a family hero of theirs. "This is for you and your family, Tim. God bless you all." Sweet lady. And having raised a barnful of boys, knew well that I probably wouldn't crack it all that often. But having it on hand, well, close enough.

"You know, I'm so proud of the boys," she said between mouthfuls of chili and Saltine crackers. "They aren't drinking at deer camp this year." I tried to keep a straight face at hearing this astonishing news. That just wasn't like them. And if that was the case, it was going to be one weird-ass hunt.

Craig came in a few minutes after we killed the chili, saving me from overexposure to Joannie's well-intentioned religious fervor, which she shared gladly and freely with anyone in sight, evangelist that she was. Just by showing up, he made his presence immediately known to all: like in a Western when the saloon's batwing doors suddenly swing wide open, and the bad ass strolls in. Everybody stops talking. Stops drinking. They see this is one bad hombre. Keep an eye on him at all times. Mi buen amigo.

"Ma!" he said with exaggerated mushiness but pure son-love as he enveloped her diminutive frame in a restrained bearhug, and she closed her eyes in motherly bliss. "Well, we're outta here," he immediately said, the catch-and-release program between son and mother, the usual. She protested, but was accustomed to drive-by visits from Craig. I thanked Joannie with a hug of my own and paid the tab. And we were indeed outta there.

When I trudged up the steps to the dacha and entered with my gear, my cursory investigation of the teetotaling I was warned of proved to be of no concern, as the evidence stated otherwise: two large Hefty trash bags in the corner were overflowing with empty aluminum cans—none of them soft drinks. I started laughing. "Do you know that your mom said that you guys were on your best behavior and there was no drinking going on this year at deer camp?"

"Wha-at?" Craig bellowed in laughter. "Oh, shit. Freddie must've laid it on her. Good thing we don't allow women out here once the shootin' starts. No drinkin'. That will be the day."

Before I knew it, several pop tops were opened and we were toasting my return to deer camp. After a long pull on a Blue Light, Craig announced, "Hey, goombah, you need to get in some target practice." He found a small plain white card, approximately 5" x 7", loosely drew three gradually widening concentric rings, and charged down the short flight of stairs and over to the base of a large beech tree about 30 yards from the porch. Upon his return, he handed me Fred's muzzleloader. "Here. Take a whack at that." I did as told, dialing in the target and pulling the trigger upon fully exhaling. The muzzleloader report echoed through the woods, so common a sound this time of year. "Well, you hit it; now let's see how you did," he said as he bounded down the stairs and hustled over to the target. "Nice shot, ace—bullseye!" he shouted gleefully. "Bet you can't do that again." Once he rejoined me, I loaded the gun and went through the drill once more. *Kaboom!* Craig was beside himself. "I'll be damned—you laid that shot on top of the first one! No more practice for you—you're good to go." We both drained our beers, and I felt a glow of pride in my marksmanship, as I had not shot a gun in the three years since my inaugural deer hunt.

For that hunt, Craig's brothers Fred and Paul and a family friend joined the two of us. This time, I was armed with a 12-gauge shotgun. I found a nice spot under a group of cedars along the Jordan River and stayed at my post for several hours, waiting for a deer to walk into view. The rest of our hunting party strung out in a long line east of me. After about 30 watchful minutes I read from Thomas Merton's classic spiritual work *No Man Is an Island*. Then I dozed off. I awoke about 4:30 p.m. when I heard the crack of a rifle. I jumped to my feet and ran toward the sound, knowing it was one of our group that took the shot. When I arrived at the kill zone, the other four hunters in our party were gathered around a young deer, dead from a clean shot to the heart. Craig was quickly field dressing the animal. "Isn't that a bit small for a legal kill?" I whispered to Paul. "Hell yes," he whispered back. "That's why the Craig-ster is going to town. Don't want the DNR to check this or we're screwed." Fred's best friend, a deer hunting newbie like me, had whacked the young deer, a female, which was too young to qualify, and he had no doe permit. Craig quickly dispatched of the guts, we hustled back to our pickups, and he tossed the carcass under a truck bed tarp. "Let's get the hell out of here," our ringleader announced, laughing conspiratorially, as we did in agreement. For little boys at heart, getting away with something never seems to get old.

The night was full of raucous, decidedly juvenile male behavior. Lots of bad language and impure thoughts, encouraged by the free flow of alcohol. This was the tradition, and the boys were making the best of it. There was no one around to put a leash on us; and whenever that interlude of precious free rein happens, boys who want to act like boys will be boys. After dinner, a poker game broke out, as did the cigars and whiskey. It would go on for hours. I couldn't hang, not accustomed to as much fresh air as I'd taken in all day. So I crashed in my bunk, the festivities not preventing me from falling into a deep snoring slumber, from what I heard later.

The following day, well after first light—which was the purported objective, to be out and hunkered down awaiting a deer kill—sleeping in due to dinged brains, our hunting party returned to the same location, but opted for a walking hunt. Craig got a pretty good look at a large buck and fired off a few rounds, but the whitetail zigzagged through the woods in a death-defying manner and avoided its demise, for now. About 2 p.m., we called it a day as far as the hunt went. As we were walking on a two-track back to the trucks, four abreast, I caught some movement to my immediate right. Along a hedgerow, a monster buck began to run. I was situated farthest from the deer and my hunting buddies. "Look! Look!" I shouted, my shotgun still resting on my right shoulder. The other three wheeled around toward where I was pointing, their rifles swinging into firing position. But it was too late. The deer had bounded into thick woods and out of sight. Then my fellow hunters all turned—toward me. Fred the Elder made it a teaching moment: "Timmy, next time you see a freaking deer and you're out hunting, don't bother politely pointing it out to your comrades—just shoot the damn thing! That will be all the notice we need that a deer is nearby, trust me." He chuckled at my admonishment.

"Oh, you silly bastard," Craig noted, clapping me on the shoulder. Everyone laughed, but me. It was clear to me that I was no hunter and never would be. I had the ability, as my target-shooting marksmanship showed. Yet I had no stomach for killing, which was a deeper conviction than I was previously aware. This would prove to be my last deer hunt.

❋

Every year a few weeks before Halloween, Craig emails, texts, and eventually calls to try to convince me to make another appearance at deer camp. "You need to get away from Indy and come home and kill an innocent woodland creature with us. It will do you good," my great outdoors therapist will remind me once again. "Someday you'll be in a wheelchair drooling all over yourself and moaning about all the good times you missed. It's not too late, bro. So whaddya say?"

Used to be, I'd tell him I'll see what I can do, just to keep the door open, just to give us both a little hope, yet we were kidding ourselves. For the past decade or so, my schedule has conveniently provided cover for my hunting reluctance. As a school administrator, my time off is mostly prescribed, and fall break always occurs in early October; getting away in November is out of the question. This year, Craig mentioned the invitation in passing while we were standing in Lake Michigan one late afternoon during fall break sipping a velvety Malbec as the low energy waves lapped about our thighs, the water temperature still tolerable for our thick, aging hides, catching up on the latest highlights of our lives apart.

"You oughta think about coming up for deer camp," he said, as we looked out toward South Fox Island, which could be seen on this exceptionally clear day from Good Harbor Bay Beach. And that was it. Once the offer was made, we moved on to another of the dozens of topics that we would broach for a couple of short but cherished hours: work; when we planned to retire; grandkids; wives; bartenders we worked with 35 years ago and what they were up to, if I knew, and I never did, as I had drifted far away from those people and remembrances; politics, but only for a moment; God and nature. Gales of laughter threaded our conversation. It was the only time I saw him that week of closing ceremonies for our Up North seasonal home, as he was preparing for his youngest daughter's wedding two weeks hence. I hoped luck would be with him on opening day if not the rest of the week at camp, and that he would bag a deer, a real nice buck with a huge rack. He wouldn't need me to point him in the right direction. And, he wouldn't hesitate to pull the trigger.

NOVEMBER LIGHT

Each November, usually just before Thanksgiving, I will remember to visit our seldom-used living room, prompted by that strange seasonal circadian clock we all have, and take a few minutes to consider the oil painting Craig gave my wife and me 30 years ago.

The canvas is oversized, a habit of Craig's. It measures 90" x 42", dominating the west wall of the room. When we moved into our modest home, built in the mid-1950s, here on Broadway Street on the north side of Indianapolis more than two decades ago, we mounted the painting over a couch between two windows.

The painting, titled *November Light*, is a twilight scene. Thin bare trees, all shadowy black, populate the canvas, backlit by the fading dramatic orange just above the horizon. In front of the tree line is a road, which stretches across the entire width of the painting. On the right side of the painting as the viewer faces it is a yellow sign that indicates "Warning: Straight Road." Craig added that as the final impish touch. My wife was baffled by this artistic decision. "Craig, this is a beautiful painting and we love it, but why the sign? It worked so much better without it." Years of friendship allow a level of art-critic candor not otherwise tolerated.

"The painting was too…predictable. It just needed a little extra something. You know, a little something you might expect from me." He laughed; she didn't. She didn't because the artwork was destined to be hung in our home, for Craig had presented it to us on Christmas Eve 1990 while we celebrated with him in his third story flat on Massachusetts Avenue in Indianapolis, at that time a blighted area with a few serious art galleries and dive bars; now, it's been reborn as a trendy restaurant-bar mecca for hipsters known as Mass Ave. It was a thank-you gift to Janet for putting up with him when he and his youngest brother, Matt, crashed with us for several months while he tried to make a go of it as a fine artist here in Indy. Since Matt was just in his early twenties, he tagged along to explore his career options, away from the influence of his parents.

Matt soon bailed. So for the remainder of that winter, Craig leased a studio in the Faris Building on South Meridian Street. The seven-story former warehouse found a second life as a home to dozens of artists, a number of whom Craig had studied with at Indiana University's Herron School of Art and Design in Indianapolis in the 1980s, such as Lois Main Templeton, a visual artist of distinction locally and nationally who befriended Craig. There at the Faris Building, nestled among his contemporaries, Craig painted like mad. And here in the Circle City, he nearly went mad. Distanced from his northern Michigan home—with forests to roam and a Great Lake to navigate and a generationally established family tradition of hunting and fishing to ground himself—and marooned here in Indy, the capital city of an industrial farming state with little regard for preserving nature, he rapidly came unraveled. He was an animal completely out of its element. To save himself, he needed to go home. Upon learning of his younger sibling's struggle, his oldest brother, Fred, drove down to Indy in a pickup truck, helped him pack his few belongings—mostly finished and in-progress artwork, paint, and brushes—and Craig returned to his beloved northland: forever, I'm sure.

❀

I, too, tried to relocate and start a new life years later. In 2004, I found a job as a communications specialist at a hospital in a town near Ann Arbor, Michigan. I really wanted to live in Michigan, to carry a Michigan driver's license, to be nearer to Craig and his family of outdoorsmen, to live in Grand Traverse or Leelanau County, where my heart was hooked and remained upon first experiencing the area. But the job was underwhelming both in requirements and pay, and my supervisor seemed to have an unwanted crush on me; none of it felt right. After two months, I abandoned my post, leaving a note one Saturday that they could keep my most recent paycheck, apologizing for quitting on them. They sent me the check anyway, a legal thing. Lesson learned: desperation does not make for the best decision-making.

Then in 2005, I was hired by Mercy Hospital to be an organizational development director. I felt like I had hit the lottery. My excitement began to build when I had my phone interview in early January with the woman who would be my supervisor. I liked her sharp wit, her candor, her passion for the work, and her appreciation for my love of northern Michigan. I drove to Grayling for a second interview in late January. The hospital put me up in a nearby bed-and-breakfast on the Au Sable River, one of the legendary Michigan trout streams writer Ernest Hemingway fished in his youth. The daylong series of one-on-one and panel interviews went well, and I intuitively felt that I scored the job. I spent that evening with Craig and his wife at their home on Old Mission Peninsula. We had vodka martinis before dinner to celebrate; two, in fact. I was living the dream; that is, my dream. A few days later, I had an offer.

But this short-lived dream disappeared just before summer arrived, when I awoke to the reality of my wife's understandable—though difficult for me to appreciate—inability to leave her family behind. What would prove to be her last visit to the Spider Lake cabin, which we had sold our stake in a year earlier to our partners from Indy, began with a tearful phone call from Janet while she was just 20 miles away from the cabin, driving up to spend a long weekend with me. It was a Friday evening in mid-June, and spaghetti sauce was simmering on the stove while I enjoyed a glass of red wine. "Honey, I'm sorry. I just can't leave Indy, at least right now. I'm so sorry. I know you love it here, that this is your dream. I-I…" I hate it when women cry—especially when they make me cry. I told her not to worry about it; I'd expected as much. But I just didn't want to admit it.

"I'll see you in a few minutes," I said, hung up, then filled my wineglass to nearly overflowing—and chugged it entirely. Then I said a few choice words and sauntered down to the wooden dock, wine bottle and glass in hand. Summer was about to begin. Dragonflies zigzagged just above the water. Bass and bluegill broke the surface, evidenced by the emanating circles, feeding on insects. Soon the bullfrogs would begin their amusing bellowing and the early stars would appear, heralding the gradual materializing of the Milky Way across the night sky. A few deep breaths, a few more sips. There was nothing to say. I simply listened to the night noises of the calming lake.

❋

Once in a while, I think about taking that painting down and returning it to Craig. But I haven't a clue as to how to break down the canvas and frame without damaging the painting. And besides, it's now November, early November, and there will be a few more times for me to contemplate the painting during its namesake month.

So for now, the painting will stay put, as will I. Staying as a reminder about where I think I belong, and where I will return to, at least this May, when the high, fast, snowmelt-fed river water beckons me to fish for trout, and the sunshiny morning calls me to hike the sand dunes overlooking the Big Lake, and to keep my head to the stars in the cool spring night. It is getting darker here in November. But that's when the light of longing shines most brightly, and remembrance illuminates the heart.

WINTER IS COMING

For the mega-hit HBO series *Game of Thrones*, the phrase "Winter is coming" is part of the program. As it is everywhere on Earth where winter comes in all its cold, snowy, icy glory. As it does here in Michigan's northwest lower peninsula.

Leelanau County averages 145 inches of snowfall each winter. This keeps downhill and cross-country skiers, snowshoers, fat-tire bikers, and snowmobilers happy. During the relentless winter of 2013-2014, more than 260 inches of the white stuff covered parts of Leelanau County (Maple City recorded 266 inches). Although the recreational users of snow may have been ecstatic, most drivers were far from that euphoric state of mind. By March that year, I can only imagine the number of Leelanau County Sheriff's Department runs to prevent potentially homicidal domestic disputes over who commanded the TV remote control. Winter can be deadly serious.

For now, in early October 2018, snow is not in the immediate future, but its presence is felt by locals as the temperature gradually cools and snow chances draw ever closer. Today I called our friends at American Waste to put a halt to our seasonal trash removal services while asking for one more pickup before we closed up the house for the winter. American Waste gladly blessed my request, and the charming representative wished me a "nice winter." I wished her the same. Suddenly the sweet lady on the other end took on an entirely different personality. She ended the call saying, "Yeah," in a you-have-no-idea-what-we'll-be-enduring-this-winter voice. Click. In northern Michigan, those blissful summer days don't come cheap.

We arrived for our last visit of the year on Saturday, September 29, about 7 p.m. It was in the forties. My very warm-blooded wife was freezing. "I'm just not used to this cold," Janet said in a shivery voice. Me? I could probably live comfortably in Alaska, as I carry plenty of natural padding to insulate me. However, her discomfort meant it was time for me to fire up the aging propane furnace, which we had serviced in mid-June in preparation for use in the fall. "This furnace is old but it's safe," the tech said. "It should last you indefinitely, given the handful of heating days you have each year." So I got down low and lit the pilot. The furnace clanked on. The heat flowed through the vents. Then it cycled off upon reaching the set temp of 66. Fifteen minutes later it started up again—but this time it blew only cold air. After relighting the pilot three more times after the heat quit, I left a message with the local HV/AC company we use and conveyed our disappointment. I emphasized that we hoped to see a tech on Monday morning. We did.

After listening for an anxious hour and a half to grunts, sighs, and clanging tools, we received a new verdict: "The gas valve is shot. A new one will run you about $1,000. I can get the part tomorrow. But you'd be better off with a new furnace."

"What are we looking at, cost-wise?" I asked.

"It's a small house, so I'd say in the neighborhood of $2,500 - $3,000."

This was definitely not music to our ears. The tech took photos and would have his sales manager call us with an estimate on a replacement unit. Fortunately, we have two wall-mounted electric heaters that saved the day— and most of the remaining week of R&R. Without a doubt, *winter is coming*, I realized. Some cold air is good for the soul; it helps clear the mind. When I was a child in Scranton, as we slipped on our snowsuits and black rubber buckle boots getting ready for our frequent snowy evening walks, my dad used to say being outside in winter "blows the stink off ya." But late September vacation weather with nighttime temps in the 30s and no heat is not good for a marriage when your wife isn't a cold-weather fan. Fortunately, that first night was the chilliest, and the temperatures rose throughout the remainder of the week.

※

On Tuesday afternoon, Janet dropped me off in Traverse City along the Boardman River east of the weir to indulge in some salmon fishing. The previous two days I checked Shalda Creek in Sleeping Bear Dunes National Lakeshore: no salmon. Puzzled, I asked locals about the timing of the annual run. "It's early," said some; "It's late," said others. So I tried the Boardman. I knew they were running there, as Janet and I had visited the weir on Monday. Plenty of kings and cohos. Some huge kings, in fact, in the 25-pounds-plus range. The big fish thrilled onlookers as they hurtled up the fish ladder to join other anxious salmonids in the holding tanks. My blood ran hot at the sight. So permission was granted for a few hours of wetting a line and drifting some spawn bags.

Found a spot that felt promising on the north side of the river near the North Union Street bridge; very few anglers were about. Had two hits within 10 minutes, not of the major strike variety, but they certainly got my attention. I did, however, get a chance to chat with a fair number of friendly folk happening by. Most of them were retired and seemed to never know a stranger. One gent from Manistee was obviously quite the fisherman and gave me a full report of the salmon run throughout the region. I confessed that if I caught a decent-sized salmon I would be letting it go, as I was fishing solo, was a bit of a salmon fishing novice, and didn't have a net. "Well, in that case I'll just stand here for a few minutes and see you catch one, then I'll grab it for you. I've done plenty of that in my time." Unfortunately, that strike-on-demand never happened, and he moved on, wishing me luck, as anglers are wont to do. Another fellow and his wife stopped to inquire if there would be "fish for dinner tonight?" There would be, I explained, "As long as I finish before Carlson's closes in Leland." They laughed; but that was appearing to be an increasingly realistic outcome for this outing.

Throughout the afternoon I grew more connected to the river and the spawning salmon. I also became more attuned to the peculiar juxtaposition I was immersed in: fishing during a millions-of-years-old annual occurrence while watching workers at an office building across the river come out sporadically for a smoke or to drive off for lunch, or to eat lunch in their vehicles parked along the riverside. I live a white-collared existence too. I understood the concept of doing such time, of counting down the days until one was done with "workin' for the man," as my three-year-old grandson says with amusing resignation well beyond his years, hitting on many a workingman's destiny. As the kings and cohos now running in the river feel the instinctual call of the wild to spawn, with salmon fishing noodle rod and spinning reel in hand, I was feeling the end-of-work-life call of retirement, asking myself that great existential question: What more to life is there than fishing?

I fished with my Cedar neighbor Paul the following day. Janet was feeling generous, as she was pressuring me to leave on Thursday instead of our usual Saturday, for the weather in Indy was unseasonably summer-like. We started our day fishing the Boardman River at the Union Street Dam. Shortly after my first cast, an excited 30-inches-or-so coho leapt up on the shore right next to me under the aging metal fence I was leaning on, but I was too surprised to react. In hindsight, that was a big mistake, as that would have been our only "catch" of the day. Even so, Paul and I had a nice relaxing afternoon, fishing, not catching. The temperature reached 75 degrees on the partly cloudy day, gift enough for early October fishing. We took a timeout a bit after one o'clock for a liquid lunch, downing a few pints of Guinness at nearby Brady's Bar. Afterward, we fished a few different stretches of the Boardman. After about an hour of casting, drifting, and retrieving, a splash and a shout about 30 yards east of me indicated a fish on, which the lucky fellow landed, a decent-sized coho on the end of the line. That helped my morale and gave me a resurgence of hope, which had gradually been waning as the afternoon wore on. The salmon were jittery and thrashed the surface intermittently, putting on quite the show. But they never went after my spawn bags, no matter where I cast upriver aiming for that perfect, irresistible presentation. My Polarized sunglasses revealed impressive-sized salmon working their way upstream, and I had the pleasure of seeing the largest steelhead trout in my history of fishing, surging behind a cluster of salmon, hunting for fresh salmon roe. Empty-handed fishermen like to say it's all about getting out and getting away. And so by that standard, it was a successful outing.

We ended our adventure at the mouth of the Boardman. There we met a variety of fishing experts. "The run hasn't even started here yet," one forward guy notified us, without us asking. "You should drive out to the Platte River. It's gangbusters there. Only 40 minutes from here, you know!" he said as he lit a cigarette and walked away. Another older fellow told us about his luck out on Grand Traverse Bay with lake trout and salmon. "Fishing the mouth of the river from out there is the way to go." And one gent who had been around the block a few times more than I kindly inquired how we were doing. When told that the beer was cold and so was the fishing, but at least we saw plenty of salmon up near the weir, he said, "Well, they have to swim in here to get to there. Good luck, boys."

We closed the day out at Dick's Pour House, a venerable drinking (and dining) establishment in Lake Leelanau, serving the thirsty (and hungry) since the end of Prohibition. Just one more beer, and southwestern and vegetarian pizzas with our wives, made up for a day of unintentional fasting. And, the piscatorial taxidermy mounted behind the bar and around the barroom made us feel right at home. Brook trout, perch, walleye, northern pike, lake trout, salmon…the prizes we pine for, the hope that keeps us coming back for more.

✳

It's Thursday morning about 8 a.m. Janet has been downstairs sipping hot tea for a while, greeting the new day in her usual quietly appreciative way. The 12 hours of darkness is turning me into a bear succumbing to the hibernation instinct, and the memory foam mattress doesn't help motivate me to movement. As I reluctantly open my eyes, a dark silhouette of wind-quivering maple leaves dance on the wall. I push myself up on my left elbow and turn to look out the only window in the loft bedroom, to the east. Through the trees I witness a multicolored sunrise, the thin clouds on the horizon ablaze in gradients of glowing orange against an ever-lightening blue backdrop. I adjust my pillow to watch. Breathing…watching…being…. Why don't I pause in the mornings to do this more often? Why the nonstop rush?

My trance is broken by Janet's racket downstairs as she hustles to get ready to leave. Now I'm caught up in leaving too. It really is autumn and we really are closing out this Up North season of 2018. Summer has left; it's the Southern Hemisphere's turn; darkness is entering its own rule; *winter is coming*. This sense of finality is bittersweet. Yet I remain grateful for the five extended visits to Leelanau County we had this year: from early May when the trilliums are in bloom and the trees are beginning to bud and trout season has returned, through seemingly endless blue-sky summer days, to early October with daylight growing shorter and its companion cooler temperatures and maples afire. It is inevitable and fitting that I acknowledge that we are all just passing through—autumn's ultimate message.

I give in to Janet's campaign to leave prematurely and head back to Indy on Thursday. She is tidying up in her usual thorough, energetic manner; our house-cleaning friend, Marie, has a great gig, as Janet leaves her usual cleanliness-is-next-to-godliness impression. The refrigerator gets cleaned out, and I leave Marie a few beers to help her whistle while she works. We collect our things, making sure to pack all our clothing, along with the too-many books and magazines we brought, and the loose ends, like phone-charging cords and extra keys to the truck. And we compose our to-do list for next season, including having a new furnace installed, remodeling our main bathroom, and ultimately, revisiting whether we stay put or sell and move on to something closer to or on the water of a local inland lake, even though doing so on highly sought Lake Leelanau, our favorite, is wishful thinking and only available to us by hitting Mega Millions (as is Lake Michigan frontage). "You have to play to win," Janet reminds me.

Every trace of our October stay has been dutifully erased; everything is back in its assigned place. The house is still, entering its long season of repose. The truck is packed. Janet is making some calls to work, so I take a few moments of appreciation. This is a blessing, and we never take it for granted. Not being a prosperity gospel adherent, I'm convinced that the good Lord wasn't thinking of us when we earned and set aside enough money to make this real estate transaction happen. But that doesn't lessen our sense of gratitude for having this small slice of heaven for however long it is in our care.

I double-check the window latches to make sure they're all secure; double-check that the shed is locked tight; double-check that I've turned off the propane valve on the pig; double-check the lockbox on the northeast corner of the house to ensure that the emergency key set is there. Janet knows the drill and patiently waits as she goes through her own ritual of parting thoughts. I hop in the driver's seat and we slowly roll down the gravel driveway. "Goodbye, house," I say aloud, affectionately. Janet adds, "We had another great season, honey."

"Yes, we did," I concur. "We really did."

Before we head back to Indy, we decide to take a final walk for the year through Leland; our high-spirited Pomeranian will ride better with some exercise, as will we. It's very windy and cool—in the mid-forties—the previous night's windstorm leaving fallen limbs and a power outage in the neighborhood east of "downtown" Leland. We notice that many of the homes along the shore of Lake Leelanau are closed for the winter: shades drawn, driveways empty, boats winterized and stored, properties devoid of human life until spring cycles back. The Fudgies are long gone, having returned home once Labor Day Weekend concluded. But more appreciative, better behaved, affable, and largely Medicare-eligible visitors will be making an appearance in a week or so for the Color Tour. Fishtown is at rest.

As we drive southbound for the next six hours, I ponder the long winter and the long wait until we return once more to Leelanau County, our migratory schedule akin to that of hummingbirds—appearing from May to October. "Seven months?" Janet says unexpectedly, reading my mind, as long-married couples tend to do. "Wow, I didn't realize it was that long." It is.

Until then, I'll try to make myself useful. I'll wait for the snow to fly here—all 26 inches on average for the winter. Read the weekly *Leelanau Enterprise* to keep up on local events. Text and call our friends Up North, who will report the drama of their winter conditions with only slight exaggeration and telling photographic evidence. Sit near the glowing fireplace on gloomy weekend afternoons, drop a book in my lap as I nod out, and have those sustaining Leelanau dreams of years past, and hopefully to come, to see me through. Winter must run its course.

PART V

Winter

SNOW

It's Christmas Eve morning, 2017. My adult son and daughter are texting childish happy thoughts, their excitement gradually rising like a tea kettle beginning to boil on a cold winter day, like today. Shawn sends a photo from her Instagram daily feed. It shows the Leland River in Fishtown, with one of the commercial fishing boats, *Joy*, docked and blanketed with snow, the western sky behind it an ominous white-to-gray-to-black, snowstorm a comin'. I tell them I wish I were there. I get a mild admonishment from my son, Matt, saying, "It sounds great, but then you'd miss out on seeing all your grandkids enjoy Christmas!"

My response? "Not if they were there with me."

I walk out of the Fourth Sunday of Advent 7:30 a.m. Mass at St. Pius X Catholic Church here in Indy to snow flurries. The weather forecast for Christmas Eve is one to three inches of snow. Snowstorm central Indiana style. This should get the grandkids even more jacked up for Santa's big ride.

I'm spending a quiet morning with our insecure and cuddly Pomeranian on my lap as I write. Janet is at a yoga class. The preparations for this evening's traditional shindig at my daughter's are done. The neighborhood is completely still. All up and down the street, festive holiday lights are lit. From my living room chair vantage point, I can see snow gently falling in the front yard, the hawthorn tree's red berries adding to the seasonal ambiance. The refrigerator hums. The furnace blows warmth. I tap my laptop's keyboard; the dog stretches and sighs. He keeps his eyes open, barely, as he awaits the return of his master (and mine, frankly) from yoga. My mind drifts to thoughts of snow. And I think about all the snow my friends Up North are getting on this most reflective early winter day.

＊

Our Cedar neighbors and caretakers, Paul and Marie, live on a 10-acre hillside lot. Their "driveway" is basically a serpentine two-track, with deep ruts on both sides from downhill-streaming water erosion. Driving up and down the grade requires one's attention at any time of year. But when the snow really flies, their automobiles can't negotiate the climb, so Paul and Marie park them at the foot of the hill, and our two intrepid friends make the ascent one slippery step at a time. Two years ago, when they were "having a winter," as the locals label the more severe ones, Paul's oldest brother Fred, who has worked in the automotive wholesale business throughout his career, purchased a reliable used snowmobile for runs up and down the hill. The couple became the talk of the small town for their can-do wherewithal throughout that grueling winter. But last autumn, which is a time for northern Michiganders to revert to their "winter is coming" mindset, Paul decided he had had enough. One late afternoon during our seasonal closing week in early October, a Chevy Avalanche drove up our driveway—with Paul at the wheel.

"This yours?" I said, asking the obvious. Paul beamed.

"Just signed the papers an hour ago. Marie and I will be climbing a certain driveway this winter with complete confidence. Let it snow!"

The 2005 pickup had some rust over the wheel wells, but overall it drove with that sturdy Chevy truck attitude. Checking reports from the Traverse City area weather on Christmas Eve, it looks like the lake-effect snow machine is on and there may well be nearly two feet of the white stuff on the ground in Cedar by Christmas Day. I can see Paul smiling from here as the Avalanche charges uphill, snow flying and Paul howling like one of Teddy Roosevelt's Rough Riders.

＊

As I like to remind my children at this chill time of year, and someday will share with my grandchildren, I was born in snow country, in the Appalachian

Mountains in northeastern Pennsylvania. As kids, we never considered snow a burden or something to dread. Twenty years ago, when my father was having dinner with us on a rare return visit to Indy (having retreated to his beloved "West By God" West Virginia shortly after his early retirement), I was regaling (or so I thought) our kids with tales of my childhood. I mentioned that my brother, Kevan, and I walked unescorted to St. Paul Catholic School from our house on New York Street in Dunmore, a trek of more than a mile. We did this when he was 7 and I was 9 years old, years before the disappearing children milk carton campaign. Sometimes we tromped through a foot of snow or so while happily enduring stinging winds. "Oh yeah, right," said my son, Matt, representing the other skeptics at the table. Shawn and her high school sweetheart (and eventual husband), Sean (they are known among their friends as Sean-Squared), laughed at what they thought was a preposterous exaggeration. So I turned to my expert witness: Dad. My cranky father, always a totally focused eater of few words while at the dinner table, didn't even look up from his plate when asked, "Didn't we hike through the snow by ourselves to get to school in Scranton?"

He growled, "You're goddamned right they did." The kids' amused faces turned sober. "Thanks, Dad," I noted smugly.

During those Scranton winters, whenever it snowed—which was frequently—we always played in it. In our minds, and that of our parents, that's what it was there for. I recall one Christmas Eve in the early sixties when we lived on Marion Street. My paternal grandmother, Gertie, a widow, lived upstairs, a refuge for Kevan and me whenever mom and dad were arguing, which was often. A major snowstorm was in progress, further enhancing the magical feel of that special evening of childhood. I watched, enchanted, while the wind-whipped flakes swirled downward in the darkness outside the glow of the living room window. By midday on Christmas, the snow had nearly reached the three-foot-high top of the black wrought-iron fence that surrounded our yard. Our collie loved it, prancing through the snow, his long snout dusted as if by powdered sugar.

When we moved to Indianapolis in August 1966, even though it was still summer, Kevan and I remained concerned about the coming winter. Our persistent questions were, *Would it snow?* and *How much?* We got our answer that first December, when a storm dumped nearly a foot of snow on the trembling Midwestern city. School was canceled, which we thought was ridiculous, as St. Lawrence Catholic School was just a block and a football field away from us. But we weren't arguing. As we frolicked in our driveway and yard, throwing snowballs in brotherly competition and building a snowman in familial collaboration, it dawned on us that we were virtually alone in this winter wonderland. No other kids came out to play. What a weird place Indianapolis was, it seemed to us. To me, still does.

✻

In December of 2000, Janet and I drove up to Traverse City and spent a long weekend with Craig. I checked the forecast, of course, and the drive seemed quite doable. We had clear sailing for several hundred miles—until we entered Grand Rapids about 7 p.m. As we approached an overpass on the south side of town on U.S. Highway 131 North, suddenly, three vehicles in front of us in three different lanes simultaneously went into tailspins: black ice. Somehow—thanks to our guardian angels; no other explanation suffices—we steered our way through the spinning vehicles unscathed. Once we were north of Grand Rapids, it began snowing hard and continued to pick up in intensity. We stopped for fuel at Big Rapids, and Janet took the pilot seat. But about 45 minutes later, without any warning, she pulled over into a parking lot in Manton (this is before the U.S. 131 bypass was built). "Your turn. I can't drive in this," she confessed. "It's making me nervous." We were in the midst of a full-throttle snowstorm, and a beautiful one at that. I smiled as I jumped out of the passenger seat and walked around the van. By the time we got to M-113 near Kingsley, we were in whiteout conditions. Through the driving snow I managed to spot the elusive red taillights of a semi-trailer truck just ahead, and followed just closely enough to keep them in sight while allowing for adequate braking distance. Without the truck "breaking trail" for us, chances were high that we would lose sight of the road. Yet once we arrived in Kingsley, the road conditions improved greatly, thanks to the prompt work of the Grand Traverse County Road Commission's snowplow fleet, and the letup of the furious snowfall.

We stayed in Craig's cozy bachelor pad second-floor apartment on Front Street, which overlooked West Grand Traverse Bay. The following day we cross-country skied on state land near Ranch Rudolph, and had the hilly woodland trail all to ourselves. Craig, who had once participated in the annual North American VASA 34K cross-country ski race, held each February in Grand Traverse County, had not been on skis in years and was fighting a cold, but managed to push through the snow in admirable fashion, hacking all the way. It was sunny and cold. We nibbled on orange slices and PowerBars, then took a break midway to indulge in a Guinness, a surprise that Craig had thoughtfully packed. It was a good day.

The next morning, Craig awoke to the misery of a full-blown cold and so decided to stay home and rest, while Janet and I drove out to Empire. It was snowing relentlessly, and M-72 was becoming clogged with the piling snow. But our 1998 Honda Odyssey's front-wheel drive managed well. We snowshoed on the deserted beach in Empire for an hour but cut the excursion short because of the heavy snowfall and concern about the drive back to Traverse City. As expected, the degree of driving difficulty had increased. Taking it slow and steady in such weather is usually the trick, and it was that afternoon. Once back in TC, we decided to have lunch at the Mackinaw Brewing Company downtown on Front Street and discuss our cross-country skiing destination for later in the afternoon. Sitting at the bar enjoying some hot soup and a beer, we realized that skiing was not in our immediate future. Calling my attention to the storefront window view, Janet commented, "Wow, it's really coming down." Although the snowy scene outside the brewery had a snow globe quality to it, driving in the heavy accumulation wasn't our idea of fun. So we foreclosed on our skiing ambition and retreated to Craig's to relax there before heading out early the next morning for Indy.

At 4:30 a.m., I awoke to a strange rumbling noise on Front Street—and a sight I wasn't prepared for: deep lake-effect snow, which had accumulated well beyond the forecasted amount. A backhoe loader with a special suction device was inhaling the snowfall covering the road and depositing it into dual tandem trailer beds hauled by a semi-tractor truck. Once a full load was reached, a second waiting truck rolled seamlessly in to replace it. Although I marveled at the city's ingenuity in snow removal and its aggressiveness in rising to the challenge, the drive home nonetheless promised to be exciting. And it was. Although the snow was cleared by first light, the roads had iced over. Again, we took it slowly. By the time we arrived at the on-ramp for U.S. 131 South, well over an hour later, the road conditions had improved and my white knuckles had returned to their normal color. Such is the risk assumed when traveling to and from snow country. You just never know.

❋

On Christmas Eve afternoon in 2013, our Cedar neighbor John, who lives directly across the street from us, sent a photo of our snowed-in retreat, showing the perspective from his living room windows. I smiled: at least two feet of snow covered the ground. Although the Leelanau County Road Commission road sign on Green Court claimed that the street is plowed when needed, the two-tracks in the image cut by local traffic said otherwise. The photo gave me that being-there feeling. An unexpected gift on that day of heightened anticipation for all Christians, and for many others who share the joy of the holiday season.

In my mind's eye I trudge through the accumulation of trillions of snow crystals, grinning ecstatically, childishly, amid a driving snowfall. Janet and I are stepping into our cross-country ski bindings, adjusting our ski poles' wrist bands, and pushing off for a late afternoon session at Sugar Loaf's Old (golf) Course. It is cold. Quiet. Still. The sun is tracking along its low wintertime southwestern arc as the landscape softens toward dusk. Our skis glide smoothly in the powdery snow, our ski poles' brief purchase syncing with each foot sliding forward. It's a good sweat; a fine workout.

Living the snowy dream.

CROSS-COUNTRY DAYS

Thanksgiving Day is next week. This looming reality always gets me motivated to conclude all the winter prep work around the house and yard. Changing the furnace filter is one of the chores. As I exchange the old filter for the new one, I notice our cross-country skis, poles, and boots gathering dust in the corner next to the furnace. I pause.

For the past several years, I've had several relatives interested in taking this ski equipment off our hands. My youngest brother, Chris, is in a phase of trying all things new, and cross-country skiing is on the list. Chris has sent me a few emails about this whenever the first significant snowfall occurs in Indy—which for the last three years, hasn't really occurred. But that's no permanent arrangement, as I told Chris, and the equipment is ready for him to try whenever we get five or six inches of snow. Our son, Matt, and daughter-in-law, Kelli, have also registered the same interest in giving cross-country skiing a shot, but yet the skis sit undisturbed.

The fact is, age has snuck up on my wife and me. Each of us has had a surgery that now encourages us to be more careful with our exercise regimen and so discourages engaging in this wintery pastime, much to our regret. But we had our share of snowy days out on the groomed-tracked powder. And they were very good ones too.

※

Here in central Indiana, whenever there is a threat of three inches or more of snow, the grocery stores and liquor stores are stampeded by those I call *Snow Pussies*. These people never learned how to play in the snow when growing up (although instructions or trainers aren't necessary; it's kind of like breathing). Instead, they view snow as dreadful, almost as if it's coming to harm them. Not me. Born in northeastern Pennsylvania, and lucky enough to live there for a decade before getting reassigned with my parents to Indy, I have a love of snow in my DNA. So when Janet suggested we learn to cross-country ski way back in the nineties, though initially reluctant, my inner child took to it. Well, eventually.

I never really downhill skied, which would have proven helpful to me in unhesitatingly embracing cross-country skiing. Being confident on skis would have helped me initially to handle the occasional short downhill slope that's part of the cross-country experience while avoiding full-body contact with the ground. When I was in my early twenties, on what a former bartending buddy and I referred to as "Losers' Christmas Eve," we drove down to Paoli Peaks in southern Indiana for an evening of downhill skiing under the lights. Dave had been a ski instructor in Vermont and was a diehard adventurer (having been a scuba diver on a U.S. Navy submarine, among other risky ventures). To ward off the chill and summon my courage, we sipped some Grand Marnier prior to exiting his truck.

Dave didn't give me any instructions, told me I didn't need the bunny hill training, then got to witness me slip and fall as our ski-lift chair approached and had to yell at the operator to stop the cabled chairs' movement so I could be extracted from beneath their path. It was humiliating, but it gave my buddy a good laugh. Thereafter, I managed to "snowplow" my way down the only hill I tried. Ride lift. Snowplow down. Risk actually skiing. Fall. Repeat. This mentally scarring downhill skiing experience would be my first and last.

Years later, married and occasionally coerced into expanding my horizons, i.e., doing new things my wife finds interesting, our first cross-country skiing experience took place at Shanty Creek Resort in Bellaire. It was just after Christmas, and Janet, 12-year-old son Matt, and I made our classic Nordic skiing debut. Both of them were naturals. Matt, athletically gifted, cruised down the first slope that started this particular loop. Janet, 5'2" and pushing 100 pounds, having a short way to fall and having downhill skied in her Life Before Tim, glided away skillfully. Then came 6' 3" me—and I quickly lost my balance and slid down on my posterior to join them. "Dammit!" I yelled, embarrassed and frustrated, and they laughed. It was figuring to be a long day. But the sky was clear and the trails were not being heavily used, and with hours of practice we all got better at it, including me. We broke for lunch, but spent a full day out on the trails winding in and out of wooded hills and glades. The following day our taut muscles were talking to us, but with some Advil and stretching and being eager to get back out on the skis, we were good to go. Ah, youth.

After this inaugural cross-country skiing experience, I was a convert. For the next five years or so we would schedule a cross-country skiing trip to northern Michigan every winter. Several times we stayed in Charlevoix at the Weathervane Terrace Inn and once at Pointes North Inn just across the street, both along the Pine river and near the drawbridge on U.S. 31. From there, we skied at Boyne Highlands Resort.

Once, while skiing at the resort, I met a Scandinavian Great Lakes freighter pilot. We were at the crest of a rather long hill that gave me pause; I considered stepping out of my skis and walking down. He noticed my hesitation. "You look like you're not ready for da hill, my friend," he said, interrupting my panicked thoughts. "Here, let me show you; watch carefully." The man, about my height and build who appeared to be in his sixties and in excellent shape, crouched into it, folding his ski poles behind him in a more relaxed impression of a downhill skier. At the bottom of the hill, he turned and waved me on. Janet and Matt were waiting too. I summoned my inner Bode Miller and pushed off, did as was demonstrated, concentrated— but not too hard—on holding my balance, and skied upright all the way down, arriving next to my informal instructor. "Good job, my friend. You are really catching on." I saw him several times later throughout the day as we passed one another on the trails, exchanging knowing smiles and nods as we glided by one another. Lesson learned: when cross-country skiing, technique matters. Good coaching does too.

After several cross-country skiing excursions we decided to buy our own skis, at my Up-North-friend Craig's recommendation. We picked them up on sale in February at Don Orr Ski N' Beach Haus in Traverse City. My new pair of waxless skis, poles, and boots made me feel like a pro—or, at least, a native Michigander. The great thing was, I could now take them back to Indy and use them in the winter there. And that I did: at Eagle Creek Park.

Whenever considerable snowfalls would bless Indianapolis, our cross-country skis beckoned. Although we sometimes went to nearby Holiday Park and broke our own trails, Eagle Creek Park would be the ideal destination. One of the best times I had skiing there was Christmas Day in the early 2000s. As is her custom, my mother-in-law throws a grand Christmas shindig at her house, which just happens to be located a block from the park's south property line. It was indeed a white Christmas, with nearly a foot of snow on the ground. Being curmudgeonly, especially at this most wonderful time of the year, I bargained with Janet to allow me to go skiing for a few hours if I would behave myself at this dreaded festive gathering of my in-laws. "Deal. But don't be gone all day."

It was quiet—very quiet for a city of a million. Granted, I could still hear the hum of nearby Interstate 65, but it was not as pronounced as usual, with few travelers on the road. Better yet, it seemed as though I nearly had the park to myself, at least the ski trails. I pushed off from the unmarked trailhead near the vacant children's playground and made my way into the woods.

And it was cold, about 20 degrees, with just a trace of wind. I quickly fell into a rhythm, one ski gliding in front of the other on the groomed tracks, bringing the next ski forward as the extended thrust of the other naturally lost momentum, keeping the pace quick and my breathing pleasantly deep, fogging in front of me. I stopped once for about 10 minutes to watch flock after flock of sandhill cranes, a late migratory run, headed south. Their primitive croaking call always captivates me, as do the V-shaped flocks of these birds with a seven-foot wingspan. I went on once I felt the cold air reaching the sweaty dampness of my innermost layer: cross-country skiing is a serious calorie-burning workout. After a few hours I headed back to my mother-in-law's. Opening the front door, I was greeted by an entire dining room of Janet's family in mid-dinner. They all turned and looked at me. "You're late," Janet noted flatly, saying what others were effectively communicating by their icy stares.

"Sorry. But that was the best Christmas present I ever had," I said joyfully. "Can't let good snow go to waste. As you were." And they went right back to feeding their faces, as they say in Indiana. Jingle bells and what not.

※

The second-to-the-last time I cross-country skied was in Grayling, Michigan. It was January 2005 and I was in the third and what would turn out to be final stage of interviewing for a job at the local hospital.

On the morning of my daylong interview session, deep snow blanketed the area. While sipping tea and gazing out the sliding glass door at the wintry scene, I asked the proprietress of the bed-and-breakfast where I could find some good cross-country skiing. She directed me to Hanson Hills. Once my interviewing was done, about 3 p.m., I hustled over there with my skis.

Wind-driven snow was falling hard and fast, and the cross-country skiing course was fairly empty. I was enjoying myself thoroughly, feeling good about the day's set of interviews. I skied vigorously, laughing aloud every now and then, just happy. The sky dimmed as the afternoon drifted toward a close. The temperature was in the high teens but was dropping quickly with the setting sun. I reached the closing hill of the course, flying on my skis and taking on the short downhill as if I had some expertise. I ended up losing it toward the bottom and fell hard on my right hip. Got up laughing. Back then, my joints were still fully cooperating.

Two years later, at Eagle Creek Park, I put on my skis on for what would be the final time. It was a snow day for schools in Indy, including the public charter school I worked at then as chief operating officer, with 10 inches of snow falling that night (an almost cataclysmic weather event in these parts). These were the last days of my being an athletic-kinda stud (at least in my own mind). Earlier that morning, I went to a 6 o'clock spinning class at the local YMCA for an hour. During my stationary ride, school was canceled. I returned home to shovel my lengthy driveway, a seasonal chore I actually used to look forward to. Later, I drove out to Eagle Creek Park for an afternoon of skiing. No one had been out breaking trail, so I ended up doing so myself, which introduced a much greater degree of difficulty. But I was stoked. After being out for several hours, now spent, I approached my Honda Element. Without any warning, my right leg felt as though it were glued to my left: there was no other way to describe it. I ended up seeing my general practitioner two days later, who had me get x-rayed prior to the visit. Holding the films up to the fluorescent lights to examine them, he declared, "Man, your hip is riddled with arthritis. How did that happen?"

How the hell did I know. "Doc, I don't even know what arthritis is," I answered honestly, my worry amping up.

He responded, "Well, there's a hip replacement in your future." His from-bad-to-worse diagnosis had a sobering effect on me. As it would turn out, he prescribed me a seven-day course of Prednisone which got me back up and almost running. He referred me to a hip specialist, who told me it would be a while before I needed surgery, if ever. Optimistic cuss, he was, as eight years later, the hip had eroded to a debilitating bone-on-bone condition. My cross-country skiing is now history.

Janet was ready to part with her set of skis years ago. Me? Not so fast. But now that I'm walking with a titanium hip implant (I tell my young grandkids I'm a lesser version of Iron Man), I'm ready to loosen my grip on the way we were and find the equipment a good home. Maybe we'll keep it in the family, which would be nice. Or perhaps I should just take the gear to our retreat in Cedar and display it somehow for atmospheric effect. (Come to think of it, I'm sure Janet would put the kibosh on that.) I could just hide it away in a bedroom closet here in Indy. Then I could check on it in the winter whenever enough snow falls, just to relive that urge from younger days to fetch the skis and poles and boots and get ready to glide through the woods in the glistening snow with a smile frozen on my icy face. Though I may be too fragile to snap my ski boots into the bindings—the very thought of which makes my heart ache—one thing is for sure: I will never be labeled a Snow Pussy. Never!

NATURAL CAUSES

Oh dangerman, oh dangerman…
—"Swords and Knives" by Tears for Fears

It is mid-winter 2019 and Indianapolis is pulling out of an attack by the Polar Vortex. Temperatures plunged to -11 with a -38 windchill. Harrowing. During times like these, my thoughts align with the weather, becoming cold and dark, and a sense of danger permeates the air. The sun is long gone at 7 p.m. and outdoor activity into the evening is months away. So as I eat supper and surf the web inside by the glow of incandescent bulbs and the sinus-drying comfort of gas heat, I check in on northwest lower Michigan by checking out the *Traverse City Record Eagle* and *UpNorthLive* websites for signs of life. Or death.

Folks who love the great outdoors can sometimes play great games of risk, whatever time of year. Like snowmobilers. While working in Grayling, I increasingly felt the joy of soon becoming an official resident of the state of Michigan, northern Michigan, specifically. The region is replete with the geographic features I cherish: hills, forests, nearby dunes, and water— enchanting brooks, clear rivers, and quiet lakes. While being courted as a potential employee by the hospital in January, I was, of course, given a tour of the facility. The hospital services a number of counties with a predominantly rural population. The emergency room was topnotch (and no doubt still is). Had to be. For the many farmers in the area are engaged in one of the most life-threatening occupations in the United States (typically making all the top 10 most dangerous jobs lists in America). Further, Grayling is one of the Midwest's hot spots for snowmobiling. Farmers may get seriously injured by workplace accident. Snowmobilers may get seriously injured—or worse—by pushing their snow-going machines to the limit while just out having fun.

Just last week I read of one enthusiast on his snowmobile who rounded a sharp turn in the woods a bit too fast, lost control, got tossed from his vehicle and thrown into two trees—two very unforgiving trees—with such velocity that his helmet was ripped off. He died on impact. Suspicions are, the daredevil had been imbibing alcoholic beverages, which contributed to his faulty judgment and sense of daring, putting the throttle into it at precisely the wrong time. Speed and/or alcohol along with careless decision-making are the typical factors in these crashes, as police and news reports indicate. Snowmobiles can attain speeds well over 100 miles per hour (why, I am left to ask), alcohol is insidious in overtaking rational thought, and decision-making is always compromised when at speed and awareness is dulled.

While cross-country skiing years ago in Bellaire at Shanty Creek, I had stopped for a break on a sunshiny afternoon, admiring the glaring view of a field covered by a thick blanket of fresh snow. The top of a fence line could be seen just above the pristine white surface. Another skier, an older gent, stopped to say hello for a moment and catch his breath. As we gazed at the scene, he told me about a snowmobiler who was out one evening cruising some nearby farm fields, ran into a barbed wire fence at high speed and was decapitated. Did it actually happen? Well, that's how it was packaged. As fantastic as the tale was, I didn't bother to check his sources. One should never let the facts get in the way of a good story.

My friend Craig used to be infamous in his circles for taking lots of risks, primarily during his twenties when he was tending bar in Indianapolis post-U.S. Army discharge while wrapping up his fine arts degree at the Indiana University Herron School of Art. He used to aptly refer to himself as Dangerman, part of the lyrics from a Tears for Fears tune that came out back when we courted danger because our youth engendered impulsive and bold and sometimes reckless and wild behavior. Back then, we lived life in the fast lane—and he drove on the Autobahn.

Though often appearing to be potentially terminal, most of his risk-taking was calculated and not as foolhardy as it initially appeared. Especially when it came to outdoor activity. He would push the limit, for example, sailing in a small boat in very big water, like Lake Michigan. But as much as it made me anxious, it made him elated. Time and again, we survived every outing together. He laughed like a madman as the Flying Scot would heel in the wind and I would grip my seat like a cat in a tree who suddenly realized its predicament. "Yee-ha! Say your prayers, sinner!" he would shriek, laughing hysterically. In hindsight, it was pretty damn funny; an electric moment in an otherwise dull life full of playing it safe.

Years ago, Craig pointed out the types of accidental outdoor deaths that occur in Michigan all too frequently. On snowmobiles. In kayaks. On sailboats. In air crashes. While deer hunting. Or swimming. "When it comes to saying hi up close and personal to the Grim Reaper, it doesn't get any better than this," he would say darkly of accidental deaths Up North. "We got all the best ways to go in full Technicolor." Although Indianapolis has its fill of urban deaths unforeseen that make the local news (including more than our fair share of murders), it can't compare with the more attention-getting ways to die in the great outdoors. One reason is, Michigan *has* great outdoors, which draws people out to test their mettle, especially the uninitiated and grossly untrained and unprepared.

❋

When Janet and I co-owned a cabin on Spider Lake with another couple from Indianapolis, we became familiar with an overly friendly next-door neighbor. She loved to hail us from her bedroom balcony overlooking the lake while we were out on our dock below trying to catch some rays and relax. "Hey, neighbors!" she would call out, suddenly extinguishing our solitude, and I would cringe, mumble a curse word or three, and consider going for a swim I hadn't planned on, just to avoid being drawn into a rambling, pointless conversation. Janet, ever the kind diplomat, would tell me to stop. "She's just lonely. Remember, be merciful," she would say, censoring any argument I'd have liked to wage.

One early weekend in May, we arrived about midnight to open up the cabin for the season. As we made our way down the two-track, we spotted an unexpected vehicle in our parking spot in front of the house. "Who's that?" Janet asked.

"Who the hell is that?" I emphasized. It was the neighbor lady's beater van.

"Maybe she needed to park here for some reason," Janet rationalized.

"I don't even want to go there," I commented, more concerned about it being on our property and in the way, than why.

"Stay in the truck," I warned. "I'll check it out." As I walked up to the driver's side window, I turned on my flashlight to peek in. Suddenly a huddled mass came alive, with a bright beaming face and hair all askew—which scared the bejesus out of me. "Shit!" I yelled, startled.

"Oh, hi there!" our unusual neighbor greeted me with a crazed look. "So sorry. I'll move this rig right away. I didn't expect you guys to be here already. But come to think of it, I guess it is May, after all. Haven't seen you in months. Well, goodnight. Enjoy your stay."

A year later, we learned the poor soul had died during the winter. She had been suffering from profound mental illness. As locals tell the story, she occasionally complained of hearing voices when no one was around. Late one night, while her husband was away working in Ann Arbor, she became frightened and went outside to escape her terror, inadvertently locking herself out while still in her nightclothes. Subzero cold gripped the area that February night. Instead of seeking help, she froze to death on her patio.

❈

In 1998 we were up in Traverse City in early July for summer vacation. The lighthearted entertainment news typically cranking out of the National Cherry Festival was temporarily overshadowed by a tragedy. On July 3, A Czech-built Aero L-39 Albatros jet plunged into Lake Michigan. The plane and its two-man crew—one a flight instructor at Northwestern Michigan College—vanished without a trace. The accident happened out near the Fox Islands.

Craig, a teller of tales both tall and actual, yet always riveting, outlined what he thought most likely happened. "When they lost control, that jet went straight down, nose first, and in its terminal dive shot way below the surface in hundreds of feet of cold Lake Michigan water. They'll probably never find the wreckage. Those two poor guys were just fish food." He provided his postmortem with complete confidence in the accuracy of his account. As ever is the case in such circumstances with Craig, it was a *Ripley's Believe It or Not!* moment.

※

When covering the topic of accidental death in northern Michigan, one is obligated to reference the sport of hunting. My first deer hunt in the early nineties seemed like it could be my last. Staying at my friend's family dacha, whose sole purpose was to house hunters and fishermen during the annual November deer and April trout camps, we got up early in the morning, well before first light. Craig and I left the rest of the snoring hunters and headed up to a location he favored near Dead Man's Hill in the Jordan River Valley. We went to the spot he'd scoped out two days earlier for deer sign and settled in somewhere in the woods about a quarter mile off the two-track where we parked his truck. The temperature was in the lower thirties, and we were hunkered down in a depression behind some deadfall; about six inches of snow covered the area.

Dawn was about 30 minutes away. We chatted quietly and intermittently, not wanting to give our presence away to any bucks in the area. A few minutes into our watch, Craig nudged me, whispering, "There are a couple of guys about 75 yards in front of us at about 2 o'clock. I'll let them know we're here." He got out his BIC lighter, ignited it, and waved it slowly back and forth to catch their attention. The two hunters had been in a tent and were stirring as if hunting was the least of their interests, making more racket than two bears rummaging through a campsite. "Those bastards are probably hungover downstaters from Detroit," Craig opined. "They aren't even aware of their surroundings. If we want to live another day, we'll need to move." I was relieved to hear him say that he would relinquish this preferred spot. Each deer hunting season, there are a few too many fatalities of the human kind. Falling out of tree blinds. Getting shot to death by another hunter. Being out of shape and having a widow-maker heart attack while dragging a buck weighing more than 200 pounds. Accidents happen. When the woods are crawling with rifle-toting trigger-happy fellas who typically spend their white-collar lives pushing paper, that is always cause for concern. Craig's family knows their weapons and they know how to handle themselves in the great outdoors. As with riding a motorcycle, it's not the bike nor the biker that's the worry—it's everybody else behind the wheel.

※

Janet and I kayak frequently when enjoying some down time Up North. We purchased a Wilderness Systems Pamlico, a tandem kayak, when we bought our cottage on Spider Lake. Craig encouraged the purchase, knowing our love of birds. "With a kayak, you can quietly close in on waterbirds and shorebirds without disturbing them. You'll love it." And we did.

To save our marriage, about five years later we gave the kayak to Craig, who used it out on Lake Superior each late August—until a wicked storm knocked over a maple tree and crushed the polyethylene life out of it. True, the Pamlico brought us closer to nature: one misty morning, we could almost touch a pair of feeding loons as they dove under us and surfaced nearby. But Janet and I just couldn't synchronize our paddling over long stretches, which would confound our intentions to enjoy a peaceful outing on the water. So we went our separate-but-equal ways, purchasing individual kayaks. And so we've stayed our gold-banded course.

When floating in water deeper than five feet, we wear our flotation jackets. When paddling shallower bodies of water, such as the Cedar River, we stow our flotation jackets under the bungie deck rigging on the back of the boats—within reach and meeting the Michigan Department of Natural Resources and U.S. Coast Guard requirements. Since we kayak, whenever a kayaker drowning occurs, it gets our attention, reminding of us of our mortality and to continue to take care while appreciating nature from the perspective of these wonderful non-motorized vessels. Flotation jackets: never leave shore without 'em.

◆

One cloudless early August morning out on South Manitou Island, my son, Matt, Craig, and I were strolling along the beach, Lake Michigan at rest, the shore calm. We were camping there for a long weekend, having sailed over from Leland the previous evening. A U.S. Park Ranger hailed us by megaphone from his patrol boat as it cut through the morning mist. He was slowly cruising about 50 yards offshore. "Have you seen a kayaker during the past 24 hours? He was in an orange and white sea kayak." We had not. He waved and continued his search. A few minutes later, a Coast Guard Dolphin helicopter flew out from the air station in Traverse City and went into a "Z" pattern over both North and South Manitou Islands and surrounding waters. The chopper repeated the circuit several times, then headed toward Leland, flying several hundred feet above the water. Days later, once our R&R on the island ended, we discovered that the kayaker had drowned. The Big Lake must always be respected. Kayaking solo across 14 miles or so of water that can become angry in a hurry is not necessarily a prudent plan. And yet, whenever such ill-advised adventures and awful outcomes occur, my heart goes out to the deceased and their families. Nobody plans on these things happening. It all starts out with a glorious notion to engage the elements. Ready or not.

❋

One evening during summer vacation in the nineties is etched in my memory for the element of danger that materialized so unnecessarily and avoidably. We had arrived in Leland on a Friday afternoon in August for our annual two-week stay. I had missed Craig in Traverse City on the way in, as he was working. He promised to be out to welcome us the following night.

It was about 10 p.m. Dusk. Janet and the kids and our friend Cindy were watching television, winding down from another tough day at the beach. I was sitting on the small concrete porch at the entrance of our vacation rental house and spotted Craig walking quickly, his unmistakable man-on-a-mission form appearing under a Lake Street light nearly two blocks away. He was smoking, too, which was a dead giveaway. "Hey, dude!" he shouted, hurrying up to the house. "Sorry. I stopped by the Bluebird Tavern for a quick cocktail and ran into a buddy. Anyway, let's hit the beach." He handed me a brown bag: Myers's Dark Rum. It was going to be a long night of catching up after a year's separation.

We sat in the cooling sand having our way overdue conversation, passing the bottle back and forth. So much ground to cover: kids, wives, work, ambitions, the state of the union, the state of the world, and the absurdity of everyday life, which is what we always returned to, warming our souls with rekindled brotherly laughter. We were alone, save the occasional hand-holding couple walking along the shore, having private conversations that we overheard but couldn't care less about. We had much more important things to discuss.

Around midnight and well lubricated, Craig announced, "Time for a swim."

"Whoa, wait a minute, bro," I protested. "It's way too dark for that. I'm not goin' out there; and you shouldn't either. You know I ain't much of a swimmer. You get in trouble, you're on your own." I knew that wouldn't make him hesitate, but I had to say it to clear my conscience, if possible, should his swim go south.

"I know it. And if I happen not to make it back, it was real nice knowin' ya, ace." And with that, he waded out into the dark water. I took another swig. He disappeared, the sound of his freestyle swimming gradually moving away from me.

I ceased sipping. Although I was buzzed and tried to downplay my concern, I ended up talking to myself as the minutes passed. *Dammit, get back here*, I whispered to nobody but me and the good Lord above. *This is getting old—really old.*

About 15 minutes later, Dangerman arose from the inky horizon, dripping his way up to me. "God, that felt good. Out there, away from it all. You don't know what you missed. Now gimme that damn bottle, you greedy bastard." We laughed, of course. I was glad that he didn't fill his lungs with water; glad that I didn't have to make a life-and-death decision to go after his struggling body or stay put; glad that we still had plenty of rum left and the night was ours, with no agenda the following day to curb this hard-earned annual reconvening of close friends. We talked for hours, watching the freighters, aglow with their running lights, move slowly through the Manitou Passage as the Milky Way emerged. Like the T-shirts and hats we wore back then declared, *Life is Good.* Especially when you manage to survive an undeniable instinct to flirt with disaster.

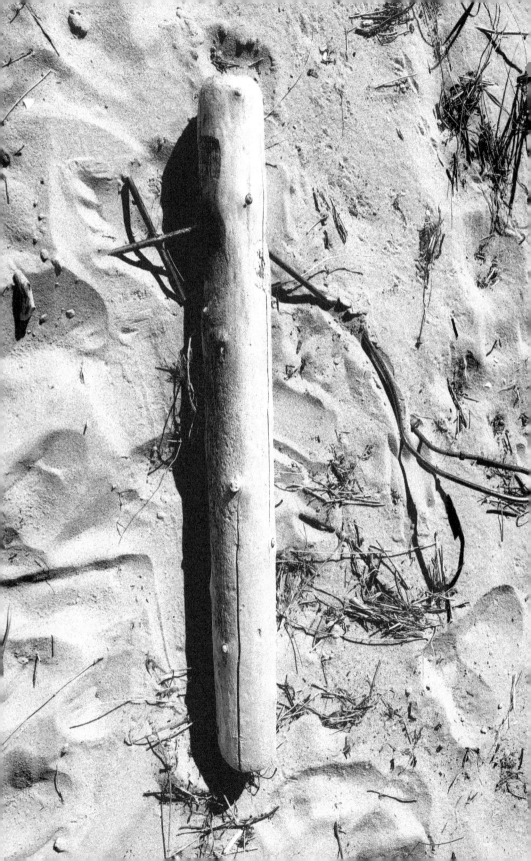

PART VI

Epilogue

AN APOCALYPTIC FRIENDSHIP

Our annual five-month season of retreating to our cabin in Cedar whenever our paid time off permitted, a 10-year practice that we hope to eventually convert into a permanent living arrangement, was wrecked in 2020: the year of the Covid-19 pandemic. Janet had made it up with me just once, for the Memorial Day weekend, as she fought through the summer and into the fall with a chronic (non-Covid-19) viral condition. At her encouragement, I attempted to get away for a week of summer vacation in late June, but ended up turning around and returning to Indy once the first weekend passed. Too much going on at work—closing out an incredibly difficult school year, being inundated with phone calls, emails, and text messages—and too much going on at home to relax. And ultimately, a vacation without Janet is no vacation at all. A decades-long love can do that to a guy. So I tried again, getting permission from my commanding officer to take a solo trip to the cabin during the first week in October. I arrived on Saturday, October 3, late in the afternoon. That evening, while sipping a welcome-home beer and watching the retreating sunlight gradually disappear through the trees, I called Craig. I had sent forewarning of my intended trip earlier in the week but didn't provide much in the way of details.

"He-ey," he greeted me musically. "Did you escape from Indy?"

"Made it. Just me this time. We should get together."

"Cool. Boys day out. I'll swing by after church tomorrow, about 10 or so. I'll take you to a beach on Good Harbor Bay you haven't seen before. It's a Petoskey-stone paradise. Bring your snorkeling gear. The water should still be warm enough for a swim."

We talked for a few more minutes, our lightheartedness increasing as we carried on. It was good to hear Craig's voice: the sound of friendship, of brotherhood, of a bond built over many years. I had something wonderful to look forward to in the morning: an outing with Craig; a much-needed rekindling.

※

More than 30 years ago, my dear friend introduced me and my family to the wonders of northern Michigan. To Traverse City, Leelanau County, to the Jordan River Valley, the Manitou Islands. To startlingly clear nights under the Milky Way and wary trout striking well-presented bait. To canvas sails sheet tight in the wind out on Lake Michigan and gunshots at first light during deer season in November. To snorkeling on shipwrecks in the Manitou Passage and swimming in the Big Lake in June when others dared not tread. To beachcombing for rocky treasures and sipping a fine cabernet on a beach near Empire on a snowy New Year's Day.

And yet, over the past decade or so, we had drifted apart. Craig became increasingly vocal about politics and more critical of all things liberal. For years, I hadn't really noticed his rightward-leaning views, instead laughing at his incredible sense of humor that appeared as he ranted about liberal idiocy and conservative righteousness. He could go off on great tangents like the late comedian Robin Williams, racing here and there with outrageously insightful and wildly funny commentary, as if in a monologue. Only his amusing stream of consciousness had become increasingly polarizing.

Janet, a tree-hugging socialist at heart, could barely take it. As the years went on, it became harder and harder for me to listen patiently to surprise attacks launched by Craig on things she and I believed in. And so we kept our friendly interactions to an increasingly reduced minimum so as not to say things that could hurt, things we might have meant. Our 40-year friendship frayed. Yet we've managed to stay in touch; we've tried to keep it together. Even with the incendiary four years of American politics leading up to the 2020 presidential election.

For the past several years, my Up North friend has shown concern for the professional life I'm living, and his belief that I'm wasting it away, working as an administrator for an urban public charter school that services a majority of students who live in poverty. Whenever I would see him—a summer Sunday afternoon when he would roar up our Cedar driveway on his Harley Davidson Sportster and converse on the deck over a cocktail; or stealing away to the Jordan River Valley for our precious annual day of trout fishing; or walking along the tourist-free Good Harbor Bay Beach in early autumn as we concluded another season of retreating in Leelanau County— he tried to convince me to pull up my Hoosier stakes, head north across the Indiana-Michigan line, and keep driving until I reached the grand understatement "Lake Michigan" sign pointing out the inland sea in front of me where South Bohemian Road ends at Good Harbor Bay. "What good is your work doing anyway? What difference are you really making?" he would ask me candidly, causing me to drink more deeply of the libation at hand. "Your heart is in the right place, bro, but the problems you face are bigger than you are. You can't cure poverty; you can't fix ignorance. You're gonna pay the price for your martyrdom—nobody else. I can see it in your face: your job is slowly killing you. And for what? When you finally leave, the door will hit you in the ass and it will be as if you never worked there. So save yourself. Get the hell out of there while you still can. Come up here and stay for the rest of your life. Haven't I told you for years that the big cities are gonna go up in flames? Armageddon is coming, sooner or later. Don't wait until the shit hits the fan. Then it might be too late." And with that said, he turned warmer, lowering his voice. "Oops, looks like I did it again. I just get a little carried away now and then. Heh-heh-heh...."

Here. In the woods. Permanently divorced from the big city and its inherent never-ending struggles: crime, traffic, pollution, noise, stress as a way of life. I would be living in a much smaller community within easy reach of Traverse City. We would be safe with Craig and his likeminded band of brothers. It was a kind, heartfelt offer. It also hurt. He really didn't understand the nature of my work and what keeps me in it. Even when I compared my situation to that of a Jesuit missionary in China more than 400 years ago, who, when exhausted by his labors, would humbly pray to God about his challenging station in life, petitioning a change of scenery:

Dear Lord, I know I am here because of you and your guiding influence. I will stay here and faithfully do your will to the best of my ability. But if you ever think me worthy of another gig where I can serve you, perhaps in Leelanau County, for example—just sayin'—please don't hesitate to send that opportunity my way. Meanwhile, of course, I'm good—very, very good!—with my mission here in Indy. Amen!

As a fellow Catholic, Craig laughed at my religiously inspired attempt at an explanation. And yet, it wasn't good enough. "You will die at your desk and nobody will care," he said. "You can be happy here, amigo." He is absolutely right. Whenever I'm Up North and chatting with a local who asks me if I'm from the area, my response reveals a personal promise: "Not yet." And it always gets an understanding smile.

❀

Ever since I laid eyes on Lake Michigan from M-72 when visiting the area for the first time, I fell in love with the Great Lake and its surrounding country. I spent my first 10 years on the planet in Scranton. Geological features like mountains and clear lakes were in my DNA. I could never attach myself to the flatlands of central Indiana; for decades, until that magical summer day in 1986 when I discovered northwest lower Michigan's incredible beauty, I felt like a foster child. My dear friend helped me in ways he never knew, not only to gain an appreciation for the countless outdoor diversions to be had in the area but the psychological healing that took place as I roamed the countryside of Leelanau and Grand Traverse counties and the Jordan River Valley in Antrim County. Recreating here also gave me temporary restorative leave from my labors. To arrive "home" in Cedar, whenever we get the chance during the warmer months, is a godsend, perhaps adding some time back on my lifespan. Here, you can get away. Big city problems don't seem so daunting, so insurmountable, so clinging. When you live in such natural splendor in the woods, when standing around a curling campfire under the Milky Way prominent in a coal-black sky, you can be judgmental about things you don't directly experience, things that are just too far out of range, or just beyond your ken. And that's okay.

＊

Come Sunday, the temperature would be in the sixties for most of the late morning and through the afternoon. It was cloudy, with some intermittent blue sky. Craig hurried up the driveway in his pickup truck. We shook hands, though I did so hesitatingly. He could sense my edginess. "How's the pandemic treating you in Indy?" he asked as I reached for the hand sanitizer.

"Well, in addition to being a charter school leader, I'm now a public health expert and an infectious disease specialist. I have to make decisions for our schools that the mayor and governor won't. It's pretty damn stressful."

"Gotcha. Now enough of that. Let's jump in the truck and go spend the day away from that crazy shit. I need to get my friend Tim back from the brink of the abyss." I pulled my black Buff neck gaiter above my nose and opened the passenger door. It was the first time I had been in a vehicle with another person, other than Janet, since early March.

"Do you want me to wear a mask?" he asked considerately, though he was in the camp of those who think of Covid-19 as "the Chinese flu."

"Your call. I'll just roll down the window and wear mine. No biggie, bro." Ten minutes and a short two-track later, we were on Good Harbor Bay Beach. All to ourselves.

Craig, always prepared for an outing, brought along an Army-issue canvas bag he used for collecting "keeper" rocks and other finds. He also pulled out a four-pack of canned Moscow Mule cocktails. "I saw these at Buntings and thought what the hell. We'll need a taste eventually, you know."

We placed our beach towels and shoes next to a 15-foot log that made for a perfect seat when we felt so inclined, then strolled westward along the people-devoid beach. This stretch obviously attracted much less traffic than the asphalted invitation to tourists on Good Harbor Trail near our cabin. Craig's secret would be safe with me.

"The water is churned up from last night's storms," he observed. "Otherwise, it's usually super clear and great for rock hunting about 30 or 40 yards out from here. But hey, there are plenty of stones right here." He had a new contraption in hand, a Sand Dipper aluminum telescoping rod with a small wire basket on the end, perfect for picking up small stones without the joint torture of bending down.

"Oh, man, are we getting old or what," I commented. "Pretty soon you'll be showing me your Clapper."

"Here, give it a try," he said, handing it to me. Soon I was scooping Petoskey stones out of the sand, comfortably hoisting them to me. With each stone picked from the rocky abundance around us, we would stop momentarily and inspect it together. We judged its unique merits based upon the definition of the fossilized material, the natural patterns, the hues, the strange features that caught our attention. Size didn't matter.

"Check that out…that's a keeper…how weird is that…" our simple geological evaluations rolled on as we began filling Craig's bag with finds. And predictably, as we sauntered on, Craig began his latest political commentary. I expected it. He couldn't help it. His pent-up rage about the attacks on the president by the leftist media on "just a simple guy like us," on the grave socialist if not Marxist threat to the country, picked up steam as we walked while scanning the ground beneath us. I didn't counter him, which, of course, would only encourage his exposition. But I never felt attacked, even though he knew that I abhorred the president's poor character that had been on full display for four long, painful years of tweeting. Craig just had to get it out, to cough up his massive fur ball of disdain for liberalism. And this liberal was fine listening to him. The running Fox and Friends-like discourse only increased the intensity of my stone search. Every now and then I would interrupt to show him a worthy find. "Oh man, that's a keeper for sure. Very cool. Nice work. Anyway, that Pelosi…." Eventually, the beach, the stones, the balmy October temperature, and the sound of moving water worked their magic, and my friend's animus cooled.

"I'm sorry, bro-ski. You know how I am. The world is going to hell (which he's been telling me for years; and of late, no argument from me), and I gotta talk to somebody about it. Whenever I go on a tear, my wife tells me to stop yelling at the TV and take it outside." Lucky me.

After wandering for about a half hour, we returned to our landing area just off the end of the trail, and Craig grunted as he seated himself on the convenient log. "Time for a drink, amigo." With a shriek of the Moscow Mule's pop-top vacuum release, he handed the can to me, then opened his own. After a swig, my Michigan wild kingdom guide shared his assessment of the drink du jour: "Hey, not bad. I could get used to this. Whaddya think?"

I gave it a thumbs-up. The classic cocktail hit the spot, as my dad, who never met an alcoholic beverage he didn't like, would say.

A few gulps and the alcohol began to work its soothing, conversation-energizing, laughter-inducing, mood-altering magic. Which is why we drink. We left politics behind. Which leads us to drink. And we returned to sharing our absurd thoughts in total brotherly confidence. One Moscow Mule down; one to go.

"So while I was up in late June, I made the mistake of texting my mother one evening after a few beers, before bed," I confided as we caught up. "I told her how pissed off I was at my sister, who had decided to tee off on me with an out-of-nowhere text about some long-simmering frustrations, most of which pointed at me not being quite the oldest son our mother deserved. Must have been a bad night at the ranch. Anyway, I said I was done communicating with her. Then my mom said, 'Tim, never quit talking to a good friend or relative over a disagreement. I did that once, and boy, I'll never do that again.'"

Craig nodded appreciatively, looking groundward, waiting to see where this was going, as we began wading into Lake Michigan, leaving our second-round cocktails on the beach. "So for some unfortunate but long overdue reason, I decided to ask Mom about why we never returned back east, to Scranton or Paterson, her Jersey home, when my dad moved us to Indy when I was 10. Within two weeks of arriving, she discovered that he had a girlfriend who worked for him at the RCA manufacturing plant on the east-side of town. Did I say we were texting?"

"You did."

"Of course. It's the new way of remote closeness."

"Oh my God, don't I know it," he concurred, as Craig and I have switched to that as our main method of communication during the past few years. It's safer to launch strikes at one another from that digital distance.

As I waded farther out, the waves crept higher on my torso, tormenting me with their chilly reach; polar bear-like Craig only sighed in increasing contentment with every step into deeper water. "So after a few exchanges, my mom texted that she never wanted to speak to me again." Craig erupted in contagious gales of laughter, and I cracked up, doubling over, barely able to talk, my eyes watering. "Now—now you see why I'm such a mental case,"

I stammered, choking on the hilarious irony. For any "normal" folks, this story really wasn't funny—it was horrifying. For me, viewed under the light of my upbringing, and for Craig, who found such human folly terribly humorous, it all made complete sense.

"I need to go to confession," I confessed.

"Yes you do," he agreed. "But make sure you don't tell the priest everything. You don't want to overwhelm the poor guy." He continued, "There's a place for me in purgatory, you know. I'm working on what will end up being at least a 10-billion-year sentence. And I must say, I think you're starting to close the distance between us. Good work, you crazy Irishman."

He turned to matters at hand. "Ready for a swim? The water feels great."

No, the water felt like winter. Craig suddenly dove in an arc, disappearing beneath the surface. I splashed water on my chest, arms, neck, and head in an attempt to acclimate, but it was no use. I didn't want to invite a cardiac event. He surfaced, swinging his head, his wet hair tossing a stream of water.

"C'mon, Ace. It's perfect! Yee-ha!"

"I'm just not the man I used to be," I admitted.

"Hell, neither of us are. But that's beside the point. It's just good to be out here with you, bro. Whether your candy-ass can take the water temp or not."

I waded back to shore while he went for his swim. I resumed drinking my Moscow Mule, retrieved my iPhone, and took a few pics of Craig in his element. As if on cue, a group of common mergansers paddled by, 30 yards or so behind him. The large ducks never spooked, never lifted into flight. Why would they? Craig was no threat, just a fellow creature immersed in the wildness that they are, that he is.

The afternoon passed quickly, as all the good ones do. "Ready to motor?" Craig asked; it was almost 3 o'clock. We had spent nearly four hours on the beach.

"Sounds good. How about a glass of a choice red wine out on the deck? The day isn't over, you know."

"Yeah, yeah—let's do that."

I had a bottle of Orin Swift 2018 Machete Petite Sirah, a gift from a

school board member that I had held onto for well over a year, waiting for just the right occasion to pull the cork: this was it.

Five minutes later, Marie and Paul unexpectedly rolled up the driveway. "I forgot to leave you some hot dog buns," Marie shouted as she opened her door. She is so good to me. These would accompany the organic hot dogs she left me as a welcome home dinner gift. Long married, she well understood the limited cooking ability of the typical unaccompanied husband.

"Pull up a chair and join us," I insisted. Paul and Craig hugged, coronavirus or not. Family.

In minutes our laughter was echoing throughout the woodsy neighborhood and dissipating into the ether. Perhaps it's what God felt like on the seventh day, when he rested and deemed that all was good. Watching my friends interact playfully, as a loving family—me something of a cousin who never really experienced such depth of familial love—warmed the cockles of my heart. No political opining, no condemnation of the libs, no apocalyptic warnings, just being in communion with one another. Despite all of the things that can get in the way of a great friendship, all was right once again with my world, even though for the world at large, it really wasn't.

A few rounds and an hour later, Marie and Paul headed home for supper. No sooner than their truck taillights disappeared from view, Craig asked: "Hey, do you mind if we heat up those hot dogs I brought from Buntings? I'm running on empty. That sounds good, doesn't it?" By all indications, hot dogs were definitely on the menu.

I was hungry too, having skipped lunch and imbibed on an empty stomach. We ravaged about a half dozen of the locally butcher-made hot dogs, slathered in mustard and pickles, buns and all. Maybe not nutritionally good for us, but definitely good for morale.

The sun was setting. "I gotta get outta here before I turn into a pumpkin," Craig announced. "Besides, I'm tempted to have another drink, but tomorrow's a workday, and I have a full schedule with lots of calls." He paused, gave me a riveting direct look, and lowered his voice: "We had a good day."

"Thanks for coming, my friend. It was a very good day indeed."

In the style of the pandemic, we elbow-bumped. Then we laughed and shook hands; caution be damned, at least momentarily. Craig waved as he rolled in reverse down our steep driveway, an old pro at executing any driving maneuver to perfection, owing to years spent in the auto sales industry—and being raised in northern Michigan to back in boat trailers at public launches on the first attempt, a skill that would ever elude me.

I poured the last sip from the wine bottle, rubbed on a generous helping of hand sanitizer, and let the gloaming settle over me.

❋

That night, before I closed my eyes to this special day, I considered that my apocalyptic friend may be right: doomsday may well be on its way. Climate change is occurring, although he would argue otherwise. Our political system is reeling. People are taking sides in ways unseen in my 64 years: brother against brother. Could be, things truly are falling apart. It may be time to acquire some weaponry to call my very own, stock up on ammo and additional gas cans, and let Craig know that if and when the feces hit the fan, Janet and I will be making a run like our very lives depend upon it for a certain rendezvous point in the northern woods.

Meanwhile, I'll hope that the country gets its act together. For now, I'll keep tending to my thankless, non-award-winning public education endeavor in urban America. I'll slowly work my way through the pandemic-shrouded winter of 2020, ever cautious, intent on staying above ground. Then one long-awaited day, the vernal equinox will bring its light-returning promise to the dormant land. And this May, when the white trillium is popping and the longer days have called us out of hibernation and our fat Walt's crawlers are tumbling toward a deep, dark hole beneath some deadfall in a cold, clear northern Michigan river, enticing a Master Angler-worthy trout to strike, Craig will resume his melodramatic discourse on the state of the country. It will come during a break in the action, late in the afternoon, as we sit in satisfied fatigue on the riverside in the sunshine while retying our fisherman's knots, sipping a cold one. I'll listen until he gets off his soapbox. He'll apologize in his uniquely comical, lovable way. And we'll laugh hard and long once again. Friends. Same as it ever was.

— END —

ACKNOWLEDGEMENTS

This book would not have come into existence had I not met a recently discharged U.S. Army veteran from Traverse City one chance evening at TGI Fridays in Indianapolis in 1980. Those were the days when Fridays was the premier nightspot in Indy, where the food was fun but the party scene way better, where all the beautiful people gathered to drink and make very merry during the decadent eighties. The antique-appointed fern bar at Keystone at the Crossing is long gone, and its nearby replacement is just another family oriented (and quite tame, by comparison to its heyday) American restaurant-bar chain location.

A mutual friend of that vet, who went by the nickname T.C., tended bar with me at Fridays while working on his bachelor's degree in painting at the Herron School of Art at Indiana University-Purdue University Indianapolis. T.C. asked me, as head bartender, if I would do him a "huge favor" and meet this "wild and crazy guy" (said while imitating comedian Steve Martin) in his art program at Herron, as we had an opening for a barback (bartender trainee). T.C. was an outstanding bartender and had my utmost respect, so I honored his request, just before starting a Friday night shift. The short of it is, I don't believe I've ever laughed so hard in my life, as this somewhat deranged and eminently lovable artist-in-the-making put on a spur-of-the-moment gut-busting show. After a few uproarious minutes, through my laughter-strained voice box I managed to utter, "You're hired." Little did I know that at that moment, a close lifelong friendship with Craig was about to begin. So my thanks to T.C. for the life-changing introduction, and to Craig for (almost) everything else between us that happened from there.

I am also indebted to my wife, Janet, for allowing Craig and me to play so much together, especially in our early years. She gave us a generous lead yet always reeled us in before we went too far. She is Craig's sister from another mother, and frankly, my savior.

My children, Shawn, Matt, and foster son, C.J., were along for a number of the adventures noted in the book. I'm so glad they got to see that their dad actually has a friend and knows how to laugh. In these pages, they'll learn more about their father—perhaps more than they care to know. At this point in my life, I'm perfectly fine with that.

I greatly appreciate having the good fortune of meeting Mission Point Press's Business Manager, Doug Weaver. I ventured a conversation with him in April 2020, which led to this publishing effort. C.D. Dahlquist, my MPP editor, reviewed the manuscript, diligently finding and correcting the errors of my writing ways. During the editing process, I was amazed and humbled by her catches. She made it all better.

Worth noting, Janet and I don't have to worry about our Up North cabin while away thanks to Craig's brother Paul and his wife, Marie, our neighbors in Cedar. They watch over our true home as if it were theirs, relieving us of the anxiety that comes with owning an out-of-state residential property. They are selfless souls, and we are in the very best of hands.

Finally, to the people who live and work in northwest lower Michigan, who truly love the area and get out in nature as much as they can, I am respectfully envious of your good fortune to call such a wonderful place home. Thank you for sharing.

Notes

Epigraph

vi   Jim Harrison, *The Big Seven* (New York: Grove Press, 2015), 43.

Before the (Gold) Rush

9   **"I've gotta be me"**: https://www.lyrics.com/lyric/25675426/I%27ve
+Gotta+Be+Me. Accessed Sept. 6, 2020.

10   **"Live only inside the grace of one single day"**: Fr. Richard Rohr, *The
Divine Dance: The Trinity and Your Transformation* (New Kensington,
Pa.: Whitaker House, 2016), 22.

11   **In 2017, 1.7 million people visited Sleeping Bear Dunes National
Lakeshore**: https://www.northernexpress.com/news/feature/strapped-times
-at-sleeping-bear/. Accessed Sept. 6, 2020.

Gone Fishin'

13   **Christ's apostles were fishermen, a thought that comes to mind
during slow fishing outings**: Jn 21:3.

Crickin'

28   **Some of us never outgrow our "grasshopper" stage:** https://www.inc
.com/james-kerr/the-leadership-wisdom-of-kung-fu.html. Accessed Oct.
15, 2020.

Hiking

35   **Eagle Creek Park is an oasis for nature-starved inhabitants of central Indiana:** https://www.indy.gov/activity/about-eagle-creek-park. Accessed Sept. 13, 2020.

Viral Vacation

51   **This popular polka tune makes me think of Cedar's annual Polka Fest:** Fredie Yankovic, "In Heaven There Is No Beer," June 22, 2004, track 5, *The Best of Fredie Yankovic,* Columbia/Legacy, 2004, LP.

Invasive Species

76   **"Aquatic invasive species in Lake Michigan":** https://www.canr.msu.edu/news/aquatic_invasive_species_in_michigan. Accessed Aug. 9, 2020.

77   **Asian carp have been discovered in the Chicago River:** https://greatlakes.org/2019/08/new-study-finds-asian-carp-threat-to-lake-michigan-is-greater-than-previously-thought/. Accessed Aug. 9, 2020.

Empire

101   **Mount Everest climber George Leigh Mallory's famous utterance:** https://www.forbes.com/global/2001/1029/060.html#1d08074e2080. Accessed Aug. 16, 2020.

102   **The huge golf ball-like radar device on a hill near Empire:** https://glenarborsun.com/when-the-world-came-to-empire/. Accessed Aug. 16, 2020.

On the Beach

110   **The bluff that slid into Lake Michigan:** https://pubs.usgs.gov/fs/1998/fs020-98/. Accessed Sept. 1, 2020.

111   **Sleeping Bear Dunes National Lakeshore project initiated:** Kalt, Brian C. *Sixties Sandstorm: The Fight Over Establishment of a Sleeping Bear Dunes National Lakeshore, 1961-1970* (East Lansing, Mich.: Michigan State University Press, 2001), vii.

Pyramid Point

121   **The unsinkable Whaler's capability:** https://www.bostonwhaler.com/the-unsinkable-legend/. Accessed Sept. 16, 2019.

Dreams I'll Never See

135   **Michigan ranked fifth in the nation for economic activity involving recreational boating:** https://www.nmma.org/press/article/22428. Accessed Sept. 7, 2020.

135   **More than one million recreational boats registered in the state of Michigan:** https://www.discoverboating.com/resources/california-grabs-top-spot-from-michigan-with-most-boat-registrations. Accessed Sept. 7, 2020.

136   **One of their early songs:** The Allman Brothers Band, "Dreams (I'll Never See)," Aug. 12, 1969, track 6, *The Allman Brothers Band*, Capricorn Records, 1969, LP.

Stones

145   **The title of Carl Sagan's last book and frequent phrase of awe of the universe attributed to him:** Carl Sagan, *Billions and Billions: Thoughts on Life and Death at the Brink of the Millennium* (New York: Ballantine Books, 1997), book title.

155   **One of Annie Dillard's classic essay collections:** Annie Dillard, *Teaching a Stone to Talk: Expeditions and Encounters* (New York: Harper & Row, 1982), 86.

One Helluva Sail

159   **French Post-Impressionist artist Paul Gauguin's** *la Orana Maria* **painting:** https://www.metmuseum.org/art/collection/search/438821. Accessed Jan. 3, 2021.

Up North Armageddon

175   **Jim Morrison and The Doors had it so right:** The Doors, "People Are Strange," Sept. 25, 1967, track 7, *Strange Days*, Elektra Records, 1967, LP.

Disappointment

186   **As the Rolling Stones' song says:** The Rolling Stones, "You Can't Always Get What You Want," Nov. 16-17, 1968, track 9, *Let It Bleed*, London Records, 1969, LP.

Salmon Run

188   **The state record Chinook (king) salmon is 46 pounds:** https://www
.michigan.gov/documents/dnr/state_records_433983_7.pdf. Accessed
Aug. 16, 2020.

Searching for Jim Harrison

194   **Gordon Lightfoot's ballad "Wreck of The Edmund Fitzgerald":**
https://www.shipwreckmuseum.com/edmund-fitzgerald/the-fateful
-journey/. Accessed Aug. 16, 2020.

199   **Jim Harrison's driveway sign in Lake Leelanau:** https://www
.theparisreview.org/interviews/2511/the-art-of-fiction-no-104-jim
-harrison. Accessed Aug. 16, 2020.

199   **"He'd died a poet's death":** https://www.mlive.com/news/2016/03
/friend_describes_how_michigan.html. Accessed Aug. 16, 2020.

Winter Is Coming

214   **Leelanau County averages 145 inches of snowfall each winter:**
https://www.leelanaunews.com/articles/leelanau-county-annual
-snowfall-totals/. Accessed Sept. 12, 2020.

214   **The relentless winter of 2013-2014:** https://www.mlive.com/weather
/2014/08/season_snow.html. Accessed Sept. 12, 2020.

220   **Indianapolis annually averages 26 inches of snow:** https://www
.weather.gov/ind/localcli. Accessed Sept. 12, 2020.

Natural Causes

237   **"Oh dangerman, oh dangerman…":** Tears for Fears, "Swords and
Knives," Sept. 25, 1989, track 6, *The Seeds of Love*. Fontana Records,
1989, LP.

240   **Czech-built Aero L-39 Albatros jet plunged into Lake Michigan:**
https://www.northernexpress.com/news/feature/21-years-ago-this-
week-a-jet-preparing-for-the-cherry-fest-air-show-disappeared/. Accessed
Aug. 13, 2020.

ABOUT THE AUTHOR

Tim Mulherin currently lives in Indianapolis. He never wanted to; and mildly complaining, he still doesn't. As happens to many children who must do what's in the best interests of parental careers, he was relocated out of state against his will. Once an adult, he fell in love with an absolutely bewitching Hoosier and stayed and raised a family there. Yet he remains convinced, after years of what he characterizes as paradisiacal visits to northwest lower Michigan, that he has been grossly misplaced. Meanwhile, he's been keeping field notes of his adventures throughout the region, and so this book: a catharsis, a tribute, and a compass bearing for future days.

Mulherin started college later in life—when he was ready and eager to learn without the distractions of youth—at the age of 26. He attended

Indiana University-Purdue University Indianapolis (IUPUI) full-time, impractically but soulfully drawn to pursuing a bachelor of arts degree in English, with a concentration in nonfiction writing. He did this in the early eighties while managing one of the then busiest bars on the north side of Indianapolis, the Pawnbroker's Pub, and raising a young family with his wife, Janet, herself a working and university-attending mom. Mulherin went on to obtain a master of arts degree in journalism from Indiana University (IUPUI) and a master of science in management degree from Indiana Wesleyan University. As well, he taught for a decade in IUPUI's Department of English.

In 1986, with his newly minted undergraduate degree in English in hand, he soon discovered that to support a family while not abandoning his academically cultivated interest in writing, he would need to compromise on his career. So he entered the sister professions of marketing communications and public relations, advancing into management and leadership positions. Mulherin worked in the fields of emergency management, insurance, healthcare, and the nonprofit sector. A one-time aspiring high school English teacher, he eventually found his way back to public education. For the past 15 years, he's had the privilege of working for Irvington Community School, Inc., a K-12 public charter school system on the east side of Indianapolis and one of the state's oldest public charters. For the past 12 years, he's served as chief operating officer and now as chief executive officer.

Mulherin and his wife have owned a cabin in the village of Cedar in Solon Township for the past 10 years. In days to come, they will return to their home Up North—for good.